By the same author:

London's Underworld: Three Centuries of Vice and Crime

London

The Wicked City

A THOUSAND YEARS OF VICE IN THE CAPITAL

Fergus Linnane

ROBSON BOOKS

First published in Great Britain in 2003 by Robson Books,
The Chrysalis Building, Bramley Road, London, W10 6SP

A member of **Chrysalis** Books plc

British Library Cataloguing in Publication Data
A catalogue record for this title is available from the
British Library.

ISBN 1 86105 619 2

Typeset by FiSH Books, London WC1
Printed in Great Britain by St Edmundsbury Press, Bury
St Edmunds, Suffolk

Contents

Acknowledgements

Herbert Pearson read the manuscript and enriched it with his suggestions. My sister Norine also read it and refused to be shocked. My debts to the many authors whose works have made this book possible are not so easily repaid, particularly the late Ephraim (E J) Burford, a true pioneer. I am grateful to the Edinburgh University Press for their permission to publish extracts from their edition of Boswell's *London Journal*, edited by Frederick Pottle (1991). This material is quoted by permission of Yale University. Also to HarperCollins Publishers Ltd for permission to publish extracts from the *Diary of Samuel Pepys*, edited by Robert Latham and William Matthews, © HarperCollins 1995. Tiggey May and her colleagues kindly let me quote from their survey *For Love or Money*, carried out for the Home Office, and Professor Roger Matthews from his *Prostitution in London*. My editor, Joanne Brooks, brought order out of chaos.

Finally I should thank my brother Barry, who made it all possible by getting me my first job as a journalist.

The incomparable courtesan: Fanny Murray, who experienced extremes of fortune before making it to the top of her profession. Her story, which reads like an eighteenth-century novel, ended in domestic respectability.

Foreword

The sex industry in London today is furtive, colourless and clinical compared to that of almost any time in the last thousand years. When London was the richest city and the greatest marketplace in the world the variety of sexual wares on offer was staggering: mollies' houses for homosexuals, expensively equipped flagellation houses, brothels with classical paintings and fine cuisine, accommodation houses where one could take one's choice of the pretty street girls for an hour or a night, with good wine and food available, bagnios or bath houses of the kind visited and described by Casanova – 'It makes a magnificent debauch, and only costs six guineas.' There were published guides to whores with descriptions of their specialities – 'a fine Woman full of Fashion and as sound as a Roach, with black piercing Eyes, much Tenderness in Looks, dark Hair and delicate Features, snowy Bosom and elegant Shoulders and Sprightly Behaviour – but she will have her Price'. Women could meet their lovers at special hotels-cum-brothels, or find male prostitutes there. 'Lady Lovevitt, who has come from the baths at Bath, and who is disappointed in her affair with Lord Alto, wants to have something better, and to be well served this evening. Capt. O'Thunder or Sawney Rawbone......50 guineas.' Thieves as young as twelve had their own 'flash women' with whom they lived in full sexual partnership. Places of entertainment were thronged with well-dressed young whores. The pleasure gardens of Vauxhall, Cremorne and others abounded in sexual opportunities. In the elegant suburbs of St John's Wood and Regent's Park courtesans such as the notorious Skittles lived in more or less discreet splendour.

This book surveys about a thousand years of commercial sex in London, from the Bishop of Winchester's licensed brothels on Bankside to the saunas and massage parlours and anonymous suburban brothels of today's city. There were attempts to suppress the industry, particularly under the Puritans, but it always emerged strengthened. It was flexible enough to respond to sudden peaks in demand, as during the Restoration and two World Wars. It reached an accommodation with gangsters and crooked magistrates and police. It survived the campaigns of moral purists in the eighteenth and nineteenth centuries.

Today it faces new challenges: singles bars, dating agencies, lonely hearts columns and sex tourism suggest that men and women can more easily find sexual solace in a franker society. Certainly commercial sex is less flagrant than it was even fifty years ago, and infinitely less so than in mid-Victorian London, when some experts estimated that there were 80,000 prostitutes in the city.

This book is not a polemic, but it is hard not to be outraged by the double standard which still blames the whore and not her customer. In a sense, London is the hero of the book, a city forever changing and forever the same. As Richard of Devizes wrote in 1177:

> I do not like the city at all. All sorts of men crowd there from every country...each brings its own vices and customs. None lives in it without falling into some sort of crime. Every quarter abounds in grave obscenities. The greater the rascal, the better man he is accounted...Do not associate with the crowd of pimps: do not mingle with the throng in eating houses: avoid dice and gambling, the theatre and the tavern...the number of parasites is infinite. Actors, jesters, smooth-skinned lads, moors, flatterers, pretty-boys, effeminates, paederasts, singing and dancing girls, quacks, belly-dancers, sorceresses, extortioners, night-wanderers, magicians, mimes, beggars and buffoons...if you do not want to dwell with evil-livers, do not live in London.

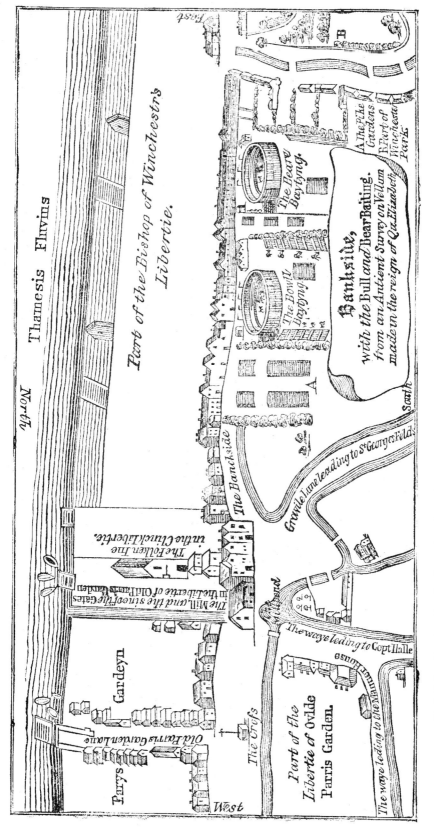

Red-light district: Bankside in Southwark, site of the first official brothels. Here Elizabeth Holland held sway.

The First Brothels

The first reference to a whore in London after the departure of the Romans was written in 1058: 'Seated on a jade mule, her locks falling over her shoulders, holding a little gilt rod in her hand...by means of indiscreet clothing she attracted the travellers' attention in the highways.'

London probably had a thriving sex industry even earlier. In 1161, when King Henry II guaranteed the Bishop of Winchester's right to exploit the eighteen brothels on Bankside in Southwark for the next four hundred years, it was said that the area had been associated with brothels or stews 'since time out of mind'. Thus was born the first official red-light district in London. At the same time, the sex trade was banned in other parts of the city. This attempt to segregate it suggests how ubiquitous it already was. As we shall see, the ban failed. To some extent the story of the sex industry in London for almost nine hundred years is of official attempts to suppress or contain it, and the resilience of the industry in resisting.

The rules regulating the way whores could practise their trade have a strangely modern ring. Women in London today are allowed to sell sex but not to solicit, which makes it almost impossible for them to operate within the law. Henry's act decreed that they were allowed to sit in their doorways, but not to solicit in any way. They were forbidden to get men's attention by calling or gesturing, or seizing them by the gown or harness. They could not swear, grimace or throw stones at passing men, 'on pain of three days and nights in jail plus a fine of eight and sixpence'.

The king's act set out what rights the whores did have, and also restrictions on their activities. The stewholders – early brothels evolved from stews, or bath-houses – were forbidden to detain prostitutes in brothels against their will. (The holding of women in closed brothels would still be a problem in Victorian London.) Perhaps to reinforce this the women were not allowed to board in the brothels. The stewholders could not charge the whores more than 14d. per week for their rooms. Women were free to give up whoring if they wished. Married women and nuns were not to be accepted as prostitutes.

The stewholders were also forbidden to keep 'any woman that hath the perilous infirmity of burning'. Sexually transmitted diseases were already a problem, although they did not get their medical names until the sixteenth century. Venereal disease is possibly one reason why the women had to spend the night with their clients – it cut down the number of sexual encounters they could have. However, it has also been suggested that this stipulation was intended to ensure that the streets around the stews were not plagued by the women and their clients at night.

The women who worked in Southwark's Bankside brothels were known as 'Winchester Geese', and the brothels had to be painted white and carry a distinctive mark: one of the best-known was the Cardinal's Hat. John Stow's *Survey of London* says that originally there were about eighteen of these brothels. Others were called the Boar's Head, the Cross Keys, the Castle, the Half Moon, the Elephant, very much as though they were inns or pubs. The men who were ferried across the river from the northern bank on frequent shuttle services during daylight would have been in no doubt about their true nature, however. The ferrymen had to keep their craft tied up at night.

Despite periodic attempts to tame it, the borough of Southwark became a lawless and dissolute area, particularly after 1181 when it was given the privileges of sanctuary. It was laid down that residence for one year and a day gave a 'thrall' his freedom. Felons and fugitives as well as 'thralls' flocked to the area. They had only to stay free for a year and a day and they were safe. These privileges were a great nuisance to the authorities, who repeatedly tried to have them revoked.

From Elizabethan times onwards the area of Southwark known as the Old Mint, where debtors could find sanctuary, was so notorious for harbouring criminals that a series of acts were enforced to suppress it. The nineteenth-century social commentators Henry Mayhew and John Binney described what happened when one of these acts came into force:

> The exodus of the refugee-felons and debtors, in July, 1723... is described as having been like one of the Jewish tribes going out of Egypt, for the train of 'Minters' is said to have included some thousands in its ranks, and the road towards Guildford (whither they were journeying to be cleared at the Quarter Sessions of their debts and penalties) to have been positively covered with the cavalcades of caravans, carts, horsemen, and foot-travellers.
>
> (Mayhew and Binney, *The Criminal Prisons of London*)

In 1240 the aptly named Cock Lane in Smithfield was also designated an official red-light district, acknowledging the fact that the area was already known for its brothels. Cock Lane is just one example of our forefathers' endearingly blunt way with words. Gropecuntlane in the parish of St Mary Colechurch is first mentioned in a document of 1276: 'in Gropecuntlane in St Mary Colechurche parish near the Bordhawe leased from St Paul's Cathedral...' Burford says in *The Orrible Synne* that the name 'signifies an area of the lowest type of prostitution, that is to say old worn-out prostitutes who catered for the poorest clientele who could not afford to pay for the full treatment, and so were charged a tiny sum just to put their hands up the old woman's skirts and grope'. Gropecuntlane was eventually gentrified by a more fastidious age as Grape Street and Grub Street, while Codpiece Alley became Coppice Lane. The Bordhawe was an area of brothels also in the parish of St Mary Colechurch. In 1405 it was called Burdellane, which meant Brothel Lane. Nearby was Love Lane, described by John Stow nearly two hundred years later as a 'street of wantons'. There was also a Love Lane in Southwark. Clearly the attempts to restrict the sex industry to a few specified areas had failed. There were whorehouses in Sopers Lane and Bread Street within the City's walls. Prostitutes were subject to a dress code, to distinguish them from 'respectable' women. In 1352 a proclamation ordered them to wear hoods of rayed – that is, striped – cloth, usually red and white. In 1437 the authorities announced that it was 'in this year ordained that strumpets should wear red hoods and white rods in their hands'.

Further futile attempts were made to control prostitutes. In 1305 the parish watch rendered a brothel run by William Cok of Cock Lane uninhabitable by breaking in and removing the doors and windows. After the Peasants' Revolt in 1381, when the rebels burnt the Bankside brothels and were welcomed 'with open arms by the commons of Southwark' the mayor ordered the constables and beadles to roam the streets and arrest 'nightwalking' women. A contemporary record says women not handsome or rich enough to bribe the officers were therefore 'carted' – driven in or behind carts with shorn heads as a mark of their shame.

In 1394 the mayor and corporation issued the *Regulations as to the Street Walkers by Night and Women of Bad Repute*. The first part ordered that nobody should be so bold as to go about by night unless he had good reason and was a respectable person. The ordinance goes on to talk of broils and affrays and murders caused by those 'consorting with common harlots at taverns ... and other places of ill-repute'. These women are to keep themselves in the assigned places, the stews on the south bank of the Thames and Cock Lane. If caught elsewhere their clothes would be forfeit, becoming the property of the City officers. In practice these officers were more likely to take the women's jewellery.

Court cases too have a modern ring. A woman named Margaret was accused of procuring a young girl named Isobel Lane and forcing her to prostitute herself with Lombards and others in the brothels of Bankside and elsewhere. Margaret, clearly a procuress, perhaps in a big way of business, was also accused of taking a girl named Joan Makelyn to a house in the parish of St Colemanstreet for sex with a Lombard who paid her 12d. Out of this Joan had to pay Margaret 4d. for the introduction. Joan was no innocent victim, however: she introduced Margaret to a 'very prodigal Venetian'.

The report of the case says that 'both women for a long time taking no thought for the safety of their souls had carried on this base and detestable manner of life'.

This case tells us a lot about whoring, including what a whore charged a customer, although we don't know exactly what service was provided. It shows that whores found good customers among the foreign community, and that there was now little hope of confining the sex industry within a few ghettoes. In January 1440 there was a case involving 'immorality, common procurers and prostitutes' in Tower Ward. Katherine Frenssh, Sibil Eddon, Katherine Clerk and Alice Moysant all admitted many acts of immorality with Ralph Hislam, Simon Strengere and numerous others in the preceding month.

Peter Ackroyd says in *London: The Biography* that vice was more prevalent, or more open, in late medieval London than at any period in the nineteenth or twentieth centuries. The Rolls of the City of London starting in 1338 give us some idea of the level of prosecutions – and also how one's status affected the punishment. In June 1338 William de Dalton was charged with keeping 'a house of ill fame' in which married women could meet their lovers. These must have been among the first 'houses of assignation', which were so important a feature of whoredom in the eighteenth and nineteenth centuries. William was a member of the spicers' guild, a liveryman and a gentleman, and so he was sentenced to only two months in prison. The following month Robert de Stratford, a cordwainer, was charged with harbouring prostitutes and was fined 6s. 8d. although the usual punishment was a carting, shaven head and an hour in the pillory.

A series of cases in 1339 show how the Holborn–Fleet Street–Chancery Lane–Shoe Lane area was an important red-light district, with a thriving business for homosexuals. At Christmas Ellen de Evesham, who lived in Fleet Street, was accused of keeping a disorderly house harbouring thieves and prostitutes. Some men from the house had attacked a passer-by in the street, beaten him up and bundled him into the house, 'she lighting their way with a candle in her hand'. A fortnight later Gilbert le Strengmaker, who lived in the Hospital Rents in Fleet Street, was charged with keeping a disorderly house harbouring prostitutes and sodomites. At the same sessions two prostitute sisters, Agnes and Juliana of Holborn, were charged with harbouring sodomites. Agnes was fined for letting her house in Shoe Lane to a 'woman of bad character'. Juliana-atte-Celere and Alice de Lincoln, both of Cock Lane, were charged with keeping a disorderly house in Hosier Lane. All of these areas continued to be associated with vice and crime for hundreds of years.

In June 1340, at a time of moral panic over a growing crime wave, the city fathers ordered a round-up of 'evildoers and disturbers of the King's peace'. Among the hundreds arrested was the 'common whore' with the very uncommon name Clarice la Claterballock, who was picked up in Bridge ward. One can only speculate on the source of Clarice's name and what special services she provided. In Cripplegate Ward Without, John Mazerer, Walter Kyng, Thomas Litelwatte, Thomas fitz Simon, Nicholas de Westsmythfielde, Walter le Tyretener and John de Wantynge, described as 'evildoers and nightwalkers and disturbers of the peace', were arrested. In the same ward John de Catton 'keepes a common bawdy-house and John le Clerke is a receiver of bawdes'.

When jurors considered cases from the wards of Tower, Bridge and Billingsgate they heard of Hugh de Staunton, who visited Alice de Stanewell's bawdy-house. Andrew and Beatrice Wrenne had wounded Alice le Shepster in the street outside their house of ill fame. A French nobleman, Sayer de Satnes, apparently 'preferred bad company to good' but got off with a caution.

In Broad Street ward John la Tapstere and William atte Pond were found guilty of keeping their brewhouse called 'Atte the Pye on the Hope' in Abchurch Lane as a brothel. Thomas le Keu ran a brothel in the Rents of the Abbot of St Albans. Le Keu was a gang leader, and the gang had its own armourer who supplied them with swords and other weapons – Master Gerard le Armourer, leader of an honourable guild. And so on.

At another court Thomas de Hundesmor, who lived in the Rents of the Church of St John, Clerkenwell, was indicted as an 'armed bully' and manager of a group of prostitutes. It seems that both men and women who lived in the houses so terrorised the area that the neighbours were afraid to go outdoors at night. Thomas was probably a pimp on a large scale. The case offers is a rare glimpse into the world of organised vice at that period.

The medieval Church was heavily involved in the sex industry. Apart from the Bishop of Winchester's interests in the Bankside brothels, one London nunnery, the Priory of St Mary Overie, let its properties in Chancery Lane and Fetter Lane to whores. In 1337 nuns acquired the whorehouse known as the Barge in Southwark. As we have seen, the Dean and Chapter of St Paul's Cathedral owned brothels in Cock Lane, and in 1321 the pope's envoy to England, Cardinal William de Testa, bought a brothel in the city as an investment for the Church, naming it 'The Social Club'. Cardinal Wolsey kept whores at Hampton Court for the use of guests. Over the door was an inscription in Latin saying: 'The house of the whores of my Lord the Cardinal'. Anne Boleyn called the Cardinal 'that old Church pander' (Nickie Roberts, *Whores in History*) The theologian St Thomas Aquinas had justified prostitution as 'like unto a cesspool in the palace: take away the cesspool and the palace becomes an unclean, evil-smelling place'. St Augustine had said: 'Suppress prostitution and capricious lusts will overwhelm society.'

So to some churchmen at least it was a necessary evil as well as a source of revenue. Others saw it as an abomination. Theologians wrestled with the problem. Thomas of Chobham argued that women had every right to sell themselves: they were acting just like any other trader. But if they derived pleasure from the transaction they should forfeit their fee, as it would no longer constitute an act of labour. He also thought that if the whore wore make-up to make herself more attractive she was cheating, and the client was paying more than the 'goods' were worth. In this case the whore should give back part of her fee, or donate it to the Church. But if whores were performing a public service, as Aquinas and Augustine suggested, the Church never accepted them. If they were still working in the sex industry when they died, they were refused burial in consecrated ground. In *The Survey of London*, Stow says that a special plot, called 'the Single Woman's churchyard', was set aside for them.

The licentiousness of the clergy was notorious. Chaucer and Langland castigated monks and nuns who lived scandalous lives, and the humanist writer Erasmus wrote:

*The persecutor: Cardinal Wolsey ordered widespread raids
to clamp down on whores and brothels.*

There are monasteries where there is no discipline, and which
are worse than brothels...a monk may be drunk every day. He
may go with loose women secretly and openly. He may waste
the Church's money on vicious pleasures. He may be a quack
and a charlatan, and all the while an excellent brother and fit to
be made an abbot...Monks of abandoned lives notoriously
swarm over Christendom...

In England the extent to which the clergy had fallen from grace is evident in an appeal from the Reverend Symon Fysshe to King Henry VIII: 'Who is she that will set her hands to work to get three pence a day, and may have at least twenty pence a day to sleep an hour with a friar or a monk or a priest? What is he that would labour for a groat a day and may have at least twelve pence a day to be a bawd to a priest or a monk or a friar?'

Many monks were illiterate time-servers without a vocation. The situation for nuns was more complicated. Women might be sent to a nunnery for a variety of reasons: they might be widows or surplus sisters or daughters from good families, unable to find a husband or a living. They might even be wards whose guardians wanted them out of the way. In these circumstances it is hardly surprising that some wanted to have a good time.

In the twelfth century the nunnery at Amesbury was run by an abbess whose wanton ways were a byword, and the nuns soon followed her example. They were merely aping their male counterparts. As one writer bitterly observed: 'bishops...may fuck their fill and be unmarried'.

In London the City's *Letter Book* for 1420 records the large number of clergymen taken in adultery in the brothels of Queenhithe and Billingsgate. The last case in that book concerns Sir Roger Watts, chaplain of the prestigious Guild of Fishmongers, 'who was taken in adultery with Alice Soureby of Bridge Ward near St Magnus Churche'.

In 1563 the City's *Letter Book* dealing with 'Priests Taken in Adultery' tells this little tale which showed the clergy had not mended their ways after the break with Rome:

On 26 June was a Minister, a Parson of Saint Mary Abchurch ...taken at Distafflane using another man's wife as his own which was the daughter of Sir Miles Partridge and wife to William Stokebregge, Grocer, he being taken in the deed (having a wife of his own) was carried to Bridewell [prison] through all the streets with his Breeches hanging about his knees...but he was not long there but was delivered without punishment and still enjoyed his Benifices...

During the Middle Ages English monarchs, some themselves dissolute, poured out a series of acts and decrees in an attempt to control the growth of prostitution. Henry V issued an ordinance in 1417 'for the abolition of stews within the city...against the many Grievances, Abominations, Damages, Disturbances, Murders, Homicides, Larcenies and other common Nuisances'.

The king's ordinance, like so many others, had little effect. This period saw the first signs of what were later called 'ancient citadels of vice and crime' which would be a problem for centuries to come. The area known as the Mint in Southwark was notorious right until the end of the nineteenth century. Another was by the banks of the Fleet river in Farringdon Ward, in Turnmill Street, later Turnbull Street. 'Many lewd persons in Turnmill street...keep common brothel houses and harbour divers impudent Queanes'. Today's Turnmill Street, which runs by Farringdon underground station, is very dull.

In 1433 King Henry VI issued an ordinance in Parliament which was in effect yet another attempt to restore order in the stews of Bankside. It seems powerful criminals – what today we might term gangsters – had used the profits from brothels to become respectable landlords by buying freeholds and land worth at least 40 shillings a year. Thus they were eligible to sit on juries, and could get their cronies off serious charges, even murder. Parliament moved quickly to decree that men who had once lived in the stews could not become landlords of taverns or hostelries elsewhere in Southwark. They were further barred from sitting on juries or inquests outside the stews.

In 1490 St Martin-le-Grand, the most important sanctuary in the capital, had become a den of thieves where 'unthrift and riot run unchecked'. Fences and thieves were using it as a base:

rich men run thither with poor men's goods. There they build, there they spend and bid their Creditors go whistle! Men's Wives run thither with their Husbands' Plate, saying 'They cannot abide their husbands for beating.' Thieves bring hither their stolen goods and live thereon. They devise new robberies; nightly they steal out to rob; they reave and kill and come in again as though these places give them not only a Safeguard for the harm they have done, but a Licence to do more again.

Rights of sanctuary in the area were not abolished until 1815.

In 1483 Edward V came to the throne and a month later the ordinance headed *For to Eschewe the Stynkynge and Orrible Synne of Lechery* was issued:

> the which daily groweth and is used more than it hath been in daies past by the Meanes of Strumpettes mysguyded and idil women daily vagraunt and walkynge aboute the stretes and lanes of this Citee of London and Suburbes ... also repairing to Taverns and othere private places ... provokynge many other persones unto the said Synne of Lechery whereby moche people daily fall to the said myschevous and horrible Synne to the grete displeasur of Almighty God and distourbance and rekyng of the King our soveraign lordes peas ...

This ordinance was aimed at brothels in Farringdon and Cripplegate, Holborn, West Smithfield and Finsbury, showing that the sex industry was breaking new ground. Under Henry VII the brothels in Southwark were temporarily closed, although 'it was not long or they were set open again'. The reason for closing them was a new and virulent wave of syphilis, first recorded when Naples fell to the French in 1496. Within ten years it had reached epidemic proportions in England. Victims were attacked by obscene abscesses which ate into bones and destroyed noses, lips and genitals.

Ten of the eighteen licensed brothels reopened after the women had a medical check-up: only those found to be free of the disease were allowed to work again. Later all the brothels reopened but by then some of the bawds and their girls had scattered across London. The poet John Skelton said in 'Hickescorner':

> Some at St Katherine's strake-a-grounde
> and manie in Hole Bourne were founde:
> Some at Saynte Giles, I trow
> also in Ave Maria Alley ...
> and some in Shoreditch drew there
> in grate lamentacion ...

and by cause they have lost that fayre Place
they will buylde at Colman Hedge a space
an other Noble Mansion.

Ave Maria Alley is next to St Paul's Cathedral; St Katherine's was
by the Tower of London. The Holborn ('Hole Bourne') area was a
criminal stronghold into the nineteenth century. Colman Hedge was
in the wilderness where the National Gallery now stands.

Within ten years, in spite of the syphilis scare and official
disaproval, the brothels had multiplied, spreading all along the High
Street in Southwark and on to the eastern side of the road to
Bermondsey. Disorder was also spreading too, and in 1513 Henry
VIII, concerned about the effects of the growing licentiousness on
his troops, decreed a new and savage punishment for whores caught
selling sex to soldiers – branding on the face with hot irons. Henry's
henchman Cardinal Wolsey ordered a search throughout the city and
suburbs for 'suspected persons', which meant all men without
occupation or masters, and immoral women. The manhunt trawled
far and wide through London. Bankside, Clerkenwell, Islington,
Hackney, Stoke Newington and Queenhithe were among the areas
raided by the cardinal's police.

The king continued to pour out a flood of ordinances against sin,
including the 1533 Act For the Punishment of the Vice of Buggery.
Sodomy was believed to be popular among the clergy, and it had
been an ecclesiastical offence since the time of Henry I. The new act
said: 'Forasmuch as there is not yet sufficient and condign
punishment appointed and limited by the due course of the laws of
this Realm for the detestable and abominable vice of buggery
committed with mankind or beast . . .' Sodomy was made a felony,
punishable by death. This malign measure continued in force until
the nineteenth century.

In 1546 Henry VIII suppressed the brothels in Southwark,
denouncing 'toleration of such dissolute and miserable persons as,
putting away the fear of almighty God and the shame of the world,
have suffered to dwell beside London and elsewhere, in common
open places called the stews, and there without punishment or
correction to exercise their abominable and detestable sin'. The

proclamation, made by 'an harold atte armes', ordered the whores and brothel-keepers out 'bag and baggage'.

Henry died the following year 'in agony of syphilitic periostitis in a stupor' at the age of 55. His vast carcass was placed in a lead coffin and carried to Syon House, where, according to a contemporary account, the coffin split and the rotten corpse leaked fluid: 'the pavement of the church was wetted with Henry's blood. In the morning came plumbers to solder the coffin, under whose feet was seen a dog creeping and licking up the King's blood.' Some years before, a friar preaching in Greenwich Church had told the king that when he died dogs would lick his blood.

Henry was not the first royal victim of the disease: John of Gaunt, uncle of Richard II, 'died of a putrefaction of the genitalls...due to carnall copulation...whiche mortification he showed (before he died) to his nephew King Richard II'. Henry VIII's successor, the sickly boy-king Edward VI,[1] ordered the reopening of the Southwark brothels in 1550. The law against sodomy was also softened slightly: convicted felons were still executed, but their property was no longer forfeited.

Not everyone welcomed the reopening of the brothels. Bishop Latimer, in his 'Third Sermon before the [new] King', fulminated:'I say that there is now more whoredom in London than ever there was on the Bank...You have put down the stewes, but I pray you, how is the matter amended? What avayleth it that you have but changed the place and not taken whoredom away?'

Some of his colleagues disagreed. They wanted the sanctions against brothels lifted completely, and their campaign gathered pace during Queen Mary's reign. A witness wrote in 1572:

The stews and public bordell houses are abolished and so continue until the time of Queen Mary, in whose days some of the clergy made labour to have them restored again: and were very likely to have gained their suit if she had lived a while longer. Such trees. Such fruit. For the Stews, saith one of them in a Sermon at Pauls Cross, are so necessary in a commonwealth as a jaxe [toilet] in a man's house.

Economic changes under the Tudors deepened the reservoir of poverty which supplied the brothels with the constant source of new girls they needed. Enclosures, rising prices, changes in agriculture all forced people off the land, and the population grew after a long period of stagnation. Women were hit worst by the drift from the land. New industries could not absorb the numbers of men arriving in the cities, and there was almost no place for their wives or children.

Some women found work as servants in noble or bourgeois houses, but they were constantly preyed on by the men of the house. The feeling that it was better to sell sex than have to give it free to an employer led to many becoming prostitutes. Others simply had no choice. Bankside, with its inns and streets of brothels, beckoned.

Although some whores continued to find comfortable lives as priests' women or as kept courtesans of the wealthy, others devised new expedients. 'Bawdy baskets' went from door to door ostensibly selling trinkets but when opportunity arose selling sex. In *Theeves Fallinge Out* the dramatist Robert Greene (1560?–92) describes them as 'women that walk with baskets or Cap-cases on their arms, they have laces pins needles white silk girdles and suchlike. These will buy Cony Skins [rabbit skins] and in the mean time steal Linen or pewter. They are fair spoken and will seldom swear while they are selling their wares, but lie with any man that hath a mind to their commodity.' 'Commodity' was the word whores used among themselves.

The rich underworld slang was already in use. Greene in a *Notable Discovery of Cozenage* (1592) gives an account of the wiles of the whores and their pimps in cheating the 'simplers' or customers. The prostitutes were 'punks', 'commodities' or 'traffic', their pimps were 'apple squires' or 'crossbiters'.

> There are resident in London and the suburbs certain men attired like gentlemen, brave fellows, but basely minded, who, living in want, as their last refuge, fall unto this crossbiting law, and to maintain themselves either marry some stale whore, or else forsooth keep one as their friend... These when their other trades fail... then to maintain the main chance, they use the benefit of their wives or friends to the cross-biting of such as lust after their filthy enormities.

It is at this time that the first mention is made of child brothels in England, which supplied rich clients with girls aged between seven and fourteen years. These children of the poor were either sold into prostitution by their parents or kidnapped for that purpose. (Parents were still selling their children into prostitution in London in the nineteenth century.) The economic pressures affecting much of society were also forcing some middle-class wives into prostitution. In Ben Jonson's play *Bartholomew Fair* (1614) the prostitute Punk Alice berates the wife of a judge for encroaching on her trade. 'A mischief on you! They are such as you that undo us and take our trade from us, with you tuftaffeta haunches!...The poor common whore can ha' no traffic for the privy rich ones. Your caps and hoods of velvet call away our customers, and lick the fat from us.'

According to the poet John Taylor (1580–1653), these middle-class whores seized the opportunity during Henry VIII's short-lived suppression of the stews:

> The stews in England bore a beastly sway
> Till the eighth Henry banished them away.
> And since the common whores were quite put down
> A damned crew of private whores are grown.

The growth of the sex industry under James I, who came to the throne in 1603, was phenomenal. This intelligent, even learned, man presided over a court of extraordinary licentiousness and vulgarity. His court has been described as 'extravagant and disorderly, with hard drinking and immorality winked at' (Godfrey Davis, *The Early Stuarts*) and personal hygiene was not scrupulous. One English lady of the court complained that she was always lousy after visiting it, and the king was a dirty drunkard who seldom washed. Even by the loose standards of the times he was fond of bawdy talk and jokes. When told by courtiers that crowds flocked to see him out of love, he replied: 'God's wounds! I will pull down my breeches and they shall also see my arse.' His weakness for pretty, Frenchified young men was scandalous.

The case books of the Middlesex Sessions show that the loose morals of the court were echoed in society at large. In 1608 Emma

Robinson was accused of being a 'Common Queane' and of sitting at her door until midnight 'to entertaine lewd persons that resort untoe her'. Ellen Allen was fined for enticing a Dutchman to lewdness. While he was kissing her, her maid stole his dagger. Elizabeth Basse 'keepeth a notorious bawdy house whereby murther was like to have been committed'.

The explosive growth of whoring was such that in 1622 even James I was moved to expostulate, issuing the ordinance *Touching on Disorderly Houses in Saffron Hille*:

> of long time hath been and still is much pestered with divers immodest lascivious and shameless women generally reputed for notorious common whores, who are entertained into divers houses for base and filthy lucre sake accruing to the private benefit of the Landlords and Tenants of such houses…such women who do usually sit at the doors…do allure and shamefully call in…such as pass by to the great corruption.

Even reinforced by mass raids this does not seem to have worked. The following year another ordinance was issued, and the list of places raided gives some idea of the spread of prostitution: Cowcross, Cock Lane, Smithfield, St John Street in Clerkenwell, Norton Folgate (just outside Bishopsgate), Shoreditch, Wapping, Whitechapel, Petticoat Lane, Charterhouse, Bloomsbury and Ratcliffe. During just one day in August 1620 at Middlesex Quarter Sessions nineteen women were convicted of brothel-keeping. Sixteen of them were located in the Cowcross area.

Charles I, who came to the throne in 1625, moved against the brothels in the same old way, and with about as much effect. His act described how wayfarers in the old brothel areas of Cowcross, Turnmill Street, Charterhouse Lane, Saffron Hill, Bloomsbury, Petticoat Lane, Wapping, Ratcliff and other places were 'pestered with many immodest, lascivious and shameless women generally reputed for notorious common and professed whores.'

In 1641, on the eve of the Civil War, Parliament decreed that prostitution was no longer a crime, but only a public nuisance, to be treated as gross indecency if committed in public. If this was a first step towards liberalising the laws surrounding prostitution it was reversed by the events of the Civil War, which broke out the following year and ended with the victorious Puritans setting up the Commonwealth.

War and its disruption are often an opportunity for whores, but the Civil Wars brought them great hardships. Some became camp-followers with the Royalist army. In 1643 King Charles I issued a proclamation abhorring the 'general licentiousness, profanity, drunkenness, and whoremongering of the army'. Some of the women were wearing men's uniform as a way of avoiding the drudgery that was the lot of the camp follower and Charles was moved to threaten: 'Let no Woman presume to Counterfeit her Sex by wearing man's apparell under pain of the Severest punishment which Law and our displeasure shall inflict.'

A whore who had accompanied the Royalist army from London to Coventry was, according to the records, 'taken by the soldiers, and first led about the city and then set in the pillory, after in a cage, then ducked in the river, and at last banished from the city'. However a warmer welcome usually awaited the London whores who flocked to the Royalist army. An order published at the head of every regiment spoke of 'the prostitute impudency of some women . . .'

Although the victorious Puritans quickly proscribed both brothels and whoredom, there were some who still saw a place for it. In 1649, the first year of the Commonwealth, a certain Dr Chamberlain proposed to Parliament that registered brothels should be opened across the country. This was against the spirit of Puritanism, however, which set about suppressing all popular entertainments. Brothels, of course, had to go, and also theatres, gambling houses, racecourses, even maypoles. The death penalty was decreed for a second offence of adultery.

The asperities of Puritanism were sometimes abated in the private lives of its leaders. The music-loving Cromwell was persuaded that opera was untainted by the scandals that marred the theatre, and at the wedding of his daughter Mary Cromwell there was a masque with pastorals by Marvell. Mary Cromwell appeared in it, and her father may even have played a part.

However, the Commonwealth was a disaster for entertainers and pleasure seekers of all kinds. Actors were persecuted and found themselves in the dock with whores and bawds. People were fined for swearing.

> Fines and corporal punishment shut out, even from children, games, dancing, bell-ringing, rejoicings, junketings, wrestling, the chase, all exercises and amusements which might profane the Sabbath...It seemed as though a black cloud had weighed down the life of man, drowning all light, wiping out all beauty, extinguishing all joy, pierced here and there by the glitter of the sword and by the flickering of torches, beneath which one might perceive the indistinct forms of gloomy despots, of bilious sectarians, of silent victims.

A blight descended on the country: maypoles were cut down, the bears used in the popular sport of bear-baiting were shot. The whores' favourite haunts, including alehouses and taverns, were strictly controlled. A contemporary observer wrote:

> If you step aside into Covent Garden, Long Acre and Drury Lane, where these Doves of Venus, those Birds of Youth and Beauty – the Wanton Ladies – doe build their Nestes, you shall find them in such a Dump of Amazement to see the Hopes of their tradeinge frustrate ...[before Puritan times] Ten or Twentie Pound Suppers were but Trifles to them...they are now forc'd to make doe on a diet of Cheese and Onions...the ruination of Whoreinge was why the London Bawds hated 1641 like an old Cavalier.

Not all taverns were closed, by any means, but they were more discreet. Some brothels, such as 'Oxford Kate's' in Bow Street, continued to trade, probably because their owners had powerful and influential customers. Sir Ralph Verney ate there despite its reputation because the food was so good. From 1652 the ever-resourceful whores found a new outlet: coffee houses became a meeting places for them and their clients.

Bathing in Luxury and Lust

Brothels ranged from vile stinking hovels to luxurious establishments such as the Hollands Leaguer on Bankside in the seventeenth century. Even modest houses would provide good food and wine: at every level, however low, drink was an invariable accompaniment to sex. How many clients the girls had each night depended on the status of the brothel. Estimates for a first-class establishment such as the Holland's Leaguer suggest that some women might have a dozen, and those in the poorest hovels an astonishing 57. Both seem rather high: the wealthy clients of the Leaguer could afford to have a girl for the night.

The George, the galleried coaching inn off Borough High Street in Southwark, gives some idea of what a seventeenth-century brothel catering for the rich would have looked like. There were restaurants and bars and private suites of rooms where wealthier clients could bring business partners to discuss affairs in the company of beautiful, intelligent and accomplished whores. Some of the women would play music and sing.

The Hollands Leaguer was a superior brothel-cum-club run by the successful whore turned bawd Elizabeth Holland, also known as Donna Britannica Hollandia, who was born towards the end of the reign of Queen Elizabeth. She was probably the first of that long succession of clever and energetic women who transformed English bawdry, insisting on high standards and prices. Elizabeth had been born into a wealthy family, perhaps in Staffordshire, and took to prostitution from sheer sexual exuberance after her parents sent her to London to acquire a veneer of metropolitan polish. Her anonymous biographer of 1632 says that eventually she decided to be 'no more a bewitching whore but a deceiving bawd: the sin of others shall maintain her sin'. Realising that, in the words of the biographer, 'every man hath a dolor [yearning] for a renowned brothel', she opened one in Duke Humphrey's Rents in the City. It was a huge success, being 'crammed like Hell itself where wicked creatures lay bathing themselves in Lust'. The food was particularly good, and 'the visitants came flocking so fast that her kitchen was ever flaming'. She became a victim of her own success. Other long-established brothels were suffering, she treated her girls badly, she was rapacious. The Lord mayor and the aldermen were persuaded to act, and Elizabeth found herself in another kind of hell, Newgate Prison. Her wealth protected her from its worst abuses, and before her trial she escaped with the help of friends in high places who had no doubt been among her customers. The freedom from vexatious City regulations drew her to Bankside, where she was advised that the Paris Gardens Manor House, then a deserted ruin, might suit her.

It was a moated mansion with a gatehouse, drawbridge and other buildings within fields with water-filled ditches spanned by small bridges. Madam Holland acquired it and turned the gardens into a pleasant backdrop for dalliance. There were walks with trees and shrubberies, prefiguring the pleasure gardens at Vauxhall and Ranelagh. She provided the best food and wine, and the prettiest and most accomplished women for her customers, among whom were King James I and his favourite, George Villiers, Duke of Buckingham. All agreed with her catchphrase 'This Chastitie is clean out of date'.

A tribute to the sumptuousness of the interior was the local nickname for the water-girt mansion, which was still known as 'the Nobs' Island' fifty years later. If the food and drink were exceptional, so were the prices.

London probably never produced a more rapacious bawd than Elizabeth Holland. She fleeced her customers more expertly and completely than a modern clip joint, but with style. A war hero of the time recalled:

At Hollands Leaguer there I fought
But there the service proved too hot!
Then from the Leaguer returned I
Naked, cold, hungry and dry.

To leave a strong gallant thus exhausted physically and financially but also well satisfied required a large and expert staff – cooks, wine waiters or 'apple squires' who would see that the customer's glass was always full, scullions, launderesses – and, of course, whores. Mrs Holland began with four of the very best. The first was a fiery giant beauty called Beta Brestonia, 'impudent above all measure and insolent beyond comparison'. For those who could stand the pace she had the reputation of being very good value for money. Next was Eliza Caunce: 'By chance her father begot her; by chance he forsook her; by chance she turned whore; and by chance Mrs Holland (the best bawd in all England) had lighted upon her.' This tiny young thing was a complete contrast in every way to Beta, except that she too was 'a wondrous wanton'. Mrs Holland's biographer suggests that Eliza was a nymphomaniac. The third woman, Longa Maria, was a tall blonde, cultured and softly spoken, a fine musician who played the viol and could sing well. 'She was not so rampant nor so rude'. Just the kind of girl a tired businessman would like to spend a few relaxing if expensive hours with after a hard day at the office. Finally there was a live wire named Maria Pettit, 'a small handful of a woman yet pleasant with all motion and action . . . nothing was more irksome to her than sleep and silence'.

This quartet was the heart of the business. Other girls were on call: their pictures and descriptions adorned the rooms. Guest whores of renown might also drop in if business was slack across the water. Almost as important was the resident doctor, whose job it was to stop the clients catching the Great Pox, or syphilis, and the Little Pox, or gonorrhoea. If an unfortunate girl caught a disease she would be expelled unceremoniously.

Madam Holland would greet each guest in person, as much to ascertain their financial status as to inquire about their special wishes. There was no credit: anyone temporarily embarrassed financially would not be admitted, however exalted. She stood for no rowdy or violent behaviour, such as ill-treating the girls. The girls paid for room and board, and handed over a percentage of their earnings. Madam Holland made a large part of her income from the sale of food and drink.

For thirty years the Leaguer was the most famous brothel in London. Its exclusiveness, efficiency, the quality of the whores and the food and drink and its formidable owner – described as a small woman, still beautiful – ensured its success. But again Madam Holland had made enemies, and when James I died and was succeeded by Charles I, who ordered the suppression of brothels, they saw their chance. Discipline also seems to have been breaking down at the Leaguer. The parties grew noisier and rowdier, the girls less genteel and ladylike. The pamphleteer Daniel Lupton expressed some of this concern when he wrote of the Paris Gardens about 1630:

> this may be better tearmed a foule Denne than a Faire Garden... heeratte foule beasts come to itt and as badde and worse keepe it; they are fitter for a Wildernesse than a Cittee: idle base persons...the Swaggering Roarer, the Cunning Cheater, the Rotten Bawd, the Swearing Drunkard and the Bloudy Butcher have their Rendezvous here.

Officials across the river had been watching and with the change of monarch they swooped. It was by no means the first time Mrs Holland had trouble with the authorities. The playwright Shakerley Marmion, a contemporary of Shakespeare and himself a customer of the brothel, wrote a play called *Hollands Leaguer*. In it he has Mrs Holland say:

> Pox on the Marshall and his Constable!
> There cannot be a mystery in this trade
> but they must peep into it! Merciless Varlets
> that know how many fall by our occupation
> and yet would have their venery for nothing...
> But we must give them good words!
> Show them a Room.

She was not prepared to be so welcoming when in December 1631 a troop of soldiers was sent to close down the Leaguer. The story goes that Madam Holland, who was now about sixty but as fiery as ever, first enticed them on to the drawbridge, then suddenly dropped it downwards so that the men were plunged into the stinking moat. As they floundered about in the slime her jeering whores pelted them with missiles and poured the contents of their chamber pots on their heads. The soldiers regrouped several times but were repulsed and eventually withdrew in disarrray.

A larger force was later sent but it too was driven off several times, while Mrs Holland 'derided [them] beyond sufferance'. It was this 'beleaguering' of Madam Holland's fortress which may have earned it the name the Leaguer. The whores' victory was short-lived, however; by the following year the Leaguer was successfully closed down. About thirty years of running the most expensive brothel in London – what the court wit Sir John Harington called making 'sweete gaynes of stynkynge wares' – had left Mrs Holland very wealthy. Her last stand with her whores before slipping away was probably motivated by her strong sense of mischief rather than fear of losing her livelihood. That is the last we hear of Madam Holland and her girls, but the house kept the name. On a map of 1746 it is called Holland Leger. Today Hopton Street runs through the site.

Some whores followed Madam Holland's path to wealth, and a few found aristocratic husbands. But for the 'common whore' life could be short and unpleasant. They might appear to have a degree of freedom in choosing sexual partners, but in fact hard necessity meant they could seldom turn away a customer, however depraved or diseased. And the whore was a prey to all: tradesmen would overcharge her and everyone would try to get their cut of what they saw as her too easily acquired money. There was the pimp and the parish beadle or constable to be paid, and the pox doctors for the treatment of venereal disease, or to cover up the fact that the girls were infected. Some of these quacks were Dutchmen, a fact mentioned in *The Poor Whores' Complaint to the Apprentices of London*:

> Our rents are great, our clients go apace
> And we forsaken are in every place.
> None pities us or hearkens to our moan,
> But every shag-bag casts at us a stone.
> Besides all this, with hot encounters
> Too many of us scab'd and mangy be;
> our Leeches who would us to health advance,
> hasten away to France ... confounded Dutch-men
> only you we curse with all our heart ...

Pox doctors were decamping to France with the girls' money, leaving them broke and uncured, because of course there was no cure.

Girls who worked in brothels at least had a roof over their heads and regular meals, but in some ways they were worse off than the street whores. They too could not refuse a customer, however obnoxious, drunk or violent he might be, and whatever disgusting demands he might make. Not only had they to keep their equanimity in the face of all these perils, they had to be careful not to upset wealthy but ageing *roués* whose failing powers made them particularly sensitive to ridicule. And to start with, these were simple country girls: certainly not innocent, since sharing the same bedroom or even bed with parents, brothers and sisters while growing up introduced them early to the realities of the relations between men and women, but not yet hardened and coarsened by the unremitting commerce of sex.

They learned quickly, taught by the bawds and the older whores. There were training manuals and the girls were also taught to be greedy and to keep relations with their customers on a purely commercial basis. One old bawd observed: 'When Fortune deserts a Man, let the Whore do so too ... the destruction of credulous whores attests to the disregard of this Rule.' The girls were taught sexual techniques: how to give the maximum of satisfaction for the minimum of effort. They were also trained in crisis management: how to deal with difficult or dangerous clients, and how to get away when violence seemed unavoidable. One important aspect of the training was the maximising of the take – getting the client to pay for extras, whether sexual services or exotic food and drink.

Some girls took to the life. Others were worn down by the long, irregular hours, the 'need to be constantly obliging', the constant drinking, the psychological strain and venereal diseases. All were coarsened and hardened, not least by the exactions of the whoremasters, who tried to cheat them of their earnings.

For those who did not find husbands or wealthy protectors the future was grim. When they were worn out and lost their looks or were simply too diseased to find customers among even the poorest, they might become procuresses for the young girls who replaced them in the brothels. Some might end their days as the diseased and semi-imbecile hags in Gropecuntlane.

A Pox on You

Venereal diseases are ancient, and it is still not clear whether the syphilis wave of the fifteenth century was a new disease or just a much more virulent strain. In 1717 the surgeon Dr William Becket published an article *On the Antiquity of Venereal Diseases Long Before the Discovery of the West Indies*, and remarked that Henry II's ordinance of 1161, which legitimized the Bankside brothels, had referred to 'the perilous disease of burning'.

The noted physician Thomas Sydenham (1624–98) described the progress of the disease:

> The patient is affected with an unusual pain in the genitals . . . a spot, about the size and colour of a measle, appears in some part of the glans . . . a discharge appears from the urethra . . . the aforesaid pustule becomes an ulcer . . . Great pain during erections . . . Bubos in the groin . . . Pain in the head, arms and ankles . . . Crusts and scabs appear on the skin . . . The bones of the skull, shin-bones and arm-bones are raised into hard tubers . . . The bone becomes carious and putrescent . . . ulcers destroy the cartilage of the nose. This they eat away; so that the bridge sinks in and the nose flattens . . . At length, limb by limb perishing away, the lacerated body, a burden to earth, finds ease only in the grave.
>
> (Maureen Waller, *1700: Scenes from London Life*)

In 1541, the year that Henry VIII died, Dr Andrew Boord published his *Breviary of Health*, which recommended washing the genitals in 'white wine or ale or else with Sack and Water.' However, if the disease took hold he suggested recourse to an 'expert Chirurgeon'. Abstinence was even better. Dr Boord's prescription against 'Erection of the Yerde to synne' was: 'Leap into a great vessel of cold water or put Nettles in the Codpiece about the yerde and the stones.'

Apart from Henry VIII other victims of that time are said to have included Archbishop Stephen Gardiner and Dr Hugh Weston, Dean of Windsor. In 1556 Weston was stripped of his office for adultery, and it was written: 'Lecherous Weston, who is more practised in the art of Brench [breech] Burning than all the Whores of the Stewes... hath been bitten with a Winchester Goose and was not yet healed thereof.'

Quacks might try plant remedies, and there were old wives' tales which recommended improbable cures. Sarsaparilla, opium, ammonia, sulphuric and nitric acids were thought efficacious. Some whores believed vigorous urinating was the answer. The seventeenth-century pamphlet *The Wand'ring Whore* describes 'Pissing... till I made it whurra and roar like the Tide at London Bridge to the endangering and breaking of my very Twatling-strings [sphincter] with straining backwards for I know no better way or remedy more safe than pissing presently to prevent the French Pox, Gonorrhoea, the perilous infirmity of Burning or getting with Child which is the approved Maxim amongst Venetian Courtesans.'

From about 1496 syphilis was treated with highly toxic mercury. 'A night with Venus, a lifetime with Mercury' was a popular adage. It was administered orally or applied in ointments to rashes, scabs and ulcers. Mercury would be also be injected into the nose and genitals. It was a drastic remedy whose side effects included loss of teeth, gum ulcerations, bone deterioration, nausea, diarrhoea and stinking salivation. All in all it was a distressing, doubtful and expensive treatment.

By the time of the Restoration venereal diseases were widespread and don't seem to have carried the stigma they acquired later. The poet and courtier Dorset wrote to a whore who had given him a dose: 'A little Advice and a great deal of Physick may in time restore you to that health I wish you had enjoyed a Sunday night instead of — your humble suffering servant.'

Royal decree: Henry VIII closed the Bankside brothels after an outbreak of syphilis. He is said to have been one of its victims.

Samuel Pepys's casual attitude to sex with maidservants and other men's wives was not uncommon in high places, and the result was widespread venereal disease. The poet Dryden said

Charles II caught one from Lady Shrewsbury, and his mistress Louise de Kéroualle, Duchess of Portsmouth, accused the king of infecting her. Pepys wrote that Dr Alexander Frazier, physician-in-ordinary, 'was helping the ladies at court to slip their calves, and great men of their Clap'. John Aubrey recalled that the playwright Sir William Davenant 'got a terrible clap of a black [dark-haired] handsome wench that lay in Axe Yard, Westminster...which cost him his nose'. Davenant got little sympathy, Aubrey writing that 'with which unlucky mischance many wits were too cruelly bold...'

In Leather Lane off Holborn a Madame Fourcade offered mercury baths and they were used by wealthy and noble sufferers. This establishment may have been known to Rochester's friend Henry Saville, who wrote to him in July 1678 as he was undergoing a cure so drastic and painful that 'he would rather have turned Turk'. There was a Dr Fourcade, who may have been related, a specialist in venereal diseases, who was sent by the King 'post-haste to Newmarket to help out' in June 1675.

Condoms were first manufactured commercially in the seventeenth century.[2] They were usually made from sheep's intestines and were used to avoid infection rather than pregnancy. Uncomfortable to wear, they were probably unknown to most whores and their clients, but they caught on in court circles and were hailed by the Earl of Rochester. In 1667 he published a pamphlet entitled *A Panegyric Upon Cundum* prophetically praising its efficacy against both disease and pregnancy: 'happy is the man who in his pocket keeps a well-made cundum...nor dreads the Ills of Shankers or Cordes or Buboes dire'. As a contraceptive it prevented 'big Belly and the squalling Brat'. He recommended it 'not only for the chaste Marriage Bed but the Filthiest Stews and Houses of Kept Dames'. The famous brothel-keeper Mother Wisebourne, or Wybourn, herself a sufferer from syphilis – she lost her looks because of it – recalled the importation of a gross of 'right Dutch cundums, newly imported from Holland by Mr Mendez the Jew' for the Duke of York. In 1708 a satire said 'Cundums were sold openly in St James's Park, in the Mall and Spring Gardens.' Earlier Pepys wrote that 'cundums could be bought in King Street almost outside the wall of St James Palace'. Some of these may have been made in London: the noted bawd Mother Douglas was said to have protected her clients' interests with 'Cundums' bought wholesale from J Jacobs of Oliver's Alley in the Strand. It is interesting that in the late eighteenth century they were known as 'English overcoats': for much of the twentieth century they were called 'French letters' in Britain.

James Boswell used condoms, and complained that the first time he wore one it gave him little satisfaction. This is how he described the encounter in his 1763 diary:

As I was coming home this night, I felt carnal inclinations raging through my frame...I went to St James's Park and... picked up a whore. For the first time did I engage in armour [a condom] which I found but a dull satisfaction. She who submitted to my lusty embraces was a young Shropshire girl, only seventeen, very well-looked, her name Elizabeth Parker.

Boswell used condoms again from time to time, but greatly preferred not to, which may account for the many infections with VD he suffered. He resolved to abstain until he found a girl he could be sure was disease-free, or was 'liked by some woman of fashion'. However, he was unable to keep his resolution. Later that same year he picked up a 'strong, jolly young damsel':

and taking her under the arm I conducted her to Westminster Bridge, and then in armour complete did I engage her upon this noble edifice. The whim of doing it there with the noble Thames rolling below us amused me much. Yet after the brutish appetite was sated, I could not but despise myself for being so closely united with such a low wretch.

Yet another encounter shows him again taking risks, and suffering the pangs of remorse for his recklessness:

so I sallied to the streets, and just at the bottom of my own, I picked up a fresh, agreeable young girl called Alice Gibbs. We went down a lane to a snug place, and I took out my armour, but she begged that I might not put it on, as the sport was much pleasanter without it, and as she was quite safe. I was so rash as to trust her, and had a very agreeable congress ...

Boswell bought his condoms from Mrs Phillips of Half Moon Street (now Bedford Street in Covent Garden). She also sold dildoes. Mrs Phillips had been the mistress of the Earl of Chesterfield when she was only thirteen, and ran through a legion of lovers before opening her sex shop in 1738. The great Georgian bawd Charlotte Hayes was another of her customers, supplying her clients with the 'famed new *Engines*, Implements for Safety of Gentlemen of Intrigue'. Mrs Phillips sold three different sizes of condom, and had an international clientele. In 1776 she 'hath lately had several orders for France, Spain, Portugal, Italy and other foreign places'. Her equivalent of the discreet barber-shop 'something for the weekend, sir' went: 'Captains of ships and gentlemen going abroad' could procure 'any quantity of the best goods on the shortest notice'. Later the shop was run by a woman named Perkins, who may have been Mrs Phillips's niece. She advertised 'all sorts of fine machines called cundums'.

James Boswell tells in his diary for 1763 how he caught a venereal disease from an actress called Louisa, with whom he had a brief affair. 'Too, too plain was Signor Gonorrhoea.' He was treated by his friend, the surgeon Andrew Douglas, who cured him with the use of mercury. The treatment took about a month and Boswell was charged five guineas, which he thought rather high.

Venereal diseases were rife. The anonymous author of the cumbersomely titled pamphlet *Some Considerations upon Street-walkers, with a Proposal for Lessening the Present Number of them* ... written in the second quarter of the eighteenth century, says:

The greatest Evil that attends this Vice, or could befall Mankind, is the propagation of that infectious disease called the *French Pox*, which in two centuries has made such HAVOCK all over *Europe*. In these Kingdoms, it seldom fails to attend Whoring, nowadays mistaken for Gallantry and Politeness, that a hale robust Constitution is esteemed a Mark of Ungentility and Illbreeding, and a healthy young Fellow is looked upon with the same View, as if he had spent his life in a Cottage...Men give it to their Wives, Women to their Husbands, or perhaps their Children; they to their Nurses, and the Nurses again to other Children; so that no Age, Sex or Condition can be entirely free from the Infection...

Cundum queen: the beautiful Constantia Phillips, child mistress of the Earl of Chesterfield and later owner of a shop selling sex aids.

Life was bleak for prostitutes who could not afford treatment, however ineffective. In *Roderick Random* (1748) Tobias Smollett described their descent into destitution:

I have often seen when I strolled about the streets at midnight, a number of naked wretches reduced to rags and filth, huddled together like swine in the corner of a dark alley; some of whom, but eighteen months before, I had known the favourites of the town, rolling in affluence and glittering in all the pomp of equipage and dress. And indeed the gradation is easily conceived: the most fashionable woman of the town is as liable to contagion as one in a much humbler sphere: she infects her admirers, her situation is public: she is avoided, neglected, unable to sustain her usual appearance, which however she strives to maintain as long as possible: her credit fails, she is obliged to retrench and become a night-walker, her malady gains ground, she tampers with her constitution and ruins it, her complexion fades, she grows nauseous to everybody, finds herself reduced to a starving condition, is tempted to pick pockets, is detected, committed to Newgate where she remains in a miserable condition, till she is discharged because the plaintiff will not appear to prosecute her. Nobody will afford her lodging, the symptoms of her distemper are grown outrageous, she sues to be admitted into a hospital where she is cured at the expense of her nose, she is turned out naked into the streets, depends on the addresses of the lowest class, is fain to allay the rage of hunger and cold with gin, degenerates into a brutal insensibility, rots and dies on a dung-hill.

The Victorians were obsessed with prostitution and venereal diseases. A series of studies and surveys examined every aspect of the problem, particularly health. An important and sympathetic Victorian commentator, Dr William Acton, in *Prostitution Considered in its Moral, Social and Sanitary Aspects*, one of the most reliable accounts of Victorian prostitution, wrote of 'rouged and whitewashed creatures, with painted lips and eyebrows, and false hair, accustomed to haunt Langham Place, portions of the New

Road, the Quadrant [in Regent Street]...the City Road, and the purlieus of the Lyceum' who were 'a mass of syphilis.' (Nash was warned that his elegant Quadrant would be used by prostitutes for street sex, but hoped that by using round pillars he would deter them. The Quadrant was eventually pulled down to stop the prostitutes using it for business, a sad loss to the city. The prostitutes continued to have sex there.)

Infection with syphilis and gonorrhoea was widespread, but guilt and secrecy made it difficult to gauge the true scale. The toll was great: in the 1830s, it was reckoned that 8,000 people died of venereal diseases each year, and in the capital's hospitals 2,700 children aged between eleven and sixteen were treated for syphilis annually. In 1856 three hospitals – Guy's, St Bartholomew's and King's College – treated 30,000 cases of VD between them. The children of infected parents were among the victims. In 1855, 269 babies under a year old died of syphilis in England and Wales. William Acton noted that syphilis was particularly deadly in children under a year old. Hereditary syphilis, which haunted the Victorian imagination, blighted generations. 'The innocent victims of syphilis are infinitely more numerous than the guilty; for it is a disease which follows vice down to the [third and fourth] generation...' (*The Lancet*, 1846). Victorian medical statistics have to be used with caution, but venereal diseases were certainly widespread, and there may have been some truth in the belief among doctors that the country was suffering an epidemic.

Lock Hospital, the first of the lock hospitals for the treatment of venereal diseases had been opened in Grosvenor Place in 1746 by William Bromfield, Surgeon to the Prince of Wales and to St George's Hospital. There was no revolutionary treatment, just a place where sufferers could find succour and soothing ointments and drugs. The need was immediately obvious – in 1758 442 patients were admitted, one hundred of them 'married women, many of whom were admitted almost naked, penniless and starving'. By 1808 the hospital was claiming it had cured 20,222 patients and by 1836 it had treated 44,973. Gaining admission was difficult: patients had to deposit the substantial sum of £1. 11s. 6d. and once 'cured' could not apply for readmission, which meant that reinfected prostitutes had little choice but to go on whoring and spreading infection. Most victims of venereal disease were treated as outpatients, although, as we shall see, whores could seldom find the privacy in their lodging houses for the recommended regime of personal hygiene which helped cure some venereal disease or keep it at bay. Hospitals allocated few beds to VD patients, and confined them in what were known as 'foul wards', as if to compound their shame. Certainly inmate whores were subjected to a regime of severity and penitential work.

There was no cure for syphilis until the discovery of Salvarsan early in the last century. So what could the lock hospitals do for their patients? The women were admitted as syphilitics, but many were suffering from a range of infections, particularly gonorrhoea. By teaching them basic personal hygiene the hospitals could at least alleviate some of their discomforts, and even cure others.

In 1864 the War Office and the Board of Admiralty, worried about the effects of syphilis on the efficiency of the armed forces, acted to stop the spread of the disease. The Contagious Diseases Acts of 1864–9 authorised the detention and medical examination of suspected prostitutes near barracks and dockyards. If they were found to be diseased they could be detained for a cure. After protests from women's rights campaigners these acts were repealed in 1886, although to judge by some observations of Bracebridge Hemyng, Henry Mayhew's collaborator on *London Labour and the London Poor*, the danger was great. A woman was pointed out to him as she solicited in the Knightsbridge Music Hall, 'who my informant told me he was positively assured had only yesterday had two buboes lanced ... she was so well-known that she obtained the soubriquet of "the Hospital" as she was so frequently an inmate of one, and she had so often sent others to a similar involuntary confinement'.

'It was estimated that in a seven-year period in the middle years of the century one-fifth of the army quartered in Britain and one-seventh of the navy based on British ports was infected with syphilis or gonorrhoea. In London the estimate was that 50,000 patients were treated each year for VD' (Fernando Henriques, *Prostitution and Society*, vol. 3). For comparison, in 1963 there were 1,099 cases of syphilis in England and Wales, and 31,547 cases of gonorrhoea.

During the public debate over the Contagious Diseases Act of 1866,

Berkeley Hill, surgeon to the Lock Hospital, made a valuable contribution in the *British Medical Journal* about the measures prostitutes in London took to cure themselves when infected. Hill, by the way, thought there were fewer than 15,000 prostitutes in the capital:

> But, passing to the question of disease among them, the result of my inquiries convinced me that nearly all of them sooner or later suffer from venereal disease of one kind or another. The women admitted this themselves; and the greater number could tell me what means they had employed to cure their disease, when they had it. The poorer ones, of course, had recourse to the hospital or workhouse; the richer had paid medical men to attend them. They all, nevertheless, use means of cure very inefficiently, and simply seek to get rid of pain or discomfort, without assuring themselves that their malady is cured before they return to prostitution... Even the women with whom men of the highest classes in society associate are nearly as careless in this respect as the wretched outcast of the street...
>
> The poor women have to contend with many difficulties to procure treatment. Most of them are very ignorant of all parts of London, except that in which they reside, or to which they resort to solicit the other sex. For instance, in the Ratcliffe Highway I found several women who had never heard of the Lock Hospital or the Royal Free Hospital; and some were even ignorant of the London Hospital close to them.

Berkeley Hill goes on to say that there were only about 150 beds in the whole of London for VD sufferers. Women who applied for help as outpatients had 'no convenience where they dwell for carrying out the directions of the surgeon'. For instance, in the low lodging houses of Drury Lane they were barred from the bedrooms until the night, and spent the day in crowded communal kitchens:

> water is scanty, and soap and towels are costly... Perhaps the best way of demonstrating the state of the women is to narrate a part of what I saw when visiting the several low districts of London...

On my visit to Drury Lane, I entered a street in which, I was told, 300 thieves and prostitutes live ... The first house I entered was a common lodging-house, and contained seventeen prostitutes ... Nine women were sitting round the room for warmth; most doing nothing, one or two sewing; one, very drunk, was talking in a loud voice, and munching a crust. I first interrogated the deputy. She said the women were very reckless; and though they always concealed their disease as long as possible, sooner or later she found it out, and they were sent off. When turned out, they usually applied for admission at the Royal Free Hospital ... otherwise they continued their prostitution, and attended as outpatients till they either recovered, or were admitted. When asked if the girls ever refrained from walking the streets while diseased, she said ''Tain't likely; if they did they must starve.'

In a court off Gray's Inn Lane, we visited four houses entirely occupied by prostitutes. In one of them, we found in a small room, two girls of 20 and 21 years old ... The first one told me that up to a year and a half ago she worked at the mantle trade; but their work became scarce and she eked out her living with prostitution. Last winter she caught the disease ... She remained in the Royal Free Hospital three months, in which time she had a sore throat and tongue, spots on the skin, and scabs in her hair. Since leaving the Royal Free Hospital she had attended the Lock Hospital as an out-patient, but continued her prostitution at the same time ...

Assistance is denied many through their being diseased, for the houses of most of the [reclamation] societies have no accommodation for such persons, and accordingly they are rejected. At the Magdalene Hospital (where applicants are at once cautioned that they cannot be admitted if they are diseased) in 1866, 284 women were examined previously to being sent before the committee; forty-five were rejected for being diseased, and of 131 admitted in an apparently healthy state, fourteen afterwards showed signs of syphilis. Again, out of 1,050 women who applied in one year to the Rescue Society for admission, 314 were or had previously been diseased.

A Merry Monarch

In 1660 the Restoration brought an inevitable reaction against kill-joy Puritanism. In an act of powerful symbolic significance, a gigantic maypole was erected in London after the arrival of Charles II. With the king came the exiled Cavalier aristocracy whose natural appetite for debauchery had been whetted, and who now set about making up for lost time. The king was by temperament and inclinations perfectly suited to take the leading role. The Earl of Rochester wrote of him:

> Peace is his aim, his gentleness is such,
> And love he loves, for he loves fucking much.
> Nor are his high desires above his strength;
> His sceptre and his prick are of a length...
> Restless he rolls about from whore to whore,
> A merry monarch, scandalous and poor.

The court quickly became 'one vast brothel'. The king, easygoing and cynical, had little patience for affairs of state, and spent much of his time with a string of mistresses, most of them aristocrats. His pander William Chiffinch also supplied him with whores and actresses. These women parade through the *Memoirs of the Count de Grammont*, their follies recorded along with those of the king. Barbara Villiers, Duchess of Cleveland, a faithless, rapacious and scheming nymphomaniac; the empty-headed and exasperating Frances Stuart, later Duchess of Richmond and Lennox, who resisted all Charles's attempts at seduction; the pious and hypocritical Frenchwoman Louise de Kéroualle; and Nell Gwyn, the orange girl who rose to command a king. Here is how de Grammont describes Frances Stuart:

> Her figure was more showy than engaging: it was hardly possible for a woman to have less wit, or more beauty. All her features were fine and regular, but her shape was not good: yet she was slender, straight enough, and taller than the generality of women, She was very graceful and danced well, and spoke French better than her mother tongue. She was well-bred, and possessed in perfection that air of dress which is so admired, and cannot be attained unless it be taken when young in France.
>
> (Memoirs, trans. Horace Walpole)

When Frances Stuart caught the king's eye he was already embroiled with Barbara Villiers, whose husband had been made Earl of Castlemaine. Pepys paid tribute to Villiers's beauty in August 1662: 'I glutted myself with looking on her' and two years later he wrote of 'Lady Castlemaine whom I do heartily adore'. He had dreams about her, in one of which he was 'admitted to use all the dalliance I desired with her'. She was widely disliked and feared, the diarist John Evelyn calling her 'the curse of our nation'. When Charles's wife Catherine of Braganza heard that Lady Castlemaine was to be one of her ladies of the bedchamber she fainted.

But her beauty could not hold the susceptible king's whole attention when Frances Stuart appeared at court. Villiers felt so confident of her hold over the king that she befriended Stuart: 'In confidence of her own charms, with the greatest indiscretion she often kept her to sleep. The king, who seldom neglected to visit the countess before she rose, seldom failed likewise to find Miss Stuart in bed with her... being confident... she could triumph over all the advantages which these opportunities could afford Miss Stewart: but she was quite mistaken' (de Grammont, *Memoirs*). Pepys called Stuart 'the greatest beauty I ever saw I think in my life; and if ever woman can, do exceed my lady Castlemaine'.

This challenge to Lady Castlemaine's hegemony over Charles disappeared when in 1667 Miss Stuart suddenly eloped with her cousin the Duke of Richmond, having resisted the king's good-natured but relentless attempts at seduction. Castlemaine over-played her hand: her extravagance, rages and greed all but destroyed Charles's affection. For a while her sexual stamina, enthusiasm and expertise completely infatuated him and made him oblivious to the harm she was doing to his reputation. There must have been another side to her. On occasion she must also have been an interesting, witty and charming companion, for the king, who was a bibliophile, music lover and patron of the great painters of the day, would have needed mental stimulation when sexually jaded. But she became a termagant, once forcing him to beg forgiveness on his knees. Finally he was willing to pay almost any price to get rid of her, lavishing sums from the privy purse, houses and a pension of £4,700 a year from the Post Office revenues on her.

Castlemaine had many lovers besides Charles. They included the Earl of Chesterfield, John Churchill, later to become the nation's greatest soldier and Duke of Marlborough, the playwright William Wycherley and the rope-dancer Jacob Hall. She was indiscreet enough as to have herself painted with Hall, and to pay him a salary. She was said to have seduced the running footman who accompanied her coach.

> She through her lackey's drawers, as he ran,
> Discerns love's cause, and a new flame began...
> Full forty men a day have swiv'd this whore,
> Yet like a bitch she wags her tail for more.

After she went to live in Paris in 1676, much to Charles's relief, she had affairs with the English ambassador Ralph Montague and, it was rumoured, the Archbishop of Paris. Another lover was an actor and highwayman named Cardonell Goodman, nicknamed Scum, who was found guilty of trying to poison two of her children.

This 'lewd imperial whore' had accumulated riches and titles, one estimate being that she consumed half a million pounds of public money. Much of it went in gambling, or was wasted on favourites.

She was described by Bishop Burnet as 'enormously vicious and ravenous'. In spite of all Charles made her Baroness Nonsuch, Countess of Southampton and Duchess of Cleveland. As she grew older her life became, if anything, more scandalous. When the body of Bishop Robert Braybrook, who died in 1440, was exhumed, it was found to be remarkably well preserved. The Duchess is said to have gone to see it and asked to be left alone. Afterwards it was noticed that the penis was missing. A document in the British Museum quotes a witness: 'and though some ladys of late have got Bishopricks for others, yet I have not heard of any but this that got one for herself' (Brian Masters, *The Mistresses of Charles II*).

But of course when we think of the king's mistresses we think first of Nell Gwyn, the incomparable commoner. Nell's origins are obscure. She was born about 1650 in London: her mother, who was often drunk on cheap brandy, kept 'something very close to a bawdy house'. Before she found employment at the King's Theatre as an orange girl, Nell sold fish in the streets and worked as a servant in a brothel. 'Her original profession, that of orange girl at the theatre, was one distinguished from prostitution more by its additional duties of fruit-selling than anything else'. (Antonia Fraser, *The Weaker Vessel*). Nell was next the mistress of the leading actor Charles Hart, who trained her to be an actress. Samuel Pepys, who saw her in John Fletcher's *The Humorous Lieutenant* in January 1666, wrote in his diary: 'Knipp took us all in, and brought to us Nelly, a most pretty woman, who acted the great part of Celia today very fine, and did it pretty well: I kissed her, and so did my wife; and a mighty pretty soul she is.'

She was at her best in comedy. Pepys was 'most infinitely displeased' to see her as the emperor's daughter in Dryden's tragedy *The Indian Emperour*, but he was bowled over when he saw her in the same author's *The Maiden Queene*: 'there is a comical part done by Nell ... that I can never hope ever to see the like done again ... so great performance of a comical part was never, I believe, in the world before as Nell do this ... '

There are many pictures of Nell, in words and paint. Sir Peter Lely's coquettish nude portrait of the recumbent beauty shows her long chestnut hair, inviting hazel eyes, fine breasts and unabashed sexuality. It cannot even hint at her ready wit and charm, sense of fun and total lack of pretension. Her time in a brothel and as an orange girl had equipped her to look after herself in a man's world, with a gift for instant repartee and a sometimes wounding sarcasm.

By July 1667 Nell was the mistress of the rake Lord Buckhurst, who made her independent of the theatre with an allowance of £100 a year. They soon fell out, as Pepys discovered from Orange Moll, a notorious bawd who had the licence to organise the orange girls at Drury Lane Theatre:

> Sir W. Pen and I had a great deal of discourse with Moll: who tells us that Nell is already left by my Lord Buckhurst, and that he makes sport of her, and swears that she hath had all she could get from him: And Hart, her great admirer, now hates her; and that she is very poor, and hath lost my Lady Castlemaine, who was her great friend also; but she is come to the House [the theatre] but is neglected by them all.

This was a brief setback for Nell. The king had seen her act, and although he was still embroiled with Castlemaine and two actresses, Moll Davies and Elizabeth Farley, he interrupted these affairs for a liaison with Nell. She moved from her lodgings in Drury Lane into rooms in Lincoln's Inn Fields, where her first son by Charles was born in 1670. This was virtually the end of her stage career. She next moved into Pall Mall, where she had another son by the king in 1671. Bishop Burnet wrote:

> Gwyn, the indiscreetest and wildest creature that ever was in court, continued to the end of the king's life in great favour, and was maintained at a vast expense. The Duke of Buckingham told me, that when she was first brought to the king, she asked only five hundred pounds a year: and the king refused it. But when he told me this, about four years after, he said she had got of the king about sixty thousand pounds. She acted all persons in so lively a manner, and was such a constant diversion to the king, that even a new mistress could not drive her away. But after all he never treated her with the decencies of a mistress, but rather

Pretty, witty Nellie: Nell Gwyn, the orange girl who became the mistress of Charles II. Bishop Burnet called her 'the indiscreetest and wildest creature that ever was in court'.

with the lewdness of a prostitute; as she had been indeed to a great many: and therefore she called the king her Charles the third. Since she had formerly been kept by two of that name.

(Peter Cunningham, *The Story of Nell Gwyn*)

While Nell was giving birth to her first son, Charles was being introduced to the enchanting young Frenchwoman Louise de Kéroualle by his sister Henrietta d'Orléans. The king's weakness for feminine charms was marked, and this elegant, refined and very beautiful woman was to become one of the great loves of his life. Apart from anything else, she was a welcome change from the raucous and vulgar Villiers and Gwyn. She was also proud, pompous, pious, virtuous, pretentious and greedy, faults that Nell Gwyn would exploit mercilessly. John Evelyn wrote of her 'childish simple baby face', and she exploited this pubescent quality, pouting and crying, especially when she saw how her tears affected the king. Her dark eyes had a slight cast, which led Nell to nickname her 'Squintabella', but many contemporaries were agreed that she was a great beauty.

It took Louise de Kéroualle a long time to succumb to Charles's seductions, and when she did it was on her terms. She was to be his official mistress, his *maîtresse en titre*, succeeding Castlemaine in that role. She thought she could cope with Nell, and perhaps eventually drive her from the king's affections. Louise was a patient woman, but the goading of the cheeky, vulgar Cockney actress drove her to distraction. In a letter Madame de Sévigné quotes Nell talking about Kéroualle's pretentiousness:

The duchess, says she, pretends to be a person of quality: she says she is related to the best families in France: whenever any person of distinction dies, she puts herself into mourning. If she be a person of such quality, why does she demean herself to be a courtezan? She ought to die with shame. As for me, it is my profession: I do not pretend to be anything better...

When Louise went into mourning for a French nobleman, Nell similarly mourned 'the Cham of Tartary', pointing out that she was as closely related to him as Louise was to the Frenchman.

Nell made constant fun of Louise, making up nicknames for her such as 'Weeping Willow'. She played on the public distrust of her French Catholic rival. Once Nell's coach was stopped in Oxford by an angry mob who mistook her for Louise; Nell put her head out of the window and called out, 'Pray, good people, be civil – I am the *Protestant* whore.'

When Louise unwisely bandied words with her Nell crushed her. On one occasion Nell appeared at Whitehall richly dressed, and Louise, who had been made Duchess of Portsmouth, said, 'Nelly, you are grown rich, I believe, by your dress. Why woman, you are fine enough to be a queen.' Nell replied, 'You are entirely right, madam, and I am whore enough to be a duchess.'

Nell didn't meddle in politics, unlike the other royal mistresses, and she was faithful to the king, which was almost unheard of. She was engagingly frank about her relationship with him, calling out 'Charles, I hope I shall have your company at night, shall I not?'

Poor Louise found others in royal circles even more insulting if less witty than Nell towards someone they regarded as little better than a whore and a French spy. After she caught a venereal disease from the king, doctors advised her to take the waters at Tunbridge Wells. She found that the house she had hoped to occupy was being used by the Marchioness of Worcester and asked her to leave on the basis that a duchess had priority over a marchioness. The marchioness replied that titles conferred as a reward for prostitution didn't count, and refused to leave.

Louise was to suffer two great shocks in her otherwise fairly untroubled relationship with Charles II. The first was the arrival at court of one of the most dazzling women in Europe, Hortense Mancini, niece of the French statesman Cardinal Mazarin. As wild and ungovernable a beauty as Nell Gwyn, she left a trail of lovers, male and female, wherever she went. Her husband was a madman who told Louis XIV that the angel Gabriel had told him to pass on to his majesty the instruction that he must immediately break off relations with Mademoiselle de la Vallière. Louis replied: 'The angel Gabriel has told *me* that you are mad.'

Soon Charles II and Hortense were having an affair, and Louise was inconsolable. Nell Gwyn pretended to go into mourning for

Louise's lost status. There were floods of tears, but it was not emotional blackmail that brought the king round. Hortense offended the king by throwing herself at the Prince of Monaco when he visited London. It was a brief fling, and Hortense's relations with Charles were soon restored, but he had by now had come to value Louise's loyalty and she resumed her supremacy in his affections. When James II, Charles's successor, fled England in 1688 Hortense lost her pension of £4,000 a year and was plunged into poverty. She died in 1699 in a Chelsea lodging house. John Evelyn said her end was hastened 'by the intemperate drinking of strong spirits'.

Louise's second great shock was the Popish Plot. Charles, who didn't believe a word of the lies that Titus Oates and Israel Tonge spread against Catholics, was almost the only man in the kingdom who behaved like a statesman, yet even he had to pretend to take the matter seriously. A rage against Popery gripped the nation and people lost their liberty and even their lives. Louise feared for hers, and several times said she wanted to go back to France. For a time she was terrified, and her natural discretion and caution served her well, keeping her out of the public eye. There were attempts to indict her, but gradually the terror died away as suspicions about Oates and his motives hardened and he was arrested, flogged and imprisoned for life. Louise felt that she had come through a very difficult period, with her relations with the king strengthened.

Then Louise, so faithful, so discreet, suddenly almost threw it all away. She fell in love with the most vicious man in Europe, Philippe de Vendôme, Grand Prior of France, a cynical ravisher of men, women and children who boasted that he had never been to bed sober. Their affair annoyed the normally complacent king, who ordered Vendôme out of England. The French nobleman refused to go, even to the king's face. Louise, painfully aware at last how she had compromised herself and fearful lest the Frenchman release their letters, pleaded with the French ambassador to help get rid of him. Eventually it was not Charles's order but a summons from Louis XIV that got Vendôme out of the country.

As usual, Charles forgave Louise. He understood that, now in her mid-thirties, she needed confirmation of her attractiveness by having an affair with a famous seducer. The affair if anything made Charles love her more, and on his deathbed in 1685 he told his brother, the future King James II, 'I have always loved her, and I die loving her.'

When Charles died things might have gone badly for Nell. A brilliant mimic, she had often made James the butt of her wit, and nicknamed him 'dismal Jimmy'. But Charles's last words had been 'Let not poor Nelly starve'; and eventually James granted her £1,500 a year for life, as well as paying off all her debts. The king's gifts had left her with a large estate: her house in Pall Mall was worth at least £10,000. Nevertheless, she still had financial problems.

Nell had made strenuous efforts to get the king to ennoble their first son, Charles. She would ostentatiously call her son 'you little bastard' and when the king remonstrated, would reply: 'Why, I have nothing else to call him.' No wonder Charles found her irresistible. He took the hint and although he bestowed no titles on Nell, he made the boy Duke of St Albans.

Nell's life effectively ended when the king died. She lingered on for two years, in increasingly poor health and in the end partly paralysed. Some attribute this to venereal disease caught from the king. There is no evidence for this, although, as we have seen, the king did give VD to Louise de Kéroualle. Nell was also under intolerable pressure to become a Catholic and dismiss her son's Protestant tutor. Her end was made more painful by the desertion of friends. She died in November 1687, aged about 37, and left money to the poor; although she remained a staunch Protestant to the end, this included £50 for the Catholic poor.

After Charles died Louise retired to France, and was soon in trouble with Louis XIV for criticising his mistress Madame de Maintenon. He was with difficulty dissuaded from sending her into exile. He gave her a generous pension, but her ungovernable extravagance – she was a reckless gambler – meant that she slowly sank into poverty. Time and again she asked Louis XIV to stop her creditors pursuing her, and time and again he obliged. She lived to be 85, and Voltaire, who saw her when she was a very old woman, said that she was still a beauty.

Charles II's male companions vied with him in sexual extravagance. Lord Rochester, wit, rake and poet of genius, was described by the Count de Gramont:

His manners were those of a lawless and wretched mounte-
bank; his delight was to haunt the stews, to debauch women, to
write filthy songs and lewd pamphlets; he spent his time in
gossiping with the maids of honour, broils with men of letters,
the receiving of insults, the giving of blows...For five years
together he was said to be drunk...Once with the Duke of
Buckingham he rented an inn on the Newmarket Road and
turned innkeeper, supplying the husbands with drink and
defiling their wives...

Rochester's verse is obscene even by the standards of his times.
Here is a sample which has the merit of giving some idea of how the
more dissolute members of the court spent their days and nights:

> I rise at eleven, I dine at two,
> I get drunk before seven, and the next thing I do
> I send for my whore when, for fear of the clap,
> I come in her hand and I spew in her lap.
> Then we quarrel and scold till I fall fast asleep,
> When the bitch, growing bold, to my pocket doth creep.
> She then slyly leaves me, and to revenge my affront,
> At once she bereaves me of money and cunt.
> I storm and I roar, and I fall in a rage,
> And, missing my whore, I bugger my page.

Bishop Burnet wrote that Rochester was 'naturally modest till the
court corrupted him'. He also paid tribute to his wit, which had 'a
peculiar brightness to which none could ever arrive'. Burnet
described some of the pranks Rochester got up to. Once the earl
dressed a footman as a sentry and posted him outside the apartments
of some high-born women involved in 'intrigues'. When the man
had gathered enough evidence Rochester would repair to the
country for a period in order to write up 'libels' or satires against the
women. He presented one of these to the king, hoping to amuse him.
But Rochester was drunk, and by mistake he handed over a satire he
had written about the king. As Burnet wrote: 'The king loved his
company for the diversion it afforded, better than his person, and

there was no love lost between them.' Rochester died aged 33, apparently after seeking the consolations of religion on his deathbed. He had shown conspicuous courage in battle against the Dutch, and some of his lyrics have a sincerity and feeling he was at pains to hide in his everyday life.

Another of Charles's cronies was George Villiers, the Duke of Buckingham, who acted as his pander. He became the lover of the Countess of Shrewsbury, and when her husband objected he killed him in a duel, with the countess looking on.

The depravity of the court is illustrated by a story told of Lord Southesk. His wife became the mistress of the Duke of York, and when he found out Southesk plotted revenge. According to the tale he sought out a prostitute with venereal disease, and after catching it gave it to his wife, hoping she would pass it on to the duke. But the duke had already ended the affair. After Southesk had gone to great trouble and expense to cure his own infection he caught it again from his wife. However, versions of this story have been told about other famous libertines.

The first King George came reluctantly to the throne from his kingdom of Hanover in 1714, bringing with him his mistresses the countesses von Platen and von der Schulenberg. The mountainously fat von Platen was known as Elephant and Castle; von der Schulenberg, tall and thin, was the Maypole. George had shut his wife away in a German castle because of an affair. Londoners hated the rapacious royal mistresses, and jeered them in the streets. On one occasion Schulenberg called out to an angry crowd, 'Goot peoples, vy you abuse us? Ve haf come only for your goots!' and got the perhaps predictable reply: 'Aye, damn ye! and for our chattels too!' The court recovered a little of the gaiety it had lost under Mary and Anne. That merciless chronicler of upper-class folly Horace Walpole told of a palace function in 1716: 'Happening to meet the Duchess of Portsmouth and the Duchess of Orkney, My Lady Dorchester exclaimed "Damme! Who'd have thought we three whores would have met here!"'

Towards the end of his life, in 1726, George I took as a mistress the 'pretty, slim and wilful' Ann Margaret Brett, daughter of the profligate Countess of Macclesfield. He did not enjoy her long, dying of apoplexy in June 1727.

His successor, George II, was a more thorough-going womaniser. He inherited from his father a *maîtresse en titre* in the Countess of Suffolk and had many affairs, the most important with Amalie Sophia von Walmoden, the lovely niece of Countess von Platen, described as 'blonde, sprightly and amiable'. He was absent so often visiting her in Hanover that in 1736 a wag placed a notice on the gate of St James's Palace:

> LOST OR STRAYED out of this Parish:
> A MAN who has left a wife and six children on the Parish.
> WHOEVER will give any Tidings of him
> to the Churchwardens so as he may be got again, shall receive
> Four Shillings and Six Pence REWARD
> Note: This REWARD will not be encreased,
> Nobody judging him to deserve a Crown [five shillings]

The period known as the Regency was not more depraved than the late eighteenth century, but it displayed in abundance all the aristocratic vices: gambling, whoring, gluttony, political chicanery. In the Prince of Wales himself, later Regent and then George IV, it had a symbol worthy of the age.

The story of the prince's youthful involvement with the actress Perdita Robinson will be told in the next chapter. Next he had an affair with the attractive and provocative Countess von Hardenburg, wife of a diplomat. When King George III was told about it the German couple were sent packing back to the Continent, but not before the prince had the opportunity to display the full gamut of his emotional hysteria and blackmail, including floods of tears, fainting, illnesses real or imagined: in a word, the vapours.

Burford in *Royal St James's* tells of the prince visiting the brothels of the West End, particularly those in King Street and King's Place, in the company of the Whig leader Charles James Fox and other raffish friends. There is a caricature of the prince being dunned by brothel-keepers who are holding up itemised bills, including £1,000 for 'first slice of a young tit only 12 years' and

£1,000 for 'uncommon diversions'. At the edge of the crowd a young girl holds a paper asking for payment for her lost maidenhead. The prince and his brother the Duke of Clarence were said to be regular visitors to Mrs Windsor's brothel in King's Place. He and another brother, the Duke of Cumberland, were reputed to be guests at the wealthy bawd Charlotte Hayes's Epsom mansion. Robert Huish, in his *Memoirs of George IV*, published not long after his subject's death, wrote: 'Previously to the attachment of the Prince to Mrs Fitzherbert, the passions, it was well known, treated him with as little reserve as the meanest of their votaries; and under their influence, he was continually seen in those pavilions of pleasure, where honour is not known, and female virtue for ever vanished.' The *Morning Post* informed its readers, when the prince was paying one of his many visits to Brighton: 'The visit of a certain gay, illustrious character at Brighton has frightened away a number of old maids, who used constantly to frequent that place. The history of [his] gallantries...has something in it so voluminous, and tremendous to boot, that the old tabbies shake in their boots when his R— H— is mentioned.'

One of the women the prince is believed to have made advances to was Georgiana, wife of the Duke of Devonshire. He lost interest when she became the mistress of Charles Grey. Georgiana wrote a shrewd and candid portrait of the twenty-year-old prince, which foreshadowed many of the troubles to come: 'The Prince of Wales is rather tall...He is inclined to be too fat, and looks too much like a woman in men's cloaths...His face is very handsome and he is fond of dress even to a tawdry degree...From the usual turn of his character and some shabby traits to his mistresses one should imagine he was more inclined to extravagance than generosity...'

Mrs Maria Fitzherbert set the pattern for the prince's mistresses: her full figure matched his taste, a taste that grew more opulent with the years. She had been twice widowed, and was a Roman Catholic, six years older than the prince. He first saw her in a box at the theatre and was soon 'really mad for love'. She was attracted and flattered, but would not live with him as his mistress. Since the Royal Marriage Act forbade him to marry a Catholic, there was an impasse, broken by his tears, tantrums, threats of suicide and finally a staged suicide attempt. They married in secret in 1785, when the prince was 22, and their association lasted on and off until 1803, often passionate on his side, less so on hers.

In April 1795 the prince married his cousin Caroline of Brunswick. They had not met before the wedding. The woman sent to accompany Caroline from Greenwich was the attractive and malicious Lady Jersey, with whom the prince had been dallying for some time. The prince and his bride disliked each other at first sight. She thought him too fat: he famously turned to James Harris, Lord Malmesbury, and whispered, 'Harris, I am not well; pray get me a glass of brandy.' Soon they were leading separate lives.

While still living with Mrs Fitzherbert the prince fell for Lady Hertford, a Tory grande dame, handsome, haughty, of more than ample figure and still beautiful, although she was getting on for fifty and a grandmother. Lady Stafford commented that 'elderly dames' seemed 'to be his taste', and from now on he pursued large and masterful older women. He had no luck with the prissy Lady Hertford, however, and had the usual hysterics, as Lady Bessborough, who suddenly became the object of his distracted passion, told her lover, Lord Granville Leveson Gower: 'Such a scene I never went through . . . [he] threw himself on his knees, and clasping me round, kissed my neck before I was aware of what he was doing. I screamed with vexation and fright; he continued sometimes struggling with me, sometimes sobbing and crying . . . and then that immense, grotesque figure flouncing about half on the couch, half on the ground.' Lady Bessborough realised that it was not she but Lady Hertford that had aroused this passion. Mrs Fitzherbert also knew, and might have overlooked his infatuation as she had his flings with the dancer Louise Hillisberg, the courtesans Elizabeth Armistead and Harriette Wilson, Lucy Howard, the singer Mrs Crouch and others. But the situation became impossible and they parted for good.

A long-standing complaint during the years they lived together was his love for Lady Jersey, another grandmother and nine years older than the prince. She was described as 'clever, unprincipled but beautiful and fascinating'. She was Lady of the Bedchamber to Princess Caroline and made malicious reports to the prince and his mother about Caroline's behaviour. She intercepted letters in which

Caroline referred to the queen as 'de old Begum' and 'Old Snuffy'. These were passed on to the queen, confirming her dislike of her daughter-in-law. Eventually Caroline had Lady Jersey dismissed from her household, which simply gave her more time to spend with the prince. When inevitably he tired of Jersey's over-blown charms he found her very hard to shake off. She ignored the high-born emissaries he sent to tell her the affair was over, embarrassed him in public and became a violent supporter of Caroline, by then queen, at her trial in 1820.

The last of George's matronly loves was Lady Conyngham, wife of an Irish peer who did very well out of the liaison, rising several ranks in the aristocracy. It is unlikely she ever became George's mistress, as they were both too fat.

> 'Tis pleasant at seasons to see how they sit,
> First cracking their nuts and then cracking their wit:
> Then quaffing their claret – then mingling their lips,
> Or tickling the fat about each other's hips.

She Gets the Money;
He Gets the Clap

The coming of the commercial theatres in the middle of the sixteenth century gave a new focus to the sex industry. The earliest of these inn-playhouses were the Cross Keys in Gracechurch Street in 1552 and its neighbour the Bell in 1560, then the Bull in Bishopsgate and the Belle Sauvage on Ludgate Hill in 1570. The latter was still standing in 1782, when the diarist Parson James Woodforde stayed there and was 'bit terribly by the Buggs last Night, but did not wake me'. Soon professional 'companies of players' were giving regular performances in the yards of inns, to the annoyance of the Common Council, which in 1574 decreed that no inn or tavern keeper should stage such shows.

Like so many attempts to curb popular pleasures this seems to have failed, for in 1580 the Privy Council ordered the destruction of the 'playing and dicing houses within the Liberties' and the expulsion of the players from the city, because 'the presence of private Rooms' led to 'immorality, gambling, intemperance, gathering of Vagrants and masterless Men, Thieves, Horse-stealers, Cozeners, practisers of Treason . . . leading to drunken affrays and bloodshed and [riots by] Apprentices and Factions'.

After more harassment from the City authorities some playhouses moved to Southwark and here the close association between whores and theatres which was to last for hundreds of years was reinforced. Two of the men most closely involved in the theatres on Bankside, Philip Henslowe and his son-in-law Edward Alleyn, were also whoremasters. Henslowe, a joiner who married a rich widow, bought up many of the Bankside brothels in a shrewd business move because, he reasoned, 'when play-houses are closed the stews flourish'. He had fingers in many pies: 'Freeholder, leaseholder, dyer, maltster, pawnbroker, stew-holder, banker, playhouse owner and bear gardener.' (W Rendle and P Norman, *Inns of Old Southwark*, 1888.) Eventually he and Alleyn managed the Rose theatre.

Alleyn, son of an innkeeper of Gray's Inn Road, was an actor, musician, usurer, property speculator and founder of Dulwich College. And whoremaster. His marriage to Henslowe's step-daughter Joan Woodward in 1592 meant that eventually all the family's brothel interests would be consolidated. Just how close to the wind these sex industry tycoons sailed is shown by the fact that while her husband was absent Joan and some of her whores were 'carted'. Alleyn does not seem to have been greatly troubled that his wife was treated like a common whore. In a letter he told her he was sorry that she had been 'by my lord mayor's officer made to ride in a cart'. After Joan died in 1623 Alleyn married Constance, daughter of the eminent poet and divine John Donne. Three brothels, the Bell, the Barge and the Cock, went into the marriage settlement of this Christian lady, and on her death the revenues went to charities.

Alleyn had become a churchwarden of St Saviour's in Southwark in 1610. Part of his revenues from the brothels was given to the churchwardens to distribute. Thus were the wages of sin sanitised.

Soon the theatres were themselves little better than brothels, thronged as they were with whores looking for pick-ups. Dryden commented bitterly in 'Poor Pensive Punk':

> The Playhouse Punks, who in a loose undress
> Each Night receive some Cullies' soft address;
> Reduc'd perhaps to the last poor half-crown
> A tawdry Gown and Petticoat put on
> Go to the House where they demurely sit
> Angling for Bubbles in the Noisy Pit...
> The Playhouse is their place of Traffic, where

> Nightly they sit to sell their rotten Ware.
> Tho' done in silence and Without a Cryer
> Yet he that bids the most is still the Buyer:
> For while he nibbles at her am'rous Trap
> She gets the Money: he gets the Clap...

(Punk is one of the many terms for prostitutes which have dropped out of use. Others included wagtails, jilts, doxies, cracks, mawkes, brims, brimstones, brown besses, trulls, trugmoldies, molls, blowsabellas, buttock-and-files, wagtails, tails, twiggers, judies and punchable nuns. Fireships were diseased prostitutes. Bawds were known as Mother or Mother Midnight. At one stage they were called lenas and nappers.)

Some of our best sources for the daily lives of whores are the plays of the period. John Marston's *The Dutch Courtesan* (1605) has the bawd Cocledemoy giving us a bawd's-eye view of the profession:

> List then: a Bawd, first for her profession or vocation, it is the most worshipfull of all the twelve companies;[3] for as that trade is most honourable that sells the best commodities – as the Draper is more worshipfull than the pointmaker, the Silk man more worshipfull than the Draper and the Goldsmith more honourable than both – so the Bawd above all. Her shop has the best ware, for where these sell but cloth satin and jewels, she sells divine virtues, as virginity, modesty and such rare gems: and those not like a petty chapman, by retail, but like a great merchant, by wholesale. And who are her Customers? Not base corn-cutters or sow-gelders, but most rare wealthy knights and more rare bountiful lords are her Customers. Again, whereas no trade or vocation profiteth but by the loss and displeasure of another – as the Merchant thrives not but by the Licentiousness of giddy and unsettled youth: the Lawyer but by the vexation of his client; the Physician but by the maladies of his patient – only my smooth-gummed Bawd lives by others' pleasure and only grows rich by others' rising. O! Mercifull gain! O! Righteous income!... 'tis most certain they must needs both

live well and die well, since most commonly they live in
Clerkenwell and die in Bridewell.

This play on words is clearly an old joke, as we shall see later.

Restoration theatre was marked by genius and obscenity. A
typical example is Wycherley's *The Country Wife*, in which a man
pretends to be a eunuch to wreak havoc among the ladies. In his *The
Plain Dealer* Widow Blackacre says: 'I say you are a worn-out
whoremaster at five and twenty, both in body and fortune: and
cannot be trusted by the common wenches of the town, lest you
should not pay 'em; nor by the wives of the town lest you should
pay 'em: so you want women, and would have me be your bawd to
procure 'em for you.'

To hear these words spoken by beautiful young actresses who
were known to be available added immensely to the fun. Until 1660
most women's parts were played by men. There were some
actresses, but they were foreign and hence suspect. When a troupe
of French actresses performed in the Red Bull and Fortune theatres
in Blackfriars in 1629 they were hissed off the stage as immoral.
Then in August 1660 a royal warrant allowed Englishwomen on to
the stage for the first time, so that plays might be 'useful and
instructive representations of human life'. The historian Macaulay
comments in his *History of England*: 'The fascination of sex was
called in to aid the fascination of art: and the young spectator saw,
with emotions unknown to the contemporaries of Shakespeare and
Jonson, tender and sprightly heroines personated by lovely women.
From the day on which the theatres were reopened they became
seminaries of vice . . . '

The two Wycherley plays and Vanbrugh's *Provoked Wife* were
castigated in Jeremy Collier's *A Short View of the Immorality and
Profaneness of the English Stage* for their 'smuttiness of expression
. . . swearing, profaneness and lewd application of scripture . . . abuse
of clergy . . . making their top characters libertines and giving them
success in their debauchery'.

It was at this time that the association of loose living and the
theatre, which had begun on Bankside in the days of Edward Alleyn,
became particularly evident. Masked whores prowled the theatres in

search of clients. Ladies of fashion also wore masks, and the ambiguity seems to have appealed to all. The theatres were divided by class and price into three sections, and the whores too: the pit, patronised by the most fashionable people, attracted the most expensive whores, the middle gallery attracted the middle class and their whores and the upper gallery, where the poorest playgoers went, was infested by common whores. This section was notorious for brawls over women. In fact the theatres were constantly in an uproar, and dramatists complained:

> Last, some there are, who take their first Degrees
> Of Lewdness, in our Middle Galleries:
> The Doughty BULLIES enter Bloody Drunk,
> Invade and grubble one another's Punk:
> They Caterwaul and make a dismal Rout,
> Call SONS of WHORES, and strike, but ne'er lugg-out:
> Thus, while for Paultry Punk they roar and stickle,
> They make it Bawdier than a CONVENTICLE.
>
> (quoted in Montague Summers,
> *The Restoration Theatre*, 1934)

The situation in the theatres, which have been likened to 'commodious brothels', was so bad that in 1704 Queen Anne issued an order for their better regulation. 'We do hereby strictly command, that no person of what quality soever presume to go behind the scenes, or come upon the stage, either before or during the acting of any play, that no woman be allowed or presume to wear a vizard mask in either of the Theatres, and that no person come into either House without paying the price established for their respective places...'

Mixing with the whores, patrons and actors were the orange girls, who sold oranges, playbills and, sometimes, themselves. Some hoped to become actresses, and perhaps the mistresses of rich men, and some succeeded in both. None succeeded like Nell Gwyn, the most famous of the orange girls, but there were others of note. Among those named in a list of common whores published in 1660 were Orange Nan and at the Theatre Royal Orange Betty Mackarel,

Play time: Hogarth shows orange girls and a prostitute touting for custom in an eighteenth-century theatre.

called 'the giantess Betty Mackarela'. Nobody took liberties with Betty, renowned for her strength, promiscuity and impudence. She could hold her own with the wits in the pit, 'hot at repartee with Orange Betty'.

In the 1660s two maids-of-honour, Frances Jennings and Goditha Price, disguised themselves as orange girls so that they could consult a fortune-teller anonymously. As Antonia Fraser says in *The Weaker Vessel*, it was easy to disguise the dumpy Mrs Price, but Frances, because of her 'brilliant fairness' and her 'particular grace of manner', was more difficult. The two women bought oranges and started selling them as a prank. The lovely Frances attracted the attention of a famous libertine, Harry Killigrew. When asked if he would buy some oranges he told Mrs Price, whom he mistook for a bawd: 'Not just now, but if you like to bring me this little girl tomorrow, it will be worth all the oranges in the shops to you.' He had kept his hand under Frances's chin, and now let it slip towards her bosom. When she angrily rebuked him he replied: 'Ha! Ha! but this is strange upon my honour! A little whore who tries to raise her fee by being ladylike and unwilling.'

Most women of low birth who achieved social distinction chose the same route as Nell Gwyn – the theatre. One such was 'Black Bess' who attracted the Earl of Dorset. Bess, who came of peasant stock and was a notorious prostitute, was called 'Dorset's whore' by a noblewoman. She replied that she was proud that she had pleased 'one man of wit' – and 'let all the coxombs dance to bed with you'.

By now the words actress and whore were synonyms. J H Wilson compiled a list of eighty women who appeared on the Restoration stage, and only roughly a quarter of them seem to have lived respectable lives:

> twelve who enjoyed an enduring reputation as courtesans or 'Misses' included the most celebrated performers such as Elizabeth Barry and Betty Boutel, an innocent-looking Fidelia, but off stage known as 'Chestnut-maned Boutel, whom all the Town F—ks'. The ladies, it should be said, thrived on this combination of public and private acclaim: Betty Boutel spent twenty-six years on the stage and Elizabeth Barry thirty-five.

As for Mrs Bracegirdle, who made a special parade of her virtue, she was described as one that had got 'more Money out of dissembling her Lewdness than other by professing it'; and it seems that she was kept at different times by both Congreve and Lord Scarsdale.

At least another twelve, either lazier, unluckier or less successful, are known to have left the theatre to become straightforward kept women or prostitutes. Another thirty are mentioned so briefly as being on the stage, that it is likely that many of them also vanished into prostitution.

(All The King's Ladies)

One of the greatest Restoration actresses, low-born Elizabeth Barry, made a disastrous stage debut in 1674 at the age of sixteen. Lord Rochester laid a wager with a friend that he could make a real actress of her. It wasn't the first time he had attempted such a transformation: Sarah Cooke, for all her ravishing looks, never amounted to anything even with Rochester's help. A satirist of the 1680s wrote after a performance by her: 'Mistaken Drab, back to thy mother's stall'. Elizabeth Barry seemed even less promising. She was no beauty, and had no discernible talent. Anthony Aston wrote of her: 'For some time they could make nothing of her; she could neither sing nor dance.'

For six months Rochester laboured with this unpromising material, to such effect that the actor-manager Thomas Betterton said he trained her 'to enter into the meaning of every sentiment; he taught her not only the proper cadence or sounding of the voice, but to seize also the passions, and adopt her whole behaviour to the situations of the characters'. The public agreed. Betterton described her triumphant return to the stage as 'incomparable'.

If on stage Mrs Barry was an ornament to her profession, off it she did little to improve its reputation. Gildon wrote: 'She has been a Rioter in her time.' She was described as 'the Finest Woman in the World upon the Stage, and the ugliest Woman off on't'. Her hardheartedness was notorious. Tom Browne said 'should you lie with her all night, she would not know you the next morning, unless you had another five pounds at your service.' The satirists were particularly bitter about the 'slattern Betty Barry':

> At thirty eight a very hopeful whore,
> The only one o' th' trade that's not profuse,
> (A policy was taught her by the Jews)
> Tho' still the highest bidder will she choose.

She was dissolute, bad-tempered and violent. She and her fellow cast member Betty Boutel quarrelled over a scarf just as Lee's play *The Rival Queens* was about to begin. As she uttered the line: 'Die, sorceress, die and all my wrongs die with thee!' Mrs Barry stabbed Mrs Boutel with such force that her blunted stage dagger penetrated Mrs Boutel's stays and pierced the flesh beneath.

Rochester had a long and difficult relationship with her, during which she bore him a daughter. He wrote her a series of despairing love letters, one of which complained: 'Tis impossible for me to curse you, but give me leave to pity myself, which is more than you will ever do for me.' As he lay stricken, virtually blind from disease, news was brought that she had borne him a daughter. He wrote to her: 'Madam, Your safe delivery has deliver'd me too from fears for your sake, which were, I promise you, as burthensome to me, as your great belly could be to you. Every thing has fallen out to my wish, for you are out of danger, and the child is of the soft sex I love...' Rochester later had the child removed briefly from its mother's care because of Mrs Barry's behaviour. He wrote to her: 'Madam, I am far from delighting in the grief I have given you, by taking away the child; and you, who made it so absolutely necessary for me to do so, must take that excuse from me, for all the ill nature of it... I hope very shortly to restore to you a finer girl than ever.'

After a long and successful career she retired to the country at Acton when she was in her fifties. She died in 1713, possibly from the bite of a rabid pet dog. Colley Cibber wrote in his obituary:

Mrs Barry, in *Characters of Greatness*, had a Presence of elevated Dignity, the Mien and Motion superb and gracefully Majestick; her Voice full, clear and strong, so that no Violence of Passion could be too much for her: and when Distress or Tenderness possess'd her, she subsided into the most affecting Melody and Softness. In the Art of exciting Pity she had a

Power beyond all the Actresses I have yet seen, or what your imagination can conceive.

An altogether more loveable actress-whore was George Anne Bellamy – the George was a mistake at her christening – the illegitimate daughter of Lord Tyrawley who reached the top of both professions around the middle of the eighteenth century. Baron von Archenholz wrote of her in *A Picture of England* in 1789: 'She was a most beautiful woman, an accomplished actress, and extraordinarily lascivious. Her whoring was as much from inclination as necessity.' There was clearly more to her than fleshly charms. Her intimate friends included Garrick, Fox, Lord Chesterfield and many other figures from the diplomatic and literary worlds of London. Women too were charmed, and even virtuous society women courted her and allowed their daughters to do so too. She was an early advocate of women's liberation, which may have helped.

Von Archenholz noted that 'her beauty, her wit, her intelligence, her talents, and her generosity and refined manners irresistibly attracted everyone to her'. Her friend Barney Thornton, proprietor of the mischievous *Drury Lane Journal*, wrote of her: 'Oh! the Mrs Bellamy! the fine, the charming, the Every Thing Mrs Bellamy – the best actress and the handsomest woman in the world!'

Her great success on the stage and her rich lovers could not always keep her out of the debtors' prison. The diplomat Count Haszlang tried to save her by giving her diplomatic immunity as his 'housekeeper'. But she died in poverty.

Some actress-whores nevertheless made fortunes, and several married into the aristocracy. Kitty Fisher was one of the most successful of these 'demi-reps'. According to von Archenholz, Kitty was 'indebted to nature for an uncommon portion of beauty, judgement, and wit, joined in a most agreeable and captivating vivacity'. She was also hard-headed, and despite 'the elegance with which she sacrificed to Venus' kept her mind on business.

The union of so many perfections procured the esteem, and fascinated the desires of those who prefer Cyprian delights to all the other pleasures of life. This lady knew her own merit; she demanded a hundred guineas a night for the use of her charms, and she was never without votaries, to whom the offering did not seem too exorbitant. Among these was the Duke of York, brother to the King; who one morning left fifty pounds on her toilet [dressing table]. This present so offended Miss Fisher that she declared that her doors should ever be shut against him in future; and to show by this most convincing proof how much she despised his present, she clapt the banknote between two slices of bread and butter, and ate it for breakfast.

Perhaps Kitty was given to exaggerating this episode. Casanova wrote: 'We went to see the well-known procuress Mrs Wells, and saw the celebrated courtesan Kitty Fisher who was waiting for the Duke of — to take her to a ball . . . she had on diamonds worth 5,000 francs . . . she had eaten a banknote for 1,000 guineas on a slice of bread and butter that very day . . . '

Kitty certainly had expensive tastes. She would demand impossible presents from her lovers, ate fresh strawberries in the depths of winter and for a time slept only with members of the House of Lords. Casanova was with the Earl of Pembroke in St James's Park when Kitty passed in her finery. Pembroke told him that he might have her for ten guineas, but when he offered her this sum she snubbed him, making it clear that her minimum rate was £50. Sir Joshua Reynolds painted her again and again, perhaps trying to capture that indefinable ingredient which great whores are said to have. He failed – she looks dull and rather stupid.

In 1743 the anonymous *Tricks of the Town Laid Open* described a theatre bawd sitting in the pit at the Playhouse surrounded by her whores. 'In the pit she keeps her office by the concourse of whores and gallants perpetually crowding about her for advice and assistance . . . having a little more business among the Quality and the Gentry . . . ' The prices of the girls were as low as 'a shilling and a glass of raspberry' and as high as five hundred guineas.

Another successful actress-whore was Nancy Dawson, who was born in Covent Garden to a porter/pimp father and greengrocer mother. Orphaned at an early age, she was put on the stage at Sadler's Wells and was something of a child prodigy, dancing and

Smutty songs: the actress/whore Nancy Dawson, who found fame as a child dancing and singing naughty songs.

playing musical instruments. In 1759 she found overnight fame dancing in John Gay's *The Beggar's Opera*. Two years later this vulgar, saucy and greedy little mercenary was celebrated in 'The Ballad of Nancy Dawson', sung to the tune of 'Here We Go Round the Mulberry Bush', once a children's favourite:

> Of all the girls in town
> The black, the fair, the red, the brown
> That dance and prance it up and down
> There's none like Nancy Dawson.

Two actress–whores who married into the peerage were Harriette Lamb and Betsy Farren. Betsy, daughter of a Cork surgeon, met Charles James Fox when she was appearing at Covent Garden, and after an affair with her he introduced her to the diminutive Earl of Derby, who married her. Betsy's haughty manner made her

High and mighty: the haughty actress Betsy Farren with her husband the Earl of Derby. She had previously been the mistress of the Whig leader Charles James Fox.

enemies, and there are caricatures of her towering comically over her husband.

Others had to be content with becoming mistresses of noblemen. Peg Woffington, daughter of a Dublin bricklayer, first became an actress and quickly attracted a string of rich admirers, among them David Garrick. They met in 1742, and lived together until a quarrel parted them for ever. Although she continued to play in his theatre they communicated only by note. She was joyously promiscuous, and for a time managed to combine sex with profit, choosing only rich and distinguished admirers. A tribute to her beauty was Jack Harris's note in his 1764 *List of Covent Garden Ladies* about another woman who called herself Peg Woffington: 'This young tit takes her name from the late celebrated actress, but we cannot allow her so great a share of beauty as Peggy had.'

Another courtesan who started her career in Dublin was Mrs Billington, who captivated audiences and lovers as a singer at Drury Lane and Covent Garden. Henriques in *Prostitution and Society* (vol. 2) says that she was lucky on her debut to attract the attention of the Viceroy, the Duke of Rutland, 'who became her devoted admirer'.

There were many others: Mrs Edwards and Frances Barton, later Mrs Abington, made the transition from the brothel to the stage. Frances quickly became a famous comic actress, but felt that the want of an education was holding her back. She took music lessons from a Mr Abington and they became lovers. However, Charlotte Hazzlewood's *Secret History of the Green Room* (1790) tells how a wealthy West Indian fell for her, spending three thousand pounds on her in the course of just three or four months. His friends, afraid that he would marry her, contacted his father back home, and the young man was ordered to return. Frances accompanied him to Portsmouth where he boarded ship, first telling her he would come back and marry her, and giving her a banknote for £500. Frances immediately returned to London and married Mr Abington. The weather prevented her former lover's ship sailing, and he too returned to London, hoping to spend a last night with Frances. When he knocked at her lodgings her servant told him that she had married Abington, and that they were enjoying the nuptial bed. The West Indian made such a commotion that Frances came to the window. When the West Indian complained and presumably asked for his money back, she offered to spend the night with him, an offer he accepted.

Another actress who found she could earn more by appearing at the fashionable brothels than in the theatre was Mrs Williams of Drury Lane. Mrs Harlowe of Covent Garden Theatre was said to specialise in making old men happy. And of course there was the eccentric beauty and exhibitionist Mary 'Perdita' Robinson, with whom the future George IV fell violently in love when he saw her on the stage at Drury Lane. Mary was born in Bristol and married an articled clerk at the age of fifteen. Their extravagant lifestyle led to imprisonment for debt, with their baby. When they were released she sought out the theatrical impresario David Garrick and he launched her upon a successful stage career. George, seventeen and Prince of Wales, wooed her with the promise of a fortune of £20,000

*Prinny's girl: the actress and writer Mary Robinson, known
as Perdita, was the first mistress of the Prince of Wales, later
George IV. She died ill and poor.*

when he came of age. He repeated the promise in writing, and Mary
gave up her stage career and became his mistress.

The prince soon tired of her, and she had difficulty getting any
money out of him. Eventually she settled for a capital sum of £5,000
and an annuity of £500, half of which her daughter was to have after
her death. It is said that from time to time, when short of money, she
appeared at Mrs Windsor's brothel in King's Place. She became one
of the Toasts of the Town and was for some time the mistress of the
dashing womaniser Colonel Banastre Tarleton, MP for Liverpool. In
later years, paralysed from the waist down, she wrote numerous
poems and plays, and received guests, including the prince, at her
home in St James's Place. She died in 1800 aged forty from 'acute
rheumatic disorder...aggravated by pecuniary distress'.

Great Bawds

The great bawds of the seventeenth and eighteenth centuries were the impresarios of whoredom. At a time when capital was short they begged, borrowed and stole to found luxurious brothels and staff them with fine girls. There were few business openings for women and they were a success story that has been overlooked in the literature of women's liberation. They had to be tough and single-minded to a degree, which should be borne in mind when we consider their reputation for flinty-hearted dealings with their customers and, particularly, their girls.

In 1660 John Garfield, author of the well-known guide to London harlotry *The Wand'ring Whore*, wrote another guide with the subtitle *The Unparalleled Practices of Mrs Fotheringham* while serving a spell in Newgate Prison. Priss Fotheringham was one of the great bawds of the age, and Garfield, who also gave details of 'whores, hectors and cullyrumpers' and their specialities, provides a list of those he said were the most famous contemporary bawds: apart from Priss Fotheringham, there were Mrs Cresswell, Betty Lawrence, Mrs Curtis, Mrs Smith, Mrs Bagley and Mrs Russell. There is no mention of Mrs Holland of the Holland's Leaguer, who was presumably long dead.

Priscilla or Priss Fotheringham (née Carsewell) is first heard of at the Middlesex sessions in July 1658 when she was charged with theft. She was sentenced to be hanged but was granted a conditional pardon by the new Lord Protector, Richard Cromwell. She married into the brothel-keeping family of the Fotheringhams. Her husband Edmund was her pimp and at least ten years younger than her.

*Sign language: Patience Russell, named by John Garfield
as one of the foremost late-seventeenth century bawds, carrying
the emblems of her profession, a mask and a fan.*

Priss had been afflicted by smallpox, and the effects were worsened by the treatment she got from a quack. Her husband was a bully who gave her venereal disease and beat her. She ran away with a sword cutter, taking much of her husband's money. When it was all spent the sword cutter deserted her, and she went back to her husband, who had her tried for theft. She spent about a year in Newgate. There she met the bawds Damaris Page and Mrs Cresswell. Then as now, prisons were universities of crime, and Priss had the best tutors. She also met there her chronicler, John Garfield.

As a whore Priss specialised in a particularly successful money-spinner known as 'chucking'. One of her early chroniclers reported: 'Priss stood on her head with naked Breech and Belly while four Cully-Rumpers chucked in sixteen half-crowns into her

Commoditie.' She performed this feat several times a day to acclaim from a crowd of enthusiastic fans. It made her brothel, the Six Windmills in Chiswell Street, Cripplegate Without, popular with customers from nearby taverns and also with customers from far wider afield.

In Newgate Prison a proposal was made that she should link the fortunes of her 'Chuck Office' with the Last and Lion in East Smithfield, whose speciality was fellatio. Its popular name was 'the Prick Office'.

Garfield recounts several anecdotes of the goings-on at Priss's brothel, including that of Mrs Cupid, an expert at the 'Chuck-game'. This tells how 'one evening French Dollars, Spanish Pistoles and English Half-Crowns were chuck'd in as plentifully pour'd in was the Rhenish Wine...the Half-Crowns chuckt into her Commoditie doing lesser harme than the Wine...for its smarting and searing quality'. When Priss performed she would allow only the best sack wine to be used because it smarted less. A half crown was a considerable sum at the time, and Garfield exclaimed: 'A Cunny is the dearest piece of flesh in the World!'

Priss died wealthy about 1668, probably in her mid-fifties. Although she must have been a fit, even athletic, woman to have performed the 'chuck ceremony' several times a day when younger, she was later much afflicted by disease. Garfield wrote in 1663 that she was 'now overgrown with age and overworn with her former all-too-frequent embraces'. Her husband was dying, 'rotten with syphilis'.

Another of the great bawds listed by Garfield, Mother Cresswell – bawds were usually known as Mother – achieved fame and influence rare for any woman of her time, and it must have been at least partly because of her unmatched understanding of men and their weaknesses. 'If Privy Councillors, Judges, Aldermen, Doctors, Dukes, Lords, Colonels, Knights and Squires may be made into beasts by stupid jades, how thinkest thou such Cullies can be handled by women of Sense and Understanding?' She also observed: 'A man will pay for a Duchess, yet all the while he embraces in Reality a common Strumpet.'

Elizabeth Cresswell was born about 1625, possibly in the village of Knockholt in Kent, into a well-connected family. By July 1658 she was a bawd, 'considered without rival in her wickedness'. In a case against her the constable John Marshall testified: 'Elizabeth Cresswell living in Bartholomew Close was found with divers Gentlemen and Women in her House at divers times: some of these women were sent to Bridewell'. She had tried to bribe the constable to hush up the case.

The following October she was again in trouble. By now she had moved to St Leonard's, Shoreditch, and a large number of angry neighbours told Westminster court that she 'did entertain divers loose Persons, Men and Women suspected to have committed bawdry... the said Elizabeth having lately taken a House... whereunto many Persons well-habited have resorted by Day as by Night... continued Drinking, Ranting, Dancing, Revelling, Swearing... demeaning themselves as well on the Lord's Day and Fast Days'. Witnesses told of seeing men and women going into rooms, 'the Woman having stript to her Bodice and Petticoat going into a room where they have shut the Casement and locked the Door... on the Lord's Day at noon some Company drunk about a Dozen bottles of Wine and further that divers Women suspected of Lightness have... declined the way to the House at the fore-gate when Neighbours looked on... and did surreptitiously slip in at a back gate whereby much infamy is brought upon the Place'.

The neighbours told of other outrages. One of the whores 'in the habit of a Gentlewoman began to propose a Health to the Privy Member of a Gentleman... and afterwards drank a Toast to her own Private Parts'. The court was told that some of the neighbours were ready to move away because 'their Daughters and maidservants werre often taken for Whores by the Men who frequent that House.'

Cresswell was sentenced to hard labour in the House of Correction, provided she was well enough – she suffered from a 'hacking cough'.

By 1660, when Charles II was on the throne, Mother Cresswell was considered to be at the head of her profession. She had a gift for advertising, boasting of her 'Beauties of all Complexions, from the cole-black clyng-fast to the golden lock'd insatiate, from the sleepy ey'd Slug to the lewd Fricatrix'. To find these beauties she corresponded with agents far and wide. No doubt London's slums provided her with many of the girls she needed.

She had a house among the brothels in Whetstone Park by Lincoln's Inn Fields where she sold 'Strong Waters and fresh-fac'd Wenches to all who had Guineas to buy them with', although this was not her principal place of business. That was in Back Alley off Moor Lane in Cripplegate – Moorgate Underground station stands on the site. This substantial building was described by the conman and wencher Richard Head in 1663. He and a companion went to Mother Cresswell's, 'formerly famous for the good Citizens' Wives that frequented her house . . . she still rode Admiral over all other Bawds about the Town'. They were led into a handsome room, and a servant brought them French wine and meats. Presently Mother Cresswell, described by Head as the 'old matron' although she was only in her forties, came in, greeting them by chucking them under the chin. She asked to see their money and then sent in a 'nice young girl' who touched his 'needle'. They could not agree a price, so she sent in 'a raving beauty'. Mother Cresswell claimed she was of 'superior birth serving only Persons of Quality'. Richard Head and Francis Kirkman in *The English Rogue* (1665) state that the girl asked for a guinea. Head offered half a crown and they agreed on half a guinea.

Five years later Mother Cresswell received the highest accolade. According to the Chevalier Phileas de Charles, 'His Majesty Charles II personally honoured her with his Presence and deigned to inspect her house . . . he saw that she had established a sound Organisation which administered a Network of Emissaries and Spies in England . . . as well as France'. Mother Cresswell also ran a kind of office in Millbank, according to E J Burford in *London: The Synfulle Citie* (1990), with a couple of 'secretaries' to supply whores to noblemen from the nearby court. She also owned a mansion in Clerkenwell.

In the City she had a 'house of assignation' where randy City wives and daughters could meet their lovers, and acted as agent for fallen gentlewomen, many of them from Cavalier familes ruined in the Civil War. These women, known as 'Countesses of the Exchange' or 'side-pillows', operated from the alleys round Gresham's Royal Exchange. It was said of these women: 'They master your Britches and take all your Riches'.

Mother Cresswell was one of the sponsors, along with Damaris Page and other madams, of the seditious pamphlet *The Poor Whores' Petition to Lady Castlemaine*, a sly blow aimed at the king's vicious and greedy mistress Barbara Villiers, Countess of Castlemaine and Duchess of Cleveland. The pamphlet, thought to have been written by the diarist John Evelyn, who detested Castlemaine, is ostensibly an appeal on behalf of poor whores 'in Dog and Bitch Yard, Lukener's Lane, Saffron Hill, Moorfields, Chiswell Street, Rosemary Lane, Nightingale Lane, Ratcliffe Highway, Well Close, Church Lane, East Smithfield &c'. It implores Castlemaine, because of her great experience in whoring, to help her poorer sisters whose houses had been pulled down and set on fire in the great apprentices' riots on Shrove Tuesday. In 1668 thousands of Londoner apprentices attacked and destroyed brothels in what became known as the Bawdy-House Riots. Apprentices traditionally attacked bawdy houses in an excess of moral zeal on Shrove Tuesday, their holiday. The riots of 1668 lasted five days. The rioters saw the bawdy-houses as symbolic of Charles II's 'flagrantly debauched' court. Pepys wrote that 'these idle fellows' regretted only that they had destroyed small bawdy houses and not 'the great bawdy house at Whitehall'. Charles II pertinently asked why the apprentices frequented the bawdy-houses if they wanted to pull them down. Eight of the riotous apprentices were executed.

Mother Cresswell was the lover of Sir Thomas Player, the city chamberlain, a man of turbulent political inclinations, and she stood by him in adversity. This rabble-rousing anti-Catholic frequently visited Mrs Cresswell's country house in Camberwell and gave lavish parties for political associates 'which turned into sexual orgies' (Burford, *London: The Synfulle Citie*). Mother Cresswell is said to have provided three hundred girls for one of these parties, a considerable feat of organisation. This party is described in the ballad 'Oates' Boarding School in Camberwell'. It concerns a fund-raising function for the anti-Catholic perjurer Titus Oates, the man who concocted the Popish Plot.

> There shall all Provision be made
> to entertain the Best.

Old Mother Cresswell of our Trade
For to rub-down our Guest.
Three hundred of the briskest Dames
in Park or Fields e'er fell
Whose am'rous Eyes shall charm the Flames
of the Saints at Camberwell.

Sir Thomas supported the succession to the throne of the Protestant Duke of Monmouth, bastard son of Charles II, which angered the Catholic heir, James Duke of York. Sir Thomas's support for Titus Oates was eventually to ruin him, and in the meantime he was borrowing large sums of money from Mother Cresswell for the cause. She tried to distance herself from these scandals, and retained a power in the underworld and among certain courtiers. A regular visitor was the king's confidant Sir Anthony Ashley-Cooper, later Lord Shaftesbury, who oscillated between whores and homosexuals. When the king declared James Duke of York his successor, there were riots in the City of London and Sir Thomas attacked the duke, saying the City would 'raise no more Money to pay for the Whores at Whitehall . . . and not for arbitrary government . . . the Crown is at the disposal of the Commons, not the King.' The authorities struck at Mother Cresswell, Player's financial backer. The *Imperial Protestant Mercury* reported in November 1681: 'The famous Madam Cresswell was on trial . . . at Westminster convicted after above thirty years practice of Bawdry . . . some of her Does most unkindly testifying against her.' Mother Cresswell later claimed that 'a malignant jury' had dispossessed her of her 'lovely habitation . . . which I have many years kept in Moorfields to the joy and comfort of the whole Amorous Republic'. But she was soon back in business.

Sir Thomas Player died in 1686 and a £300 bond Madam Cresswell had guaranteed for him was called in. For some reason she does not appear to have paid, although her will showed her to be still wealthy. Nathanael Thompson's *Loyal Songs* contained the line: 'Not being paid, the worn-out Cresswell's broke'. Her health too was broken, and the 'hacking cough' which was probably tuberculosis was getting worse. A contemporary portrait of her by Marcellus Laroon shows her face lined and careworn. She was sent to the Bridewell, where she died. She left £10 in her will for a sermon at her funeral, stipulating that it must speak well of her. James Grainger, who included her in his *Biographical History of England*, tells this improbable story of the sermon:

> A preacher was found with difficulty to undertake this task. He preached on the general subject of Mortality and concluded with saying: By the will of the deceased it is expected that I say nothing but well of her. All that I shall say of her therefore is this: she was born well, she liv'd well and she died well for she was born with the name Cresswell, she liv'd in Clerkenwell and she died in Bridewell.

As we have seen, this play on the word 'well' was far from new.

Mother Cresswell left substantial legacies to relatives and others, and two of her girls were given three years to pay off the debts they owed her. George Shell dedicated his book *The Whore's Rhetorick* to her 'because of her recent misfortunes': it is subtitled *Mrs Cresswell's Last Legacy*, and is a satirical manual for the instruction of whores. The fictional Mother Cresswell it depicts is described as livid in appearance, with hoary eyebrows, yellow gummy eyes, sagging breasts and a beard. It contains this passage satirising her instructions to young whores:

> You must not forget to use the natural accents of dying persons ... You must add to these ejaculations, aspirations, sighs, intermissions of words, and such like gallantries, whereby you may give your Mate to believe that you are melted, dissolved and wholly consumed in pleasure, though Ladies of large business are generally no more moved by an embrace, than if they were made of Wood or stone.

Not so improbable, really. Mother Cresswell was known to insist on her girls being sober, elegant, well-spoken and above all fragrant.

By the time she died Clerkenwell had become respectable, populated by immigrant Huguenots, and the high-class brothels had moved westwards to Covent Garden and St James's. There other madams would maintain the high traditions associated with Madam Cresswell, who would be long remembered for her bawdy cry of 'No money, no cunny.'

Finally, and briefly, this list of seventeenth-century bawds must include Damaris or Damarose Page, known to Pepys as 'The Great Bawd of the Seamen'. She operated in the Ratcliffe area, an ancient haunt of vice, and imported and exported whores, the former including Venetian women who were among the most expensive and expert in Europe. Her brothels at Ratcliffe were for poor seamen, but she also operated at the luxury end of the trade nearer the court. After her death in 1669 her will showed that she had made a fortune from vice.

THE SIN MAP OF FASHIONABLE LONDON IN THE EIGHTEENTH CENTURY. THIS RELATIVELY SMALL AREA PROVIDED EVERYTHING THE MAN OF PLEASURE REQUIRED — SEX, FOOD, DRINKING AND GAMBLING.

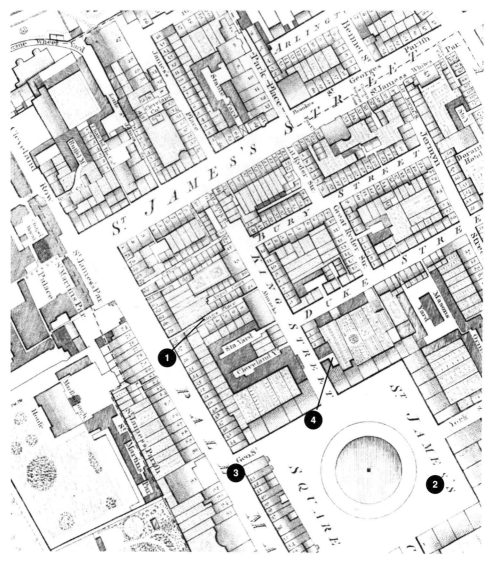

1. King's Place, epicentre of sin in Georgian London. This insignificant alley housed the brothels of, among others, Sarah Prendergast, Sarah Duberry, Mother Windsor, Black Harriott and, most celebrated of all, Charlotte Hayes.
2. St James's Square, an enclave of aristocracy. Less respectable inhabitants included Viscount Bolingbroke, 'a profligate tawdry fellow [who] swears that he will seduce any innocent girl whatsoever'. His wife was the promiscuous aristocrat Lady Diana Spencer. Lord Baltimore, who kept a harem and kidnapped and raped a shop girl, also lived there.
3. Pall Mall, a well-lit and popular fashionable promenade for two hundred years. At various times it housed Charles II's mistresses Nell Gwyn and Hortense Mancini as well as Almack's and Brooks's Club.
4. St James's Street housed clubs (including Boodle's and Crockford's), bagnios and brothels. The latter included Miss Fawkland's Temples of Love.

The Wild Eighteenth Century

We know nothing of the fourteenth-century whore Clarice la Claterballock except her extraordinary name, and for the medieval period as a whole and the centuries immediately following there are few records other than court reports. The eighteenth century is by contrast confessional and revelatory; the records of whoredom are profuse and London was if anything more profligate than in Stuart times. There was a gusto about eighteenth-century vice unmatched before or since. It had something to do with the size of the city. The fashionable worlds of vice and entertainment were contained within a few square miles, small enough for a sober man to cover on foot. It was an age of getting and spending. As the historian Sir Lewis Namier has written, every age has dominant terms which seemed to obsess men's thoughts, and those of Georgian England were property, contract, trade and profits. He might have added pleasure. More men were making more money from trade, banking, the stock market and the growing sales of luxury goods, and they, or in many cases, their sons had no moral scruples about how they spent it.

The pioneer criminologist and magistrate Patrick Colquhoun reckoned that around 1800 there were 50,000 women living partly by prostitution. As the population of London was just under one million this is a very high figure. Here is how he broke it down in his *Treatise on the Police of the Metropolis* in 1796:

1. Of the class of Well Educated women it is earnestly hoped the number does not exceed 2,000

2. Of the class composed above the rank of Menial Servants perhaps 3,000
3. Of the class who may have been employed as Menial Servants, or seduced in very early life, is conjectured in all parts of the town, including Wapping, and the streets adjoining the River, there may not be less, who live wholly by Prostitution, than 20,000
4. Of those in different ranks in Society, who live partly by Prostitution, including the multitude of low females, who cohabit with labourers and others without matrimony, there may be in all, in the Metropolis, about 25,000

This is just an informed guess, and Colquhoun is tentative in his conclusions, but his estimate is close to that reached by others. In 1789 the German visitor Baron von Archenholz in *A Picture of England*, said 'London is said to contain 50,000 prostitutes, without reckoning kept mistresses'. Von Archenholz, an acute and well-informed observer, continues:

The most wretched of these live with matrons, who lodge, board and clothe them. The dress worn by the very lowest of them is silk, according to the custom which luxury has generally introduced into England. Some times they escape from their prison, with their little wardrobe under their arms, and trade on their own bottoms, when, if they are unfortunate or happen not to be economical, they are soon dragged to gaol by their creditors.

The uncertainty of receiving payment makes the housekeepers charge them double the common price for their lodgings. They hire by the week a first floor, and pay for it more than the owner gives for the whole premises, taxes included...Their apartments are elegantly, and sometimes magnificently furnished; they keep several servants, and some have their own carriages. Many of them have annuities paid them by their seducers, and others settlements into which they have surprised their lovers in a moment of intoxication...

Besides the immense number of women who live in ready-furnished apartments, there are many noted houses in the neighbourhood of St James's where a great number are kept for people of fashion...

Let it be recollected, however, that I speak only of a few, for it is very uncommon to find such precious qualities among those vile prostitutes whose kind of life stifles in their breasts every seed of virtue. At all seasons of the year they sally out towards the dusk, arrayed in the most gaudy colours, and fill the principal streets. They accost the passengers and offer to accompany them; they even surround them in crowds, stop and overwhelm them with caresses and entreaties. The better kind, however, content themselves with walking about till they themselves are addressed...

I have beheld with a surprise mingled with terror, girls from eight to nine years old make a proffer of their charms; and such is the corruption of the human heart, that even they have their lovers.

Von Archenholz has here surveyed the late eighteenth-century sex industry in London. When we look in greater detail it is even more varied and colourful, or wretched. When Colquhoun wrote of the 'profligate state of Society in vulgar life', he could have pointed to Covent Garden, for long the centre of the capital's vice and entertainment industries. In the eighteenth century there were public houses in the area where a kind of striptease was performed by 'posture molls'. They 'stripped naked and mounted upon the table to show their beauties' and also offered flagellation. The Rose Tavern was called 'that black school of SODOM' by the satirical writer Thomas Brown, who said it was a place where men 'who by proficiency in the Science of Debauchery [are] called Flogging Cullies...these unnatural Beasts pay an excellent Price for being scourged on their posteriors by Posture Molls.' The entertainments were not for the squeamish: women would wrestle with each other, stripped to the waist while the customers, who included homosexuals and transvestites, cheered and took bets. At the Shakespeare's Head there was a 'Whores' Club' which met every Sunday, presided over by a 'Pimpmaster General'. There were also 'mollies' houses' and clubs for homosexuals, among them the Bull and Butcher, the Spiller's Head, the Fountain, the Sun and the Bull's Head. Respectable City businessmen would go there to pick up young homosexuals.

Covent Garden swarmed with criminals of all kinds, pickpockets, footpads – violent robbers – fraudsters, even on occasion highwaymen. Many of the nearby courts and alleys were home to thieves and prostitutes, and the rich pickings also attracted criminals from outside the area. According to the *Tatler*, every house in Covent Garden itself 'from cellar to garret is inhabited by nymphs of different orders so that persons of every rank can be accommodated'.

For men of the town and sex tourists there were guides to the charms on offer. John Garfield's *The Wand'ring Whore* of 1660 had listed the best-known women of the town, including the Queen of Morocco, Peg the Seaman's Wife, Long-Haired Mrs Spencer of Spitalfields, Mrs Osbridge's Scolding Daughter (how could this possibly be a turn-on?) and Mrs Osbridge herself, said to have practised within Bedlam. Other well-known whores were Jenny Middleton, Moll Hinton (who may have given the Earl of Dorset a venereal disease), Sue Willis and Doll Chamberlain. Garfield mentions the veteran whore Fair Rosamund Sugarcunt, and Burford says she operated around the Law Courts. London pullulated with brothels: in some areas tents were set up and the customers queued outside.

In 1691, among other guides to vice, *A Catalogue of Jilts, Cracks & Prostitutes, Nightwalkers, Whores, She-friends, Kind Women and other of the Linnen-lifting Tribe* appeared. It was a list of 21 women who could be found in the cloisters of St Bartholomew's Church during Bartholomew Fair in Smithfield. It listed the women's physical attributes: 'Mary Holland, tall graceful and comely, shy of her favours but may be mollified at a cost of £20. Elizabeth Holland [her sister] indifferent to Money but a Supper and Two Guineas will tempt her.' Dorothy Roberts could be had for a bottle of wine; Posture Moll, a flagellant, wanted only half a crown; Mrs Whitby, who had obviously come down in the world, had previously charged more than five guineas but would now accept ten shillings from 'any ordinary fellow'. There are two black women in the list: 'Bridget Williams, a pretty little Negress ... not yet mistress of her profession so can be offered half-a-crown ... and bullied out of her

Tricks of the trade: a pack of whores and pickpockets rob a susceptible young man under the Piazza in Covent Garden.

money again' and Mrs Sarah Heath, 'a Negress...her fee is higher...will make no concession about fee'.

Von Archenholz writes in *A Picture of England*:

A tavern-keeper in Drury Lane prints every year an account of the women of the town entitled Harris's *List of Covent Garden Cyprians*. In it the most exact description is given of their names, their lodgings, their faces, their manners, their talents and even their tricks. It must of course happen that there will be sometimes a little degree of partiality in these details; however, notwithstanding this, 8,000 copies are sold annually...

Jack Harris is believed to have been head-waiter at the Shakespeare's Head tavern in Covent Garden. He began to circulate handwritten lists of whores in the 1740s. Soon he was indeed selling

8,000 printed copies of each edition. Not all the descriptions are flattering, but the list launched many young women into fame and fortune. Harris was charged with being a pimp, a charge he was proud to admit. 'The whole amount of the Charge against me is that I am a Pimp . . . I grant it. I need not be ashamed of the Profession from its Antiquity. Nay!' Harris described himself as 'insinuating, dissembling, flattering, cringing, fawning, conniving, with philosophy enough to bear a kicking and a face as great a (seeming) barrier to incontinence as eunuchism'. He had agents all over London seeking out new faces for his *List*, every stage coach and waggon would be met, and once a year he went to Ireland, where he said the girls were among his most beautiful recruits. He was proud he was responsible for seeing that London was so well stocked with fine whores, whom he had taught himself to become 'perfect adepts'. For this service he charged the whores a fifth of their income, and set up a kind of whores' trade union, one of whose main functions seems to have been collecting his fees. He died in 1765, probably wealthy, as he had many irons in the fire. One night he heard one of the foremost women on his *List*, Fanny Murray, arguing with a client who couldn't afford her price of two guineas, as he had only 5s. 6d. Harris lent him the remainder on the security of his sword and peruke. No doubt he made a profit on this transaction.

Harris's book bears the title *List of Covent Garden Ladies Or The New Atlantis*, and the sub-title *Containing an exact description of the Persons, Tempers and Accomplishments of the several Ladies of Pleasure who frequent COVENT-GARDEN and other Parts of the Metropolis*. In the introduction, presumably written by Harris himself, he says that 'were there no common women, young fellows would be more earnest and assiduous in their attacks on the virtuous'. This theme, that the world is full of vice and that virtuous women would be ravished or seduced but for the safety valve of the whore, is repeated:

It cannot be denied by anyone, that is not utterly unacquainted with the world, that public stews are an absolute necessity for the preservation of chastity and virtue; and it must be acknowledged that there was never a greater occasion for such licence than at present, in order to oppose the prevailing schemes of gallantry, the intent of which seems to be to corrupt all without distinction, and to make a grand seraglio of the whole nation. May then both Laws and Magistrates be kind to those public-spirited Nymphs, who contribute to stem the torrent of corruption ...

Attach yourselves with constancy to your keepers, soothe their amorous flames, preserve their ardour unabated. With every artifice rouse ancient desire, and make them young once more. Reflect, that if you neglect your keeper, your lusty gallant must lack his necessary supply. Keepers are the sinews of your trade; may they multiply instead of decreasing; may they always be ready and willing to keep up the call as honest Nature bids; so shall the public good be invigorated, the cause of virtue promoted, and the most abominable of all vices entirely rooted out.

Jack Harris had a weakness for *doubles entendres*, as his appeal to the susceptibilities of seafarers over the charms of a Miss Devonshire of Queen Anne Street shows: 'Many a man of war has been her willing prisoner, and paid a proper ransom; her port is said to be well-guarded by a light brown chevaux-de-frieze ... the entry is rather straight; but when once in there is very good riding ... she is ever ready for an engagement, cares not how soon she comes to close quarters, and loves to fight yard arm and yard arm, and be briskly boarded.' Or he could be more frankly pornographic. This is Miss Wilkinson of 10 Bull and Mouth Street:

a pair of sweet lips that demand the burning kiss and never receive it without paying interest ... Descend a little lower and behold the semi snowballs ... that want not the support of stays; whose truly elastic state never suffers the pressure, however severe, to remain but boldly recovers its tempting smoothness. Next take a view of nature centrally; no folding lapel; no gaping orifice; no horrid gulph is here, but the loving lips tenderly kiss each other, and shelter from the cold a small but easily stretched passage, whose depth none but the blind boy has liberty to fathom; she is a native of Oxfordshire, and has been a visitor to the town about one year, is generally to be met with at home at every hour excepting ten at night, at which time she visits a favourite gentleman of the Temple.

His description of a Miss South, who lived in Thatched House Court, St James's, makes her sound rather lively. 'Young, genteelly educated, a fine Woman full of Fashion and as sound as a Roach, with black piercing Eyes, much Tenderness in Looks, dark Hair and delicate Features, snowy Bosom and elegant Shoulders and Sprightly Behaviour – but she will have her Price.' Her price started at five guineas. His description in the 1764 edition of Lucy Seales of York Buildings, Duke Street, is less enthusiastic: 'very genteel and well-made Lass, with black eyes and light brown hair . . . she has not seen much service yet . . . she shows little passion in her amours'.

Many of the entries are ambiguous. 'Mrs Paterson alias Jackson. Haymarket. This piece of affectation is the daughter of a strolling player and was for some time an actress . . . returning to England was taken into keeping by a Jew whom she soon left . . . because the Israelite, who was not one of the richest, paid her but poorly.'

Harris also tells us that Lord Chesterfield, urbane writer of the famous Letters liked to have his eyelids 'licked by two naked whores'.

After Harris died hack writers were employed to keep the *List* going. Some of the later entries are more like hatchet jobs than advertisements. For example, it is difficult to believe that Miss Grafton of Bow Street paid for this:

that bubble vanity has so elated her that self alone engrosses all her thoughts, and little I, the heroine of all her thoughts, is sure eternally to be her table talk . . . a woman of her cast is hardly worth notice unless for mere amusement; no intimate acquaintance or connection should be made with her, as she is well known to have as tender a regard for the male part of the sex as a wolf for a lamb . . . a poor ignorant Irishman piping hot arrived, fell into her clutches and she fleeced the poor devil so much that she scarce left him with a coat to his back, and insolently laughed at him in prison where he was confined for debts contracted for her use; she may be found at the Cat in the Strand almost every evening, and sometimes at the Blakeney's Head in Bow Street, though this house is not calculated for this lady, as they preserve decency and good order.

The later editions make it clear that Covent Garden was no longer the main focus of high-class harlotry, as many of the women have addresses elsewhere. This is Mrs Griffin with an address near Union Stairs in Wapping. The entry indicates clearly that she is a sailor's woman, and her price, five shillings, gives the game away.

Come on: a Jewish customer is welcomed by a fashionable young whore to an eighteenth-century brothel. Her maid holds the door discreetly half-open.

This is a comely woman, about forty, and boasts she can give more pleasure than a dozen raw girls. Indeed she has acquired great experience in the course of twenty years of study...She is perfect mistress of her actions, and can proceed regularly from the dart of her tongue, the soft tickle of her hand, to the ecstatic squeeze of her thighs; the enchanting twine of her legs; the elaborate suction of her lower lips, and the melting flood of delights with which she constantly bedews the mossy root of the tree of life... 'tho past her meridian, she is still agreeable, her eyes are black as well as her hair...Five shillings is her price, and she earns it with great industry...

The *List* for 1788 advertises a Miss Johnson of Goodge Street:

The raven-coloured tresses of Miss Johnson are pleasing, and one characteristic of strength and ability in the wars of Venus. Indeed this fair one is not afraid of work, but will undergo a great deal of labour in the action; she sings, dances, will drink a cheerful glass and is a good companion. She has such a noble elasticity in her loins that she can cast her lover to a pleasing height and receive him again with the utmost dexterity. Her price is one pound one and for her person and amorous qualifications she is well worth the money.

These later entries lack Jack Harris's playfulness, suggesting that a change had come over the business of selling sex. In 1795 two booksellers were jailed for publishing Harris's *List*.

Towards the end of the eighteenth century another guide book was *The Ranger's Magazine*. 'This published, among a great deal that was scatological, a "Monthly list of the Covent Garden Cyprians; or the Man of Pleasure's *Vade Mecum*"'. (Henriques, *Prostitution and Society*, Vol 2).[4]

The choice for the man of pleasure in the eighteenth century was breathtaking, and makes the modern city with its sex shops and massage parlours seem dull. Apart from the posture molls, the mollies' houses, the brothels and bagnios, there were taverns with rooms full of prostitutes. When customers asked for the company of a woman these whores were sent out one at a time. Taverns which kept these women included Bob Derry's School of Venus in Maiden Lane and the Golden Lion in the Strand. The girls were known as 'tavern players'.

Casanova encountered this interesting custom at the Star Tavern in Pall Mall. The landlord told him that if he rejected a girl he had to give her a shilling. After he had rejected twenty he complained to his profligate friend Henry Herbert, Earl of Pembroke, an expert in the ways of vice in London. Pembroke explained how the racket worked. The women were kept in a back room 'like sheep in a fold waiting to be let out', and the landlord, who got a cut from the shillings of those who were rejected, naturally sent the least attractive out first. Pembroke told Casanova that he should have made it clear from the outset that he was prepared to pay four, eight, or even twelve guineas for a high-class whore.

The sign of the Dog and Duck tavern, a haunt of
criminals and prostitutes for many years.

London abounded in tea-gardens and pleasure gardens, of which Vauxhall and Ranelagh were the most famous. Some were noted for the licentiousness of their clients. The Dog and Duck in St George's Fields south of the river shared the low reputation of the whole area. It continued in business from 1642 to 1812. Here aspiring young criminals would go to watch the highwaymen mount up and say goodbye to their 'flashy women' before setting off to earn their living on the highways. Henriques says that it was a favourite resort of whores and their ponces. Another author wrote that 'some of the most beautiful middle-class women of the town, their bullies and suchlike young men, who came there, with no thoughts for the consequences, refresh the thirsty throats of their girls with fiery drinks' (J P Malcolm, *Anecdotes of the Manners and Customs of London During the Eighteenth Century*, 1810). David Garrick in his *Prologue to the Maid of the Oaks* described the riotous goings-on:

> St George's Fields, with taste and fashion struck,
> Display Arcadia at the Dog and Duck;
> And Drury Misses here in tawdry pride,
> Are there 'Pastoras' by the fountain side;
> To frowsy bowers they reel through midnight damps,
> With fauns half drunk and Dryads breaking lamps.

Vauxhall, one of the most popular of all the pleasure gardens, had its origins in the seventeenth century. Pepys, who is frank about his own weaknesses, was shocked by the behaviour of the visitors. His diary entry for 27 July 1688 reads: 'Over the water with my wife and Deb and Mercer...and eat there and walked; and observed how coarse some young gallants from the town were. They go into the arbours where is no man and ravish the woman there, and the audacity of vice in our time much enraged me.' Things had certainly not improved in the next century.

Vauxhall had many shady and secluded arbours which were ideal for prostitution. 'Those who purposely lost their way in the bushes did not bother to be discreet and made a tremendous uproar, no doubt added to by the screams of respectable women being raped.' (Henriques, *Prostitution and Society*, vol. 2) Yet the gardens were also popular with respectable Londoners of all classes and remained open until 1859. Vauxhall, where the entrance charge was 1s., was seen as more democratic than Ranelagh, which cost 2s. 6d. and was more exclusive and also more raffish. Vauxhall was similar to Cremorne Gardens, which opened on a riverside site in Chelsea in 1830. By day they were typical pleasure gardens used by families for picnics, fireworks, concerts and so on, but at night the atmosphere changed. The *Saturday Review* commented that 'none but an idiot' could fail to notice that at dusk the women there were augmented by 'a large accession of fallen [women] characters'. Cremorne fell victim to Victorian values: it lost its licence in 1871, and closed six years later.

Moll King, Coffee Queen

Covent Garden had many attractions besides its 'posture molls' and the 'mollies' houses' for homosexuals. Coffee houses began as bastions of male exclusivity, then were gradually invaded by whores looking for pick-ups. The most notorious was Tom and Moll King's coffee house, located in the wooden shacks running the length of one side of the Piazza. It attracted fashionable whores 'all dressed up fine and pritty and elegantly as if going to a box at the Opera'.

In the 1720s and 1730s Moll King's was the most important meeting place for the worlds of fashion, harlotry high and low, crime and bohemian intellectualism, the haunt of 'bucks, bloods, demireps and choyce spirits of all London'. Though never a brothel it was certainly disorderly, and gullible men who had too much to drink might awake to find themselves with a large bill for breaking the crockery – a supply of broken crockery was kept hidden for this confidence trick.

As a young girl Moll had been a street fruit-seller in Covent Garden market, loved for her good looks and peculiar sweetness of temper. She lost both eventually, as the anonymous *Life and Character of Moll King* of 1747 makes clear. Among her friends were celebrated whores, including Sally Salisbury, the most famous of her time. Moll married another street seller, Tom King, but left him when he began to beat her and briefly became a whore. After they were reconciled Moll said she had always loved him, and had only left him because he was having an affair with a vicious prostitute who beat her up.

They went into business in a small way selling coffee at a penny a dish in Covent Garden from 'a little hovel' in front of the church. Their shop soon expanded, becoming a magnet for 'young rakes and their pretty misses ... Every swain, even from the Star and Garter to the coffee house boy, might be sure of finding a nymph in waiting at Moll's Fair Reception House, as she was pleased to term it, and the most squeamish beau, surely, could not refuse such dainties and the very sweetest too that ever Covent Garden afforded.' Many of the criminals and their molls talked flash, the underworld vocabulary, because informers were ever ready to 'peach' for money.[5]

Moll herself was no longer so sweet. She had become a hard businesswoman, interested in little except money, of which she was making a great deal. She lent money to prostitutes at high interest. 'Notwithstanding her temper, we do not find that she ever put anyone in prison [for debt] unless they used her very ill'. She also lent money to the poor market traders at two shillings or half a crown in the pound. 'Town Misses', as whores were sometimes known, had to pay more: Moll, now become oddly hypocritical, 'made a great distinction between industry and vice'.

Her coffee house was now the most talked-about resort of whores and their customers. The owners of nearby brothels were dismayed to find their girls taking time off to have a drink there, or worse, meeting men there and taking them somewhere else to seal their bargains. 'The Paphian Grove', a satire of 1738, says:

> Refrain from tears, ye Haggs of Hell, refrain
> Each girl will soon return and bring a swain
> Loaded with gold – who at vast expence
> For to support your cursed extravagance!

After midnight things became riotous. Drunken whores fought over customers, swords would be drawn and cudgels swung, desperate fights would spill out into the piazza. According to *The Nocturnal Revels*, an anonymous work of 1779:

From this gambling set many a broken gamester has repaired to Moll King's to snore out the remainder of the night, for

Mistress of the revels: Moll King, proprietor of the riotous Covent Garden coffee house. She is shown late in life, after she had taken to drink.

want of a shilling to obtain a lodging. If he should chance to have a watch or a pair of silver buckles remaining, while he was paying his devotion to Morpheus the nimble-handed gentry of either sex were labouring in their vocation, and the unhappy victim of fortune became the still more unhappy victim to Mercury and his votaries. From this receptacle the son of Bacchus reeled home at day-break, the Buck took his doxy to a bagnio, and the Blood carried off his moll in triumph in a chair, himself at the top of it with a broken sword and a tattered shirt, escorted by link-boys, watchmen and pick-pockets.

After three men were assaulted, Moll was charged with keeping a disorderly house where sexual offences were committed. Moll, two of her bouncers and another woman were fined. Moll's evident success and sharp tongue riled the owners of nearby brothels, and they stirred up more trouble by informing against her. Her coffee house was often raided by that scourge of prostitutes and procuresses, the magistrate Sir John Gonson, but because Moll had always insisted that there should be no beds in her shacks he could not accuse her of running a brothel.

The Kings became so wealthy that Tom bought an estate at Haverstock Hill on the way to Hampstead and built 'a very genteel country house'. In fact it was a row of houses, which still exist. Moll was looking from a window of the mansion one day when a party of gentlemen came by and one remarked: 'Look, there's Moll King's folly.' Moll called back: 'No, ye bantling, it's your folly and some more Jack-an-Apes as silly as yourself, for you know fools' pence flew fast enough about, and they helped to build it.' Having drunk himself into a decline, Tom died in his country house in 1739.

Moll refused to retire, saying 'I love to be in town because I shall see what my pretty Birds are doing.' She too took to drink and became quarrelsome, having long been renowned for staying sober when all around were utterly inebriated. She became a bloated termagant, her house became even more disorderly, and after a riot in June 1739 she was accused of assaulting a young gentleman whom she had thrashed. Usually Moll beat the rap by bribing the witnesses against her not to appear, but this time she was fined the enormous sum of £200 and sent to the King's Bench Prison until she paid up. She refused to pay, saying the fine was excessive, and was sent to Newgate to cool off. For three months she negotiated with the high bailiff, and eventually got the fine reduced by half. Life in prison was irksome but comfortable for someone as rich as Moll, and when she was released she found her nephew William had run the business competently. She married a man named Hoff, who was after her money, but she had already willed it to her son Tom, who had been educated at Westminster School. She died in 1747, and 'one of her favourite customers' wrote an elegy from which these lines are taken:

Late-night revels: Hogarth's engraving depicts a woman walking to church in Covent Garden past whores and their customers and a riot in Moll King's coffee house.

Here lies my love, who often drove
Wheelbarrows in the street;
From which low state, to Billingsgate,
With wickedness replete
She sold a dish of stinking fish
With oaths and imprecations;
And swore her ware were better far
Than any in the nation.
From thence she came to be in fame
Among the rogues and whores
But now she's gone to her long home
To settle all her scores.

After Moll's death in 1747 Elizabeth Weatherby's coffee house in Russell Street which was called Ben Jonson's Head but was famous simply as Weatherby's, attracted low-life clients, 'rakes, gamesters, swindlers, highwaymen, pickpockets and whores'. Some famous whores got their start there, including Lucy Cooper and the one-eyed Betsy Weems, or Wemyss. William Hickey, the memoirist and man-about-town, describes a visit to Weatherby's, 'an absolute hell upon earth', with some friends equally 'brimfull of wine':

Upon ringing at a door, strongly secured with knobs of iron, a cut-throat looking rascal opened a small wicket, which was also secured with narrow iron bars, who in a hoarse and ferocious voice asked: 'Who's there?' Being answered 'Friends' we were cautiously admitted one at a time, and when the last had entered, the door was instantly closed and secured, not only by an immense lock and key, but a massy iron bolt and chain. I had then never been within the walls of a prison, yet this struck me like entering one of the most horrible kind. My companions conducted me into a room where such a scene was exhibiting that I involuntarily shrunk back with disgust and dismay, and would have retreated from the apartment, but that I found that my surprize and alarm were so visible in my countenance as to have attracted the attention of several people who came up, and good naturedly enough encouraged me, observing that I was a young hand but should soon be familiarised and enjoy the fun.

At this time the whole room was in an uproar, men and women promiscuously mounted upon chairs, tables and benches, in order to see a sort of general conflict carried on upon the floor. Two she devils, for they scarce had a human appearance, were engaged in a scratching and boxing match, their faces entirely covered with blood, bosoms bare, and clothes nearly torn from their bodies. For several minutes not a creature interfered between them, or seemed to care a straw what mischief they might do each other, and the contest went on with unabated fury.

In another corner of the same room, an uncommonly athletic young man of about twenty-five seemed to be the object of universal attack. No less than three Amazonian tigresses were pummelling him with all their might, and it appeared to me that some of the males at times dealt him blows with their sticks. He however made a capital defence, not sparing the women a bit more than the men, but knocking each down as opportunity occurred. As fresh hands continued pouring in upon him, he must at last have been miserably beaten, had not two of the gentlemen who went with me, (both very stout fellows), offended at the shameful odds used against a single person, interfered, and after a few knock me down arguments succeeded in putting an end to to the unequal conflict.

The Nocturnal Revels says Weatherby's was a 'receptacle' for rakes, highwaymen, pickpockets, swindlers and prostitutes, 'from the charioted kept mistress down to the twopenny bunter who plies under the Piazza'.

The passport to this infernal world of vice and riot was the price of a cup of coffee. With the steaming cup in front of her a starving whore could sit and try her luck among the crooks and gentlemen of quality. *The Nocturnal Revels* draws a wretched picture of such a drab: 'the unfortunate strumpet who had been starving in a garret all day long while washing her only and last shift, upon making her appearance here, might probably meet with a greenhorn apprentice boy who could treat her with a mutton chop and a pot of porter'. With luck he might also be persuaded to take her to a bagnio for the night.

Lucy Cooper was a young fruit-seller in Covent Garden market, and Elizabeth Weatherby took her under her wing. It may have been at Weatherby's that she met the ancient debauchee Sir Orlando Bridgeman, who became infatuated with the burgeoning beauty and her repartee. *The Nocturnal Revels* indeed says her quick tongue 'was the greatest attraction she possessed'.

The feeling was not mutual, but she allowed him to set her up in a 'voluptuous manner' in an elegant house in Parliament Street with her own 'chariot'. Sir Orlando wanted to marry her, claims *The Nocturnal Revels*, but she was 'so generous as to refuse his hand that she might not bring a scandal upon his family'. Lucy did not want his company, either, and spent many drunken nights at Weatherby's. Her carriage was seen standing outside for 48 hours at a time. 'Dissipation was her motto.' She was generous to a fault with Bridgeman's money, lavishly entertaining friends and lovers who included the actor John Palmer, the poet Charles Churchill, Betsy Wemyss, the penniless hack Sam Derrick and 'some more choice geniuses...wit, frolic and fun circulated at her expence'. Her appetite for drink and sex earned this tribute from Edward Thompson's 'The Meretriciad' of 1765:

> Lewder than all the whores in Charles's reign...
> At famed Bob Derry's where the harlots throng
> My muse has listened to thy luscious song
> And heard thee swear like worser Drury's Punk...
> Cit, soldier, sailor or some bearded Jew
> In triumph, reeling, bore thee to some stew.

Bridgeman died in 1764, and Mrs Weatherby the following year. Without her protectors Lucy grew wilder and more drunken. She began frequenting that last resort of low whores, Bob Derry's Cider Cellar in Maiden Lane. One evening two Jews were murdered there, and Lucy was held partly to blame for the violence. She was sent to prison. This may have been the occasion that led William

Hickey and his friends to have a whip-round for her in 1766. 'Tomkyns... had that very day received a letter from Lucy Cooper, who had long been a prisoner for debt in the King's Bench [prison], stating that she was almost naked and starving, without a penny in her pocket to purchase food, raiment or coal to warm herself.' Hickey and his friends sent her £50: 'this seasonable aid had probably saved the life of a deserving woman who, in her prosperity, had done a thousand generous actions'. She died in poverty in 1772.

Shortly afterwards Weatherby's closed. The new owner was refused a licence because of nightly affrays and riots, and when he was indicted for causing a nuisance he was pilloried and jailed.

Lucy's friend Sam Derrick is an interesting example of the period's numerous penurious hacks. He was probably the author of the *Memoirs of the Bedford Coffee-house*, anonymously published as by 'a Genius'. He coached the actress/whore Jane Lessingham for her first appearance at Covent Garden, which was a triumph, and she repaid him by leaving him for the theatre's proprietor Thomas Harris. She became a successful comedy actress but refused to help Derrick. He was employed by the publisher H Ranger to edit the famous *List of Covent Garden Ladies* after Jack Harris died, and was then surprisingly appointed to succeed Beau Nash as Master of Ceremonies at Bath. After this sudden rise in status he called on Jane, but her servant said she 'knew no one of that name'. When Derrick forced his way in she threatened to call out the watch.

Faithless Jane continued to break men's hearts and purses. She took up with Henry Addington, later Lord Chief Justice and Earl of Sidmouth. She died in 1801.

Moll King's coffee house was taken over by George Carpenter, a Covent Garden porter, and it was renamed after him. William Hickey wrote of the unappetising beverage sold there, 'they still continued to dole out a Spartan mixture, difficult to ascertain the ingredients of, but which was served as coffee'. Carpenter's was also known as the Finish. It is noteworthy that in Victorian times the late-night boozing dens were also known as 'finishes'.

A special place in this world of fashionable vice around Covent Garden was held by the bath-houses, or bagnios, in a sense a revival of the medieval stews. They were very expensive but popular, and those who went there, both men and women, had other things on their mind than bathing or washing. Men could send out for the prostitute of their choice, or relax after the rigours of an encounter. Casanova, who visited a London bagnio, wrote: 'I also visited the bagnios, where a rich man can sup, bathe and sleep with a fashionable courtesan, of which species there are many in London. It makes a magnificent debauch, and only costs six guineas.' Von Archenholz as usual gives us chapter and verse:

In London there is a certain kind of house, called bagnios, which are supposed to be baths; their real purpose, however, is to provide persons of both sexes with pleasure. These houses are well, and often richly furnished, and every device for exciting the senses is either at hand or can be provided. Girls do not live here, but they are fetched in [sedan] chairs when required. None but those who are specially attractive in all ways are so honoured, and for this reason they often send their address to a hundred of these bagnios in order to make themselves known. A girl who is sent for and does not please receives no gratuity, the chair alone being paid for. The English retain their solemnity even as regards their pleasures, and consequently the business of such a house is conducted with a seriousness and propriety which is hard to credit. All noise and uproar is banned here; no loud footsteps are heard, every corner is carpeted and the numerous attendants speak quietly among themselves. Old people and degenerates can here receive flagellation, for which all establishments are prepared. In every bagnio there is found a formula regarding baths, but they are seldom needed. These pleasures are very expensive, but in spite of this many houses of the kind are full every night. Most of them are quite close to the theatres, and many taverns are in the same neighbourhood.

Another attraction in Covent Garden was a version of the 'chuck game' made famous by the seventeenth-century bawd Priss Fotheringham. In the following century it was played in the Rose Tavern near Drury Lane Theatre in Russell Street. One of the 'posture molls' would strip naked and dance on an enormous pewter plate, then lie on her back, draw her knees up under her chin and clasp her hands under her thighs. The descriptions of this performance invite you to imagine what happened next as the drunken customers crowded round. At some stage the posture woman would snuff out a lighted candle in an obscene mockery of sex. Plate 3 of Hogarth's *Rake's Progress* shows the room at the tavern as the act is about to begin. The posture woman is stripping off in the foreground and in the background a porter known as Leathercoat or Lethercote is bringing in the platter and the candle. Leathercoat, a man of prodigious strength, would for the price of a drink lie down in the street and allow a carriage to pass over his chest.

The Rose, although not a brothel, was another sink of iniquity: Hogarth's marvellous print shows drunken whores robbing their customers, becoming quarrelsome and getting ready for a night of riot. The Rose specialised in posture molls, women who would flog or be flogged and show off their charms, sometimes by stretching out naked on the floor. These women were not prostitutes, and resented being asked for sex. 'They had a great aversion to whoring...their function was to flagellate or be flagellated to arouse sexual desire in the gentlemen.'

The Rose had a reputation for good food. Pepys ate there with Doll Lane, and through its rooms over the generations passed the great Toasts of the Town: Sally Salisbury, Betsy Carless (known as Careless), Lucy Cooper, Elizabeth Thomas and Fanny Murray; as well as princes and paupers, poets and playwrights, merchants and broken servants, conmen, mountebanks, rakes, lawyers and distinguised foreigners. Among its most famous customers were the actors and managers from the nearby theatre, including David Garrick, Sheridan, Sarah Siddons and Peg Woffington. There were sudden riots, with groups of drunken whores attacking customers who insulted them, pimps maiming their girls, half-naked whores rolling on the floor and tearing at each other's faces

A Rake's Progress: *Plate 3 of Hogarth's series of engravings takes place in the notorious Rose tavern in Covent Garden. The drunken rake is robbed by two whores. A posture moll strips off ready to dance on the large platter brought in by the servant Leathercoat.*

Rake's hell: in the last plate of Hogarth's series the rake ends his days as a syphilitic wreck in Bedlam, where the world of fashion came to gawp at the poor lunatics for entertainment.

and bodies, and murderous attacks by bullies on their rivals. 'The
Covent Garden Eclogue', published in 1735, catches something
of the atmosphere:

> The Watch had cried 'Past One' with hollow strain
> And to their stands returned to sleep again.
> Grave Cits and bullies, rakes and squeamish Beaux
> Came reeling with their doxies from the Rose . . .

More Bawds

By the eighteenth century the most celebrated whores were stars with a fan club among the rich and dissolute, who would compete for their favours. Those who could not afford the most expensive whores would nevertheless go to the brothels where they operated just to see them, before solacing themselves with someone less costly. Prostitution had become one of the city's most important industries, and unlike many retail businesses which had to offer long lines of credit, it produced instant cash in large amounts. The building industry received a boost from the number of houses rented by bawds as brothels, the luxury trades depended on the more successful whores for sales of fine clothes and jewellery, as did the brewers and wine merchants for sales of drink in brothels and the many taverns associated with vice.

One of the energetic women who paved the way for this change was the vicious bawd Elizabeth Needham who had a brothel in Park Place, St James's. Even in middle age she was considered striking, Hogarth describing her as 'the handsome old Procuress...well-dressed in silk and simpering beneath the patches on her face...' She is the insinuating bawd in Plate 1 of *A Harlot's Progress*. She treated her girls little better than slaves. They were forced to hire their clothes from her at outrageous prices,[6] and if they couldn't pay were harried to improve their work rates. If they still weren't earning enough for their keep they might be bundled off to the debtors' prison and left there to rot until they agreed to her terms. When they were too old or diseased she threw them out.

Mother Needham got her girls from various places, including, apparently, auctions: in October 1784 the *Rambler* magazine carried this advertisement: 'TO BE SOLD by Inch of Candle at Mrs Kelly's Rooms several Orphan Girls under sixteen imported from the Countrey & never shewn before. Gentlemen of sixty-five and over are invited.' She was well-known for picking up country lasses just come to town. The essayist Richard Steele wrote in the *Spectator* in January 1712 about a visit he had made to the Bell Inn in Cheapside: 'But who should I see there but the most artful Procuress in the Town examining a most beautifull Country girl who had just come up in the same Waggon as my Things...' The girls would have been impressed by this handsome and well-dressed woman and her promises. Only later would they experience her temper and vicious tongue. Alexander Pope wrote of her in *The Dunciad*:

> Try not with Jests obscene to force a Smile
> Nor lard your Words with Mother Needham's style!

It was at Mother Needham's that Sally Salisbury, who had moved on after Mother Wiseborne's death, stabbed her lover. The Duke of Wharton and his cousin, Colonel Charteris were two of the numerous members of the nobility who patronised her brothel. She is believed to have arranged for Anne Bond to become Charteris's servant, and this may have led to her arrest in March 1731 by the magistrate Sir John Gonson, a well-known scourge of prostitutes and procuresses. She was sentenced to the pillory where, perhaps because of her friends in high places, she was allowed to lie face down and so protect her face. The *Daily Advertiser* reported that, 'notwithstanding which evasion of the Law and the diligence of the Beadles and a number of Persons who had been paid to protect her she was so severely pelted by the Mob that her life was despaired of'. The *Daily Courant* reported that 'at first she received little Resentment from the Populace, by reason of the great Guard of Constables that surrounded her; but near the latter End of her Time she was pelted in an unmerciful manner.' Several recent authorities say she died of her injuries, but the *Grub Street Journal* reported that 'Elizabeth Needham alias Bird alias Trent' was one of a number of brothel-keepers tried on 14 July and was committed to Newgate. She seems to have died shortly afterwards, for in September a satirical broadsheet entitled *Mother Needham's Elegy & Epitaph* commented:

> Ye Ladies of Drury, now weep
> Your Voices in howling now raise
> For Old Mother Needham's laid deep
> And bitter will be all your Days.

Another enterprising bawd of the early eighteenth century was Mother Wisebourne, patroness of the celebrity courtesan Sally Salisbury. Mother Wisebourne was the daughter of a clergyman and used to visit prisons, clutching her Bible, to buy the freedom of likely girls, and also looked for recruits among children whose parents rented them out to beggars for the day. Another source of recruits for her brothel was the children who were offered for sale outside the church of St Martin in the Fields. Those she chose would be 'drest with Paint and Patches...and let out at extravagant Prices...she was always calling them young milliners or Parsons' daughters'. She specialised in restoring their virginity after selling them to the highest bidder.

She taught them other tricks, such as touting for customers in church, as one of her girls recalled:

> We'd take all opportunities, as we came down stairs from the galleries, or as we past over the kennels [gutters] in the streets, to lift up our coats so high, that we might show our handsome legs and feet, with a good fine worsted or silk pair of stockings on; by which means the gallants would be sure either to dog us themselves, or else to send their footmen to see where we liv'd; and then they would afterwards come to us themselves; and by that means have we got many a good customer.

The greatest bawd of early Georgian times was Charlotte Hayes, who was born in a Covent Garden slum about 1725 and lived on into the next century, dying in her eighties after a long career of innovation which included a 'Cyprian Fete' at which gentlemen 'of the highest breeding' first watched athletic young men copulating with nubile whores and then joined in themselves.

Early in her career Charlotte was imprisoned in the Fleet debtors' prison and there met and fell in love with an Irish conman, Dennis O'Kelly. After he arrived in London in 1748 he worked as a sedan chairman. His charm and amours got him into trouble with husbands and a spell in prison for debt probably saved him a beating. He and Charlotte experienced wild swings of fortune. Charlotte set up a brothel while in prison and used the proceeds to start O'Kelly on a career which would see him become a wealthy colonel of militia and owner of the Duke of Chandos's estate, Canons, at Edgware. At least as important from the social point of view was his ownership of the wonder horse Eclipse, which never lost a race. This was an entrée to the highest levels of society, and friendship with the Prince of Wales.

The couple were freed in an amnesty in 1760, and the following year Charlotte set up her first luxury brothel, a 'Protestant Nunnery', in Great Marlborough Street. O'Kelly's racing connections helped bring in aristocratic devotees of the turf – the Dukes of Richmond and Chandos, the Earls of Egremont and Grosvenor among others. Charlotte decided she needed to be even closer to the court, and in 1767 opened another brothel at No. 2 King's Place, Pall Mall. The *Town and Country Magazine* called her 'a living saint' and said she should be canonised because she could 'make old Dotards believe themselves gay vigorous young Fellows, and turn vigorous young men into old Dotards'. Interestingly she charged clients 50 guineas for a night with one of her girls, the same amount as the famous racehorse Eclipse's stud fees.

Charlotte kept her nuns, as the girls were known, in a kind of benign bondage. Like other bawds of the time, she charged them so much for jewellery, rich clothes, food and lodging that they were always in debt to her. Their best hope was to find a wealthy husband who would buy them out. Otherwise she treated the girls well, taking them out for walks or, in bad weather, in the brothel's own carriages. She also treated her elderly and infirm clients with consideration, having special 'elastick beds' designed for their comfort.

To recruit new girls for her brothels Charlotte visited employment agencies, where girls would be lined up for the inspection of people seeking domestic servants. The most suitable would be groomed for their profession, and some became famous courtesans. These included the 'shaggy-tail'd uncomb'd unwash'd filly of fourteen ... bought from her industrious painstaking Mechanick of a Father for a Song' who as Kitty Fredericks became the 'veritable Thais amongst the haut ton, the veritable Flora of all London'. (Burford, *Royal St James's*) Then there was Frances Barton, who endured a degrading childhood to be rescued by Charlotte and turned into the actress Frances Abington, famous alike for 'so often exposing her lovely naked bosom to the gaze of lascivious leering gentlemen' and for her rich and varied love life.

Dennis O'Kelly, whom Charlotte eventually married, was always a worry. In 1769 he lost a great deal of money gambling. At York races he tried to seduce a young woman at his hotel and had to pay £500 to avoid a scandal. In 1770 Charlotte was committed to a debtors' prison once again, emerging to open London's most luxurious brothel at 5 King's Place.

William Hickey visited 'that experienced old Matron Charlotte Hayes in her House of Celebrity in King's Place'. In 1776 she was committed to the Marshalsea prison for debt. She had refused to pay £50 to a bankrupt lacemaker, although she admitted the debt. Dennis came to her rescue. He died in 1788 aged 67, leaving her £400 a year for life and much else besides, including his parrot Polly, which could reputedly sing the 104th Psalm. In 1798 Charlotte, still living at Canons, was again in a debtors' prison because of her extravagance. Dennis's nephew bailed her out and paid all her debts in return for her making over all her assets to him. She is last heard of in 1811 at Canons, and died soon afterwards. Whatever her financial straits, she is reputed to have made the substantial fortune of £20,000 from brothel-keeping. This is about the sum that William Hickey brought back after several years' successful practice as a lawyer in India.

One great bawd who managed to hang on to her money was Mother Jane Douglas, born in Scotland in about 1698 and celebrated by the playwright John Gay as 'that inimitable courtesan'. She is the buxom bawd praying for the safe return of the soldiers – her customers, after all – at the window of the brothel in Hogarth's print *The March to Finchley*. Her whores crowd the other windows and cats line the roof, a reference to the fact that one of her brothels, the King's Head in the Covent Garden Piazza, was called a 'cattery'. Hogarth drew her again for his print *Enthusiasm Delineated* of 1761, by which time drink had destroyed her once-elegant figure. The playwright Charles Johnson described her shortly before her death in that year: 'Her Face presents the remains of a most pleasing sweetness and beauty...her body bloated by drink and debauch.' Horace Walpole's correspondent, the diplomat Sir Charles Hanbury-Williams, was less kind, describing her as: 'A great flabby fat stinking swearing hollowing ranting Billingsgate Bawd.'

The Nocturnal Revels states that Mother Douglas attracted princes and peers, 'and she fleeced them in proportion to their dignity'. Noble beauties also visited incognito, but embarrassing confrontations were avoided. 'It frequently happened that while my lord was enjoying Chloë in one room, in the adjacent apartment her ladyship was cornuting her caro sposo with a pair of the largest antlers she could procure.' The book says that high-class demi-reps also frequented Mother Douglas's, and mentions Campioni and Peg Woffington as having 'often sacrificed at the altar of Venus in this chapel...'

After her death Mother Douglas's many aristocratic clients could enjoy poignant reminders of the joys of being fleeced by her when her 'fine Old Masters, rich Furniture and costly properties' were sold by auction.

According to *The Nocturnal Revels*, Mrs Gould's brothel in Russell Street was second only to Mrs Douglas's in importance. She tried to maintain a high tone: 'This lady plumed herself much upon being the gentlewoman; she despised every woman who swore or talked indecently, nor would she suffer drunken females.' Her lover was a 'certain notary public of Jewish extraction' for whom, *The Nocturnal Revels* says, she had a great passion 'on account of his uncommon parts and great abilities'. Burford identifies him as Moses Moravia.

*

Sacred and profane: the pious but drunken bawd Jane Douglas prays at a window of her brothel in a detail from Hogath's engraving The March to Finchley.

In around 1750 London gained its first brothels modelled on the sumptuous French establishments. A madam named Mrs Goadsby, who had been to Paris to see what that city had to offer, opened a house in Berwick Street, Soho, and 'catered to all tastes, at the most exclusive prices'. Only the very best whores were engaged, and they were medically examined first. A physician was retained to carry out weekly examinations. The girls were dressed in fine French silks and lace. Mrs Goadby 'brought an air of refinement into brothel-keeping'. Within a few years she had made a fortune and retired to a fine house in the country, but there were others to follow her lead. The new brothels were called seraglios, nunneries, abbeys, temples and cloisters.

The most important and expensive brothels were around the west London area of St James's. A Miss Fawkland kept three adjoining houses in St James's Street, patronised among others by Lords Cornwallis, Buckingham, Loudoun, Falkland, Bolingbroke and Hamilton, and the writers Sheridan and Smollett. She put her girls through a training course before they took up their duties. The houses were called temples, the first being the Temple of Aurora which specialised in girls aged between eleven and sixteen. Here elderly customers were allowed to fondle the girls but not to have sex with them, at least in theory. These little virgins were said to be 'handpicked from those brought to the establishment by their parents'. From here the girls could graduate to the next-door Temple of Flora, which was a luxury brothel. Finally there was the Temple of Mysteries, which catered for those interested in flagellation and other sado-masochistic practices. The charges were exorbitant, and Miss Fawkland could afford to treat her girls well.

A brothel in King's Place was operated by a Miss Harriott, known as Black Harriott, a negress from Guinea who had been captured in a slave raid as a child and shipped to Jamaica. Her beauty and intelligence attracted William Lewis, a plantation owner and captain in the merchant navy. He bought her and treated her as his wife, teaching her to read and write and grooming her to appear in English high society.

In London they lived just off Piccadilly and mixed in the highest circles. Lewis died of smallpox in 1772, leaving her penniless, and she was committed to the King's Bench debtors' prison. Freed with the help of some admirers, she was soon running a flourishing brothel where her clientele included many peers and 'fifty rich men none ever paying less than a soft Paper', that is a £20 banknote. In 1774 Black Harriott took over No. 3 King's Place where her clients included the Earl of Sandwich, one of the leaders of the Medmenham Abbey set and famous to posterity for inventing the snack which bears his name. A noted lecher, he turned against his fellow club member John Wilkes, and read out extracts from the obscene poem the 'Essay on Women', then believed to have been written by Wilkes, in the House of Lords. The intention was to discredit Wilkes's political radicalism. Thereafter Sandwich was known as Jemmy Twitcher for his unspeakable treachery. This is a reference to the line in Gay's *The Beggar's Opera*, then playing in London, 'But that Jemmy Twitcher should peach I own surprises me.' Sandwich had shouted at Wilkes, 'Sir, you will either die on the gallows or of the pox,' to which Wilkes replied, 'That, my Lord, depends on whether I embrace your principles or your mistress.' Wilkes was forced to flee the country to escape prison for libel.[7]

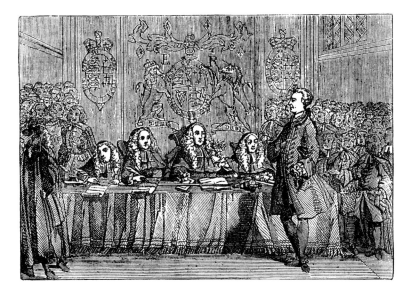

Radical rake: John Wilkes during his trial. He was thought, wrongly, to be the author of the obscene poem, 'Essay on Woman'.

Harriott's downfall was said to be a passion she developed for a Guards officer. She neglected her business and the whores sold the contents of her brothel. She was imprisoned for debt, and although she later ran another brothel in King's Place she was now seriously ill, eventually dying of tuberculosis. Harriott was the only black woman to have run a brothel in the heart of the upper-class enclave of Royal St James's, although Boswell was told of a brothel staffed entirely by black women.

Harriott's house in King's Place was taken over by Sarah Prendergast, who was involved in an amusing sexual scandal involving the Earl of Harrington, known as 'Lord Fumble' and described by the *Westminster Magazine* as 'a person of the most exceptional immorality'. Mrs Prendergast kept only three girls in her seraglio, sending out for others when business was brisk. One night the earl rejected her three resident whores, so she sent to Mrs Butler's establishment at Westminster for 'a couple of fresh country tits'. The girls Mrs Butler supplied were Elizabeth Cummins, known as Country Bet, and a girl known as Black-Eyed Susan. The doddery old earl indulged in 'manual dalliance' and was apparently well satisfied, giving each girl three guineas, which was rather less than they had been led to expect.

When they got back to Westminster Mrs Butler demanded her cut of 25 per cent. Susan paid up, but Country Bet refused. Mother Butler took her clothes, and Betty went to the police. No one could have foreseen the far-reaching consequences. Mrs Butler was convicted of stealing the clothes, and of keeping a brothel. Furthermore, she was convicted of 'causing Elizabeth to go in company with another woman of the lowest order to meet the Earl of Harrington at the house of Mrs Prendergast, who keeps a seraglio in King's Place'. Mrs Butler's husband, a sergeant in the Grenadier Guards, was convicted of helping his wife's brothel-keeping by transporting girls to the seraglios in King's Place, where they were dressed as country maids. It was reported that 'the Earl attended Mrs Prendergast's seraglio on Sunday, Mondays, Wednesdays and Fridays, having two females at a time'.

The earl was furious. A scandal sheet had picked up the story, says Burford in *Royal St James's*, and he 'flew into a great Passion, stuttering and Swearing and Shouting' that he would not be able to show his face at court. The sensible Mrs Prendergast bought up all the copies of the paper and paid Betty £5 to drop the prosecution. She assured the earl that neither girl would work again in the brothels, and moved quickly to reassure her clients that nothing like it could happen again.

To cheer everyone up she decided to hold a grand ball, at which 'the finest Women in all Europe would appear in *puris naturalibus*'. Lord Fumble, in a gesture of gratitude, started the ball rolling with a subscription of 50 guineas towards the cost. The ball was a great success. Aristocratic ladies flocked to join the professional beauties and danced nude for hours while an orchestra played facing the wall so as not to embarrass them. Afterwards there was a banquet.

Mrs Prendergast made a profit of £1,000, but she soon lost one of her best customers, Lord Fumble, who died a few weeks later in 1779. Nevertheless she retired wealthy.

The Earl of Harrington and his wife were both renowned for their immorality, the *Town and Country Magazine* saying the earl was 'as lecherous as a Monkey'. The magazine listed some of his lovers, including Kitty Brown who had 'a fair complexion, brilliant blue eyes ... with small, pouting Bubbies'; then he had a brief fling with the greedy Kitty Fisher who was succeeded by another actress, Mrs Houghton. When the Duke of Dorset died the earl took on his mistress, Jane Courteville, only to see her fall for 'the corpulent charms' of Mrs Rushton of King Street. At one stage he had a harem in his mansion, 'which comprised a Negress in a feather'd Turban, a young girl in pseudo-classical dress, another [dressed] as a Country-wench, as well as a Mandolin-player'. After his affair with a Miss Lisle, the widow of a military hero, who had become a whore, the *Town and Country Magazine* said this of the earl and his wife: 'His Lordship is an impotent Debauchee and his Lady a professional Messalina [after the cruel and debauched wife of the Roman emperor Claudius] who has little cause to be jealous – she would rather be inclined to laughter at this liaison.' Lady Harrington had a weakness for both sexes. When her lesbian lover Elizabeth Ashe deserted her for the diplomat Count von Haszlang she said she was 'quite devastated ... her character had been demolished by this desertion'. Ashe, one of the many actress-whores of the time, was twice married and had many lovers. After she died at the age of 84 Horace Walpole observed that she had 'a large collection of amours'(Burford, *Royal St James's*).

Sarah Dubery, who took over Charlotte Hayes's old brothel at King's Place, had foreign ambassadors among her clients and well-known actresses and divas among her beauties. One of these part-time whores was Isabella Wilkinson, a famous rope dancer who performed at Sadlers Wells and Covent Garden. She was the mistress of the Swedish Ambassador, Count Gustav von Nollekens. One night Mrs Dubery promised to introduce the count to a 'new nun'. The count was furious to find that the 'nun' was his Isabella, 'whom he supposed was waiting for him at home as chaste as Penelope' (Burford, ibid.). The count's *amour propre* was restored when Mrs Dubery found him a replacement for the faithless Isabella. Mrs Dubery retired in 1814, 'after a reign of thirty-six years' successful trading'.

Isabella was fond of drink and put on weight, which may account for her eventually breaking her leg. While she convalesced, says *The Nocturnal Revels*, she 'rusticated' at the coffee houses and bagnios in Covent Garden, where her pick-ups included members of the diplomatic corps, a line of clients she seems to have specialised in: ''Tis true her bulk is rather a hindrance to her agility which may in some measure excuse her not being able to get off the ground . . . she still continues to tipple to excess.'

Royal St James's was the very heart of the aristocratic red-light district. Other high-class brothels existed in Bond Street, Curzon Street, off Fleet Street and in Soho and Holborn. A popular 'house of assignation' was run by a Mrs Redson in Bolton Street, off Piccadilly. In the much-smaller city of the eighteenth century there were few places for married women in particular to meet their lovers, so these establishments provided an important service.

High-class brothels, whose whores had their own coaches and servants in livery, were prohibitively expensive. Von Archenholz, writing about King's Place in St James's, says:

The admission into these temples is so exorbitant, that the mob are entirely excluded: there are, indeed, only a few rich people who can aspire to the favours of such venal divinities... The houses were magnificent and the furniture worthy of a prince's palace... The celebrated Fox [the politician Charles James Fox, (1749–1806), leader of the Whigs] used to frequent these places often before he became a minister; and even afterwards, drunk, as it were, with the pleasures he had enjoyed, he went from thence to move, astonish, and direct the House of Commons, by means of his manly and moving eloquence.

Some idea of the prices in one of these establishments can be gained from the price-list of Charlotte Hayes's extremely successful brothel in King's Place. She called it a 'cloister', and her girls her 'choice merchandise'. Although the style is facetious, the prices are believed to be accurate. Some of the customers' names are aliases for real people.

Sunday the 9th January

A young girl for Alderman Drybones. Nelly Blossom, about 19 years old, who has had no one for four days, and who is a virgin ....20 guineas

A girl of 19 years, not older, for Baron Harry Flagellum. Nell Hardy from Bow Street, Bett Flourish from Berners Street or Miss Birch from Chapel Street.................................10 guineas

A beautiful and lively girl for Lord Sperm. Black Moll from Hedge Lane, who is very strong................................5 guineas

For Colonel Tearall, a gentle woman. Mrs Mitchell's servant, who has just come from the country and has not been out in the world..10 guineas

For Dr Pretext, after consultation hours, a young agreeable person, sociable, with a white skin and a soft hand. Polly Nimblewrist from Oxford, or Jenny Speedyhand from Mayfair ....2 guineas

Lady Loveitt, who has come from the baths at Bath, and who is disappointed in her affair with Lord Alto, wants to have

something better, and to be well served this evening. Capt.
O'Thunder or Sawney Rawbone..............................50 guineas
    For his Excellency Count Alto, a fashionable woman for an
hour only. Mrs O'Smirk who comes from Dunkirk Square, or
Miss Graceful from Paddington................................10 guineas
    For Lord Pyebald, to play a game at piquet, for titillatione
mammarum and so on, with no other object. Mrs Tredrillo
from Chelsea...5 guineas

It is significant that prices for the simple services enjoyed by Dr
Pretext and Lord Pyebald are low: those for a putative virgin high.
The highest price of all is demanded of Lady Loveitt. Henriques
says that in a well-run brothel husband and wife could pursue their
separate pleasures with no danger of an embarrassing confrontation.
But there was no equality of the sexes: the wife had to pay at least
five times as much as her husband.

    Burford, in *Royal St James's*, identifies some of these clients. Lady
Loveitt is the 'nymphomaniac' Lady Sarah Lennox, and her lover
Lord Alto is Lord William Gordon. Alderman Drybones is Robert
Alsop, Lord Mayor of London in 1752. Lord Pyebald, so decrepit that
he can only fondle girls' breasts, is Hugh, Viscount Falmouth.

    A brothel designed for the gratification of women, those with
lovers and those without, was established by Mary Wilson. She had
brothels in Old Bond Street, St Pancras and Hall Place, St John's
Wood. In 1824 she published *The Voluptarian Cabinet*, describing
an 'Eleusinian Institution'. This was divided into two sections, one
for married women and their lovers, the other for women seeking
sex. This is her sales pitch:

I have purchased very extensive premises, which are situated
between two great thoroughfares and are entered from each by
means of shops, devoted entirely to such trades as are
exclusively resorted to by ladies. In the area between the two
rows of houses, I have erected a most elegant temple, in the
centre of which are large saloons, entirely surrounded by
boudoirs most elegantly and commodiously fitted up. In these
saloons, according to their classes, are to be seen the finest men

of their species I can procure, occupied in whatever amuse-
ments are adapted to their taste, and all kept in a high state of
excitement by good living and idleness . . .

Before making their choice the women viewed the men through a
window. When they saw one they fancied they would ring for a
chambermaid and point him out. Mary Wilson wrote that the woman
client could 'enjoy him in the dark, or have a light, and keep on her
mask. She can stay an hour or a night, and have one or two dozen
men as she pleases, without being known to any of them . . . '
Two dozen men would have been extravagant in every sense.
Brothels where women were the customers were rare, and they had to
pay a premium, according to Henriques in *Prostitution and Society*,
vol. 3. Mary Wilson's establishments were decorated with pornographic paintings after the Renaissance artist Giulio Romano. Patrons
had to pay handsomely for all this: the subscription was 100 guineas,
and the fine wine and food had also to be paid for, as in a restaurant.
   Another fashionable establishment was run by Madame Cornelys
in Carlisle House, Soho Square. She was born in the Tyrol and had
once been the mistress of Casanova, by whom she had a son. She
arrived in London in 1763 and after a failed career as a singer she
rented Carlisle House where she held recitals, balls and
masquerades. These masked balls were fronts for pick-ups: 'the
whole Design of the libidinous Assembly seems to terminate in
Assignations and Intrigues'.
   William Hickey describes in his memoirs a visit to her 'truly magnificent suite of apartments . . . So much did it take that the first people of
the kingdom attended it, as did also the whole beauty of the metropolis,
from the Duchess of Devonshire down to the little milliner's apprentice
from Cranbourn Alley.' Although she maintained a high tone and her
performances attracted the haut monde, she was unable to stop
fashionable whores slipping past the doormen. As Horace Walpole
said, the house attracted 'both righteous and ungodly'. Even her friends
in the royal family and Parliament could not shield her for ever, and in
1771 a rival accused her of allowing her premises to be used for
dramatic performances without a licence. A grand jury then indicted
her for keeping 'a common disorderly house, and does permit and

suffer divers loose, idle and disorderly persons, as well men as women, to be and remain during the whole night, rioting and otherwise misbehaving themselves'. A common disorderly house was another term for a brothel.

Poor Mrs Cornelys was forced to sell off the contents of Carlisle House. She tried other covert forms of brothel-keeping, the last being a 'Purveyor of Asses Milk' in Knightsbridge. In 1772 she was committed to the Fleet Prison for debt, and she died there seven years later.

Not all bawds were inhuman leeches. Mother Willit of Gerard Street had the sense to feed and clothe her girls. 'So help her kidnies, she al'us turned her gals out with a clean arse and good tog [outfit]; and as she turned 'em out, she didn't care who turned 'em up, cause 'em was clean as a smelt and as fresh as a daisy – she vouldn't have a speck'd 'un if she know'd it' (Ronald Pearsall, *The Worm in the Bud*, 1993).

The Cyprian Corps

The great courtesans of the eighteenth century, known by the newspapers and magazines which breathlessly followed their every move and *mot* as the Cyprian Corps, the Great Impures, the Toasts of the Town, Cythereans and Paphians, were the supermodels of their day. Fans could follow their progress in newspaper columns with headings such as 'Cytherean Intelligence'.

The first to achieve Toast of the Town status was Sally Salisbury. This dazzling beauty and wit was as wild as the century, tempestuous, quick-tempered, generous and doomed. Born Sarah Pridden in 1692, the daughter of a bricklayer, she grew up wretchedly poor in the slums of St Giles, north of Covent Garden. Her biographer wrote: 'At different seasons of the year she shelled beans and peas, cried nose-gays and newspapers, peeled walnuts, made matches, turned bunter [prostitute] &c., well knowing that a wagging hand always gets a penny' (Captain C Walker, *Authentic Memoirs of the Life, Intrigues and Adventures of the Celebrated Sally Salisbury*).

She was seduced, poxed, cured, and, with the help of the famous bawd Mother Wisebourne, re-virginised by the age of fourteen. An early friend was the great actress Elizabeth Barry, who dropped Sally because of her rough manners and unpredictable temper. She then became the mistress of the notorious rake Colonel Francis Charteris, cousin of the Duke of Wharton. When he abandoned her in Bath – perhaps again because of her violent temper – she went back to work for Wisebourne, proprietor of a whorehouse in Covent Garden which was reputed to be among the most expensive in London.

Mother Wisebourne's clients included many aristocrats, and Sally was an asset. She was unabashed in high society, and counted some of the highest in the land among her conquests. They included Viscount Bolingbroke, Secretary of State in Walpole's corrupt administration, who paid 'the highest price for the greatest pleasure'. Others were the Duke of Richmond, Nell Gwyn's son the Duke of St Albans, the poet Matthew Prior and the Prince of Wales, later to become King George II. For a while she was part of the Duke of Buckingham's 'harem', and a ballad says she played the 'chuck game' (see page 105). Her madcap escapades were famous. She and another girl went to Newmarket races with George Brudenell, Earl of Cardigan, got him blind drunk, bundled him into bed and made off with all his clothes and jewels. Reunited with him in London the girls returned the clothes and he treated the whole affair as a huge joke – fortunately for them. He could have had them hanged.

After a riot at Mother Wisebourne's in 1713 the quick-tempered Sally was sent to Newgate. She was released on the order of Judge Blagney, who had fallen for her. Blagney had written to the jailer asking him not to punish Sally as he had something else in mind for her. Sally could be waspish. At a grand society ball the hostess, outshone by Sally, had the temerity to comment on the splendour of the whore's jewels.

'They had need be finer than yours, my Lady,' said Sally. 'You have but one Lord to keep you, and to buy you jewels, but I have at least half a score, of which number, Madam, your Ladyship's husband is not the most inconsiderable.'

'Nay, my Lady,' cried another guest. 'You had better let Mrs Salisbury alone, for she'll lay claim to all our husbands else, by and by.'

'Not much to yours, indeed, Madam,' replied Sally tartly. 'I tried him once and am resolved I'll never try him again; for I was forced to kick him out of bed, because his – – is good for nothing at all.' (Walker, *Sally Salisbury*)

Such a rackety life was perhaps bound to be short. Lady Mary Wortley Montague described in a letter the incident that led to her death:

Queen of hearts: the riotous Sally Salisbury, as wild as the eighteenth century, was the first working-class Toast of the Town.

The freshest news in Town is the fatal accident happened three Nights ago to a very pritty young Fellow, brother to Lord Finch, who was drinking with a dearly beloved Drab whom you may have heard of by the name of Sally Salisbury. In a jealous Pique she stabbed him to the Heart with a Knife. He fell down dead immediately but a surgeon being called and the Knife being drawn out of his Body, he opened his Eyes and his first Words were to ask her to be Friends with him, and he kissed her.

Finch lived, but Sally was sentenced to a year in Newgate and fined the enormous sum of £100. In spite of Finch's pleas she remained in Newgate, where she caught jail fever and wasted away. Here is how César de Saussure described her death there in 1723:

Jealous rage: Sally Salisbury stabs her lover the Hon. John Finch in the Three Tuns tavern in Chandos Street in 1772. She died later in prison.

You will suppose her lovers abandoned her in her distress. They did no such thing, but crowded into the prison, presenting her with every comfort and luxury possible. As soon as the wounded man – who, by the way, belongs to one of the best-known English families – was sufficiently recovered, he asked for her discharge, but Sally Salisbury died of brain fever, brought on by debauch, before she was able to leave the prison. (*A Foreign View of England in the Reigns of George I and George II*, 1902)

Sally was buried at St Andrew's Holborn in February 1724. Her coffin was followed by four coaches, and six gentlemen bore it to the church. She was about 32. Hogarth's print series *A Harlot's Progress* and John Cleland's *Fanny Hill* owe much to her life and legend. She failed to pay the fine.

Sally Salisbury's place as Premier Toast was filled for a time by Betsy Carless, known as Careless, but she was too careless of her money and her health and she died young and broke in 1739. Her place was taken by Frances Murray, who attracted superlatives such as 'incomparable' and 'celebrated'. There is a portrait of her in the British Museum: it shows a large-eyed, round-faced woman who was by common consent one of the beauties of the age.

Frances, known as Fanny, had been whoring for four years without success when Jack Harris included her in his lists. Her story, told in the anonymous *Memoirs of the Celebrated Miss Fanny Murray* in 1759, suggests that Fanny was not enough of a businesswoman to begin with to make the most of her charms. Despite her beauty it took her a long time to break into the top rank of courtesans.

Fanny was born in Bath in 1729, where her father was a poor musician. She was orphaned at the age of twelve, and became a flower-seller in the Assembly Rooms. She attracted the attention of the 'proverbial rake' Jack Spencer 'of libertine memory'. Fanny was far too young to offer more than the thrill of conquest to such a man, and he left her after a few weeks. She was taken up by Beau Nash, Bath's arbiter of taste, who was in his sixties. Given the great age difference, this too was a doomed relationship: they quarrelled and Fanny left for London. She lodged with a Mrs Softing who was little better than a bawd, introducing Fanny to randy old men, one of whom gave her a snuffbox with £40 in it. She quarrelled with Mrs Softing who threw her out, and she became a common prostitute. 'What must be the ultimate end of such variegated concupiscence? Infection.' Fanny had her first dose of the pox, she needed expensive treatment and she had no money. She had to pawn her clothes, the surgeon's last fee being produced by her last gown. At this low ebb in her career her new landlady mentioned that a procuress in Old Bailey was looking for 'any clean fresh country goods' to replace girls who had been imprisoned in Bridewell. Fanny was reluctant but really had no choice. The results of her first week's efforts were earnings of £5. 10s. 6d., and expenditure of £5. 10s. Fanny's problem, like that of many other whores, was that she had to hire her clothes at exorbitant rates from her bawd. Here is how she – or rather the anonymous author of the *Memoirs*, for it is unlikely to have been Fanny – detailed her expenditure:

Board and lodging (in a garret, on small beer and sprats) ....£1. 15s.
Washing (two smocks, 2 handkerchiefs, two pairs stockings) ....7s.
Use of brocade gown (worth a crown [5s.]) ....8s.
Use of pair of stays (not worth a shilling)..............................3s.
Use of pair silk shoes (not worth a shilling) ....2s 6d.
Use of smocks (old, coarse and patched) ....7s.
Use of ruffles (darned; worth only 2s. 6d. when new) ....2s.
Use of petticoats (all of the lowest rank) ....4s.
Seeing constables to prevent going to Bridewell (Peace officers' fees – in buckram)...10s. 6d.
Use of a hat (worthless) ....2s.
Use of ribands (unusable) ....3s. 6d.
A few pins ....6d.
Use of a Capuchin cloak ....8s.
Use of gauze aprons (rag-fair quality) ....5s.
Use of gauze handkerchiefs (the same)............................2s. 6d.
Use of silk stockings (yellow and pierced) ....2s. 6d.
Use of stone buckles (most of stones out) ....4s. 6d.
Carmine and tooth powder and brushes (brick-dust for the first two: brushes unseen)...3s.

[The author does not seem to have bothered to add up this sum.] The money thus supplied was mostly gained by apprentice boys who were seduced by the house to spend double the sum they gave to their doxy in bad punch, and worse negus. Perhaps their masters' tills were the only treasure for such debauchery, but good Mrs — the landlady never troubled herself with such reflections. If Tyburn carried off one set of her customers, which it frequently did, growing vice and the depravity of the times furnished her with another.

Fanny was in a fix. The landlady took all her money and was constantly threatening to have her imprisoned for debt if she didn't earn more. She managed to save and conceal seven guineas from her earnings, and with this money she fled the brothel and took up with some of her upper-class former lovers. Her luck had changed, and soon 'she had so much business, all in the private lodging, ready-money way, that she could not possibly drive so great a business entirely on her own bottom'. Fanny took an apprentice, and her business was so flourishing that it soon attracted the attention of Jack Harris, publisher of the *List of Covent Garden Ladies*. Mr Harris, the celebrated negotiator in women, applied to get her enrolled upon his parchment list.' The *Memoirs* show to what an art Harris had raised his pimping operation. 'The ceremony was performed with all the punctilios attending that great institution.' Fanny was examined by a surgeon to prove she was free of venereal disease, and a lawyer was on hand as she signed the solemn agreement to pay Harris a fifth of her earnings, and also to hand over twenty pounds if she lied about the state of her health. This is how Harris described her:

Perfectly sound in Wind and Limb: a fine Brown Girl rising nineteen years next Season. A good Side-box Piece – will show well in the Flesh Market – wear well – may be put off for a virgin any time these twelve months – never common this side Temple Bar, but for six months. Fit for High Keeping with a Jew Merchant – NB a good premium from ditto – then the run of the house. And if she keeps out of the Lock [the VD hospital] may make her Fortune and ruin half the Men in town.

This advertisement worked, and Fanny became the acknowledged Top Toast, at first charging a minimum of two guineas, which seems very low. Another whore in Harris's *List*, Poll Davis of Manchester Square, was said to charge a minimum of ten guineas and half a crown for her servant. Slightly later in the century the Honourable Charlotte Spencer was charging a minimum of £50 per night. No doubt Fanny soon raised her prices. She was among the more classy whores, sought after as models by some of the leading painters.

Next she became the mistress of the wealthy Sir Richard Atkins, who set her up in a fine house at Clapham. When he died Fanny, who was only 27, was arrested for debt. John Spencer, the son of her first seducer, came to her rescue, paid her debts and gave her an annual allowance of £200. She married the actor David Ross and became a respectable housewife, dying, much loved by her many noble friends, in 1778.

Fanny was a member of the Whores' Club, which met every Sunday night at the Shakespeare's Head tavern. There were about one hundred members of this mutual-aid organisation, which seems to have been the brainchild of Jack Harris. Certainly he was the main benefactor.

The brothel-keeper Mother Wisebourne had set up a 'society' or committee of whores in the previous century, apparently with the intention of establishing some kind of code for the industry. Anodyne Tanner, the perhaps pseudonymous author of *The Life of the Late Celebrated Mrs Elizabeth Wisebourn, Vulgarly Called Mother Wybourn* (1721), suggests that it carried on successfully after her death in 1720. He gives an instance of how it worked. A courtesan caught her lover in bed with another member of the society at Mrs Wisebourne's. Wisebourne suggested that the matter be put to the full committee for a ruling. They decided that no woman could claim a monopoly of a man, whatever their relationship. The good mother also proposed setting up an insurance scheme for men who caught VD from prostitutes, but the proposal was not taken up.

The aim of the Shakespeare's Head club was to help whores who were down on their luck or in prison. The apparently contradictory rules suggest what a gulf there is between us and the eighteenth century:

1. Every girl had to have been 'debauched' before she was fifteen.
2. All members had to be on Harris's *List.*
3. No modest woman to be admitted.
4. Members must not have been in Bridewell more than once.
5. Any girl tried at the Old Bailey for any crime except picking pockets could remain a member as long as she had not pleaded her belly (told the court she was pregnant).
6. Any member who became pregnant would be struck off.
7. Each member to contribute half a crown, one shilling of which to go to support members who could not earn a living because they were being treated for venereal disease, or who could not get into the Lock Hospital. Another sixpence to go to Harris for 'his great care and assiduity in the proper conducting of this worthy society'. The remaining shilling was to be spent on drink, 'gin not excluded'.
8. Any member who found a wealthy protector to make a suitable donation to the club before quitting.
9. No men to be allowed in except Harris, who could choose any girl he fancied for his bedfellow that night.
10. No religion or politics to be discussed.
11. Any member who got too drunk to walk to be sent home in a coach or sedan chair at the expense of the society, the fare to be paid back at the next meeting.
12. Any member who broke glasses, bottles etc or behaved in a 'riotous manner' to be expelled until she paid for the damage.
13. Any member 'overcharged' with liquor who in 'clearing her stomach' soiled another's clothes must replace them.

There were lively Sunday nights at the Shakespeare's Head when these spirited young women, many of them still in their teens, let their hair down. Yet the *Memoirs* tell us that this particular female naughty-pack included women of noble birth.

This catalogue of the principal figures in eighteenth-century vice is by no means complete. One name should be added, not only because of her famous conquests, wealth and long life, but also for her extraordinary marriage. Elizabeth Cane started as one of Mrs Goadby's whores, became the Great Impure of her day, married the Whig leader Charles James Fox in 1795 when she was about 45, and lived to be 91.

Nothing is known of her childhood, but Burford speculates in *Wits, Wenchers and Wantons* (1986) that she was connected to the brothel-keeper Mother Cane, who crops up in court records from the 1730s. In 1773 the *Covent Garden Magazine* said, 'Mrs Goadby, that celebrated Abbess, having fitted up an elegant Nunnery in Marlborough Street, is now laying in a stock of Virgins for the ensuing season . . . ' One of these 'virgins' was Elizabeth Cane, who called herself Mrs Armistead although there was no Mr Armistead. Incidentally, the magazine says Mrs Goadby charged 50 guineas for a virgin, and when the girl had become familiar to all the customers her price would gradually fall to the normal five guineas.

Nobody considered Elizabeth a great beauty, but she was tall and elegant, and her full, deep-bosomed figure exactly conformed to current taste. From her launching pad at Mrs Goadby's she quickly soared right to the top of her profession. The difference between a whore and a courtesan was the strength of woman's connections among aristocratic and wealthy men-about-town, and Elizabeth had the best. She passed through the arms and beds of the Duke of Dorset, the Earls of Loudoun and Cholmondeley and the Prince of Wales, later George IV.

Publish and Be Damned

The great courtesans offered more than sex. They were not always beautiful, but they were usually lively, witty, stylish, sexy, amoral. 'They were elegant, had fine manners, were passable linguists and musicians; they had learned to discuss politics and current literature as well as the latest scandal; they were witty, improvident, imprudent, the rage – and available' (Lesley Blanch, introduction to *Harriette Wilson's Memoirs*, 1964): someone a man tired of stuffy domestic respectability would be pleased to be seen out driving with in the park, or sharing a box with at the theatre.

At the end of the eighteenth century one of the most celebrated courtesans in London was Harriette Wilson, one of three prostitute sisters known as 'the Three Graces'. She had all the qualities of the successful courtesan, she was wildly extravagant, imprudent, altogether outrageous. She said 'a fifty pound note is as good as an introduction.' She cut a swathe through the aristocracy and when she fell on hard times wrote her memoirs, then sent copies of the manuscript to all her many high-born lovers with a note demanding '£200 by return of post, to be left out'. She had listed them in the index by rank: Dukes, Argyle, Beaufort, Leinster etc., Marquesses, Anglesey, Bath, Hertford, 'and so on down through Burke's Peerage to the modest Esquire' (Lesley Blanch, ibid.).

One of the few to resist this blatant blackmail was the Duke of Wellington, who is said to have scrawled 'Publish and be damned' on the manuscript before sending it back. This may account for the unflattering portrait of him in the memoirs.[8]

Harriette was born in Mayfair in 1786, one of fifteen children. It was said that of the nine who survived only three of the girls led respectable lives. Her sisters Amy, Fanny and Sophia where also whores. Sophia married Lord Berwick, and snubbed her sisters. Harriette got her revenge by taking the box directly above Sophia's at the opera, and spitting down on her head. (Because of her marriage Sophia was not considered one of the 'graces'). Here is an example of Harriette's lively style from the *Memoirs*:

I was getting into debt, as well as my sister Amy, when it so came to pass, as I have since heard say, that the — immortal!!! No; that's common; a very outlandish distinction, fitter for a lady in a balloon. The terrific!!! that will do better. I have seen His Grace in his cotton nightcap. Well, then, the terrific Duke of Wellington!! the wonder of the world!!! ... at three on the following day, Wellington made his appearance. He bowed first, then said —

'How do you do?' then thanked me for giving him permission to call on me; and then wanted to take hold of my hand.

'Really,' said I, withdrawing my hand, 'for such a renowned hero you have very little to say for yourself.'

'Beautiful creature!' uttered Wellington ... 'Beautiful eyes, yours ...'

'Aye, man! they are greater conquerors than ever Wellington shall be ...'

Wellington was now my constant visitor – a most unentertaining one, Heaven knows! and in the evening, when he wore his broad red ribbon, he looked very like a rat-catcher.

'Do you know,' said I to him one day, 'do you know the world talks about hanging you?'

'Eh?' said Wellington.

'They say you will be hanged, in spite of all your brother Wellesley can say in your defence.'

She treats her affair with Wellington as a kind of farce, but Harriette's heart could be touched: the *Memoirs* chronicle her brief affair with Lord Ponsonby, the love of her life. Fifteen years after it ended she wrote to Lord Byron: 'Don't despise me – nothing Lord Ponsonby has dearly loved can be wholly destitute of merit.'

She may have been bullied into blackmail over the memoirs by her lover, the shady and probably bogus Colonel William Henry Rochfort. The book was a bestseller, and apart from the blackmail money should have made them both rich. The publisher, Stockdale, had to erect barriers outside his shop in the Haymarket to hold back the crowds, and the pair are said to have received £10,000. Both Harriette and Stockdale paid a high price; he engulfed in lawsuits and she ostracised. In 1830 she was charged with assaulting her French maid. 'There was a lot of noisy recriminations and the newspapers made much of Harriette's vanished looks, the Colonel's doubtful ancestry and their joint inability to raise bail' (Blanch, ibid.). Nothing is heard of her after 1832 and it is not known when or where she died. There was a story, probably untrue, that one of her lovers had once tried to lure her away to live in his house in the country, but Harriette, 'never one for ruralising', turned him down. Under the terms of his will the richly furnished house has stood shuttered and empty ever since.

Kiss and tell: the courtesan Harriette Wilson, who wrote revealing memoirs and tried to blackmail the Duke of Wellington.

The Pretty Horsebreakers

After Harriette's death upper-class vice became less public for a time. Wealthy men still kept mistresses, of course, but more discreetly. In the 1850s, however, it was noticed that they were again appearing on the arms of rich men at places of entertainment such as theatres and racecourses. In 1857 a writer in *Paul Pry* said: 'There can be no disguising the fact that at the West End, at Brompton, at St John's Wood, Foley Place, Portland Road, Regent's Park and intermediate spots some of the most magnificent women in London live under the protection of gentlemen.'

Holman Hunt's painting *The Awakened Conscience* gives a good idea of how a St John's Wood *demi-mondaine*'s home would have looked. The narrative picture shows a mistress leaping conscience-stricken from the lap of her rather swell lover, who has been idly stroking the keys of the upright rosewood piano. For us it is not the strident moralising that is most interesting but the vulgar furnishings of the mid-Victorian room. Everything is bright and rather too new – the Turkish carpet, the gilt clock under the glass cover, the gilt mirror. It is all newly bought, just like the girl.

Mistresses also began to flaunt their wealth and fine clothes by riding in Hyde Park, to the annoyance of the respectable middle classes. Attractive women who would have been barred from the park if they appeared on foot were allowed in on horseback. They were called 'the pretty horsebreakers'. The author George Augustus Sala wrote in 1859:

Can any scene in the world equal Rotten Row at four in the afternoon and in the full tide of the season? Watch the sylphides as they fly or float past in their ravishing riding habits and intoxicating delightful hats... from time to time the naughty wind will flutter the skirt of a habit, and display a tiny, coquettish brilliant little boot, with a military heel, and tightly strapped over it the Amazonian riding trouser.'

Respectable opinion was outraged and newspapers compared the situation unfavourably to the licentiousness of the Regency period. There was even a music-hall song commenting on the horsewomen:

The young swells in Rotten Row, all cut it mighty fine,
And quiz the fair sex, you know, and say it is divine,
The pretty little horsebreakers are breaking hearts like fun,
For in Rotten Row they all must go
The whole hog or none.

It was a picture of one of the pretty horsebreakers that turned what was a scandal into a cause célèbre. The portrait by the leading painter Sir Edwin Landseer was ostensibly of a respectable horse-woman, a Miss Gilbert. Although it was voted Picture of the Year in 1861 it was clearly a portrait not of Miss Gilbert but of one of the leading courtesans of the day, Catherine Walters, better known as 'Skittles'. She was the mistress of Lord Hartington, heir to the Duke of Devonshire, described as the most eligible bachelor in London. Catherine had been a prostitute in Liverpool, and would go on to become one of the great courtesans of the age.

The controversy was heightened by a letter to *The Times*, ostensibly from 'Seven Belgravian Mothers'. It may have been written by James Matthew Higgins, 'man about town and a quixotic provoker of controversies' (Trevor Fisher, *Prostitution and the Victorians*, 1997).

Sir – We, seven Belgravian mothers appeal to you... to make known our present distressing condition... We are mothers – with one exception, noblewomen... we have without exception daughters at our disposal, of whom we have now for several seasons, industriously and in all propriety endeavoured to dispose. To make them eligible as wives of high rank we have spared no pain, no cost, no amount of careful study. They were carefully reared at our country seats in every principle, that we, and religious governesses at high salaries, esteemed to be good . . . We have taken every advantage – some of us – for at least seven seasons, and yet our dear girls are still at home. We cannot accuse ourselves of any neglect of our duty, as mothers with one purpose at heart – their establishment as wives; we have ever diligently sought their attachment, as far as Providence permitted us, to the 'heirs' of the day. Balls, bazaars, breakfasts, concerts, scientific *conversazioni*, the churches and chapels, where music, art, or eloquence attract the young men of the day; the Opera, Epsom, Ascot, Volunteer reviews, even the Crystal Palace – all of these gave us opportunities . . . but all has been in vain.

We seven have at this moment 24 daughters, actually what our sons call 'in running', not one of whom has had an offer that any one of us mothers for a moment could have entertained . . . However unpleasant, indelicate the truth, all dreadful as it is to us to write it, marriage in our set is voted a bore – is repudiated . . .

With all pain, and some shame, we declare it – an openly recognised anti-matrimonial element pervades good society . . . And why? Because what our simple-minded daughters call 'the pretty horsebreakers' occupy naughtily and temporarily where we should occupy *en permanence*.

Go where we will, the mother's eye has this social cruel pest intruded upon it: those bad rivals of our children are no longer kept in the background, as things we know, but, knowing, are seen not to know. Neither Row nor ring, church nor chapel, opera nor concert are wanting in their evident presence . . .

This absurd and amusing letter provoked the *Daily Telegraph* to write that it 'no more emanates from seven English noblewomen than it does from seven Irish washerwomen'. The *Annual Register* said: 'Unfortunately the picture was suggestive of one of the social scandals of the hour, and the public was as much attracted by "The Pretty Horse Breaker" as by the wonderful art of the painter.'

As Trevor Fisher says in *Prostitution and the Victorians*, 1862 brought enlightenment to those who were so far unaware of the scandal. That summer Skittles was seen with Hartington at the Derby, and *The Times* published another amusing letter, saying her notoriety was attracting such crowds to Rotten Row to ogle at her that they had become a serious obstruction to traffic. The letter refers to Skittles as Anonyma:

Up to the beginning of last year the fashionable world chiefly affected the Ladies' Mile in the Park...the thoroughfare from Apsley House to Kensington was comparatively unfrequented, save by Anonyma. But this year, when the road is more especially required to be kept open for the convenience of visitors to the Exhibition, it is daily choked with fashionable carriages – from five to seven – all on account of Anonyma. Chairs are placed along it either side; the best parties that England knows...all sit there watching for Anonyma. About 6 pm a rumour arises that Anonyma is coming. Expectation rises to its highest pitch; a handsome woman drives rapidly by in a carriage drawn by thoroughbred ponies...but alas! she causes no effect at all, for she is not Anonyma; she is only the Duchess of A—, the Marchioness of B—, the Countess of C—, or some other of Anonyma's eager imitators. The crowd, disappointed, reseat themselves and wait. Another pony carriage succeeds – and another – with the same depressing result. At last their patience is rewarded. Anonyma and her ponies appear, and they are satisfied. She threads her way decorously, with an unconscious air, through the throng, commented on by hundreds who envy her. She pulls up her ponies to speak to an acquaintance, and his carriage is instantly surrounded by a multitude; she turns and drives back towards Apsley House, and then – away into the unknown world, nobody knows whither. Meanwhile thousands returning from the Exhibition are intolerably delayed by the crowds collected to gaze on this pretty creature and her pretty ponies, and the efforts of Sir Richard Mayne and his police to keep the thoroughfare open are utterly frustrated.

Could you not, Sir, whose business is to know everything and everybody, and who possibly, therefore, may know Anonyma herself, prevail on her to drive in some other portion of the Park as long as the Exhibition lasts? If she will but do this, the fashionable crowd will certainly follow her, and the road to the Exhibition will be set free for the use of the public.

Soon afterwards Hartington's father learned of his affair with Skittles and the relationship ended. Hartington went on to a distinguished political career, becoming leader of the Liberals in the 1870s. Skittles, who had been bought off, became one of the *grandes horizontales*, as the most famous courtesans were by then known. She found time to be the lover of the minor poet Wilfred Scawen Blunt, who made her the heroine of his *Love Sonnets of Proteus*. The Prince of Wales visited her parties and Gladstone even dropped in for tea. Skittles was remembered for skating with 'memorable grace' at the new roller-skating rinks in London and Tunbridge Wells. Whores continued to parade in Rotten Row.

Hell Raisers and Rakes

London in the nineteenth century was noted for its societies for the suppression of vice: in the eighteenth century there were societies for its promotion. Some had been founded in the seventeenth century. These included the Beaus' Club, which gave lectures on the finer points of whores, and the Dancing Club, which held dances where members would partner prostitutes. For aristocrats there were the Hell Fire clubs, 'dedicated to atheism and sexual depravity'. They indulged in satanic rituals and so exasperated the establishment that in 1721 George I issued an order for their suppression. The blasphemous Order of Saint Francis at Medmenham Abbey near High Wycombe in Buckinghamshire created another scandal. There are no first-hand accounts of its activities by any of the thirteen men who formed the inner circle of 'monks' and much of what follows is speculative, although none of the principal participants ever denied any of these charges. Outside this inner core there was a constantly changing group of more or less involved visitors, anxious to take part or be scandalised.

The guiding spirit was Sir Francis Dashwood, rapist, rake, drunkard and a future chancellor of the exchequer. His mistress, the brothel-keeper Mrs Stanhope, was known as Hell-Fire Stanhope. Visitors and members included Lords Bute, Sandwich and Melcomb and many others, including the political gadfly John Wilkes, Lord Mayor of London. They hired the abbey, furnished the cells comfortably, installed a pornographic library and set about recruiting upper-class ladies for their sexual orgies. These women wore masks as they surveyed the scene in the candlelight. Only when they were satisfied that no member of their family was unexpectedly present would they reveal their identities. The monks then chose their partners, presumably by consent. There were said to be doctors and midwives to deal with pregnancies, and children of such brief couplings were called 'the sons and daughters of St Francis'. If the supply of aristocratic nuns showed signs of drying up, or the monks wanted variety, says Henriques in *Prostitution and Society*, those other 'nuns', the whores of the St James and Covent Garden brothels, were called upon.

Lesbianism was encouraged, and watched by the whole company. It was said that incest was contrived because sometimes before an orgy all the participants were blindfolded, and a monk might unwittingly make love to his sister, or even his mother. The sight of a naked young girl lying on an altar surrounded by flickering candles rekindled the sex drive of many a jaded habitué of the London brothels, especially if they drank the holy wine from her navel.

One of the bawds who 'brought her Nymphs to participate in the outrageous Orgies' was Charlotte Hayes. Among the upper-class 'nuns' were said to be Frances, Viscountess Fane, the intrepid but middle-aged Lady Mary Wortley Montague, Lady Betty Germain and Dashwood's half-sister, Mary Walcott. Some of the most important political figures of the time were involved, although how deeply is not known. Lord Bute was soon to be prime minister. Lord Sandwich, known as Jemmy Twitcher, a sadistic rapist obsessed with defloration, was first lord of the admiralty at a time when sea power was vital to Britain's interests. He was said to be 'completely depraved, as mischievous as a monkey and as lecherous as a goat'. Thomas Potter, son of the Archbishop of Canterbury, was paymaster-general and treasurer for Ireland. He was rumoured to be a necrophiliac. William Douglas, later fourth Duke of Queensberry and among the richest men in Europe, was the lecher of the age. John Wilkes, defender of democracy, was a fearless critic of the status quo. The Chevalier D'Eon, who appeared at different times as a man and a woman, and whose sex was a source of constant speculation among the monks, was too discreet to perform in public. When he died he was found to be a man.

This is how Horace Walpole described the order:

He [Dashwood] and some chosen friends had hired the ruins of Medmenham Abbey, near Marlow, and refitted it in conventual style. Thither at stated seasons they adjourned: had each their cell, a proper habit, a monastic name, and a refectory in common – besides a chapel, the decoration of which may well be supposed to have contained the quintessence of their mysteries, since it was impenetrable to any but the initiated. Whatever their doctrines were, their practice was rigorously pagan: Bacchus and Venus were the deities to whom they almost publicly sacrificed.

The spurious religiosity of the orgies owed something to Dashwood's tortured inner life. When a young man he had 'fornicated his way across Europe' on the grand tour, making his way to Rome, where he was deeply affected by the rites of the Roman Catholic Church. It was said that at one moment he would be jeering at the trappings of relics and vestments, the next he would be on his knees sobbing. On one occasion he produced a whip in the Sistine Chapel and beat those kneeling in prayer. In the rites at Medmenham he took the role of Christ.

Samuel Pepys defied convention in his relationships with many women, including his mistress Betty Lane, which did not end when she became the wife of the exchequer clerk Samuel Martin. Betty and her sister Doll were linen drapers at Westminster Hall, and Pepys bought his linen bands from them. On 29 June 1663 he writes that he took her to 'the further Rhenish wine-house – where I did give her a lobster and do so towse her and feel her all over, making her believe how fair and good a skin she had; and indeed, she hath a very white thigh and leg, but monstrous fat'. In September the affair has progressed: he took her to Lambeth 'where we were lately, and there did what I would with her but only the main thing, which she would not consent to, for which God be praised; and yet I came so near, that I was provoked to spend. But trust in the Lord that I shall not do so again while I live.'

Frank diarist: Samuel Pepys, who was candid about his affairs and his strong feelings for the great beauties of his day.

They soon become lovers, however, and on 3 June 1666 he records in his mixture of shorthand and various languages: 'And so to Mrs Martin and there did what je voudrais avec her, both devante and backward, which is also muy bon plazer'. Betty gave him these intimate sexual favours over a long period of time, and in return got what we might call a good night out – visits to taverns to drink wine and eat chicken and cake. Her readiness to please him he repaid with pious scorn. 'I perceive she is come to be very bad and offers anything', he wrote in February 1666. There were many other women of the same class: one, a Mrs Bagwell, he continued to use even though he came to despise her.

Pepys was infatuated with Charles II's mistress Lady Castlemaine, and would listen to any gossip about her. His employer Lord Sandwich's maid Sarah was a source of such gossip, which on one occasion so excited him that he made a pass at her. 'I went up to her and played and talked with her and, God forgive me, did I feel her, which I am much ashamed of, but I did no more, though I had so much a mind to it that I spent in my breeches.'

The voyeur: when he was too old to take an active part Old Q still spied on the sexual commerce outside his Piccadilly mansion. Guildhall Library, Corporation of London

SPY'S Taken at GREENWICH on EASTER-MONDAY.

Two veterans: The Duke of Queensberry
with the celebrated bawd Mother
Windsor and two of her girls in
Greenwich Park. He was one of
her best customers.

Right: Buy my goods: an old man is importuned by street sellers and prostitutes as he knocks at the door of a brothel.

Below: Fore play: a sedate audience at Covent Garden Theatre. Many of the women went there looking for wealthy pick-ups. They took boxes to advertise their charms as widely as possible.

Previous left page: Rough justice: two men await their fate at the hands of the mob in the pillory at Charing Cross.

Previous right page: Trial and error: an apprehensive prisoner watches as a woman gives evidence at the Old Bailey. Trials often lasted just a few minutes.

Below: Sin and sophistication: a masquerade at the elegant Pantheon in Oxford Street. It was impossible to stop gallants taking in celebrated courtesans.

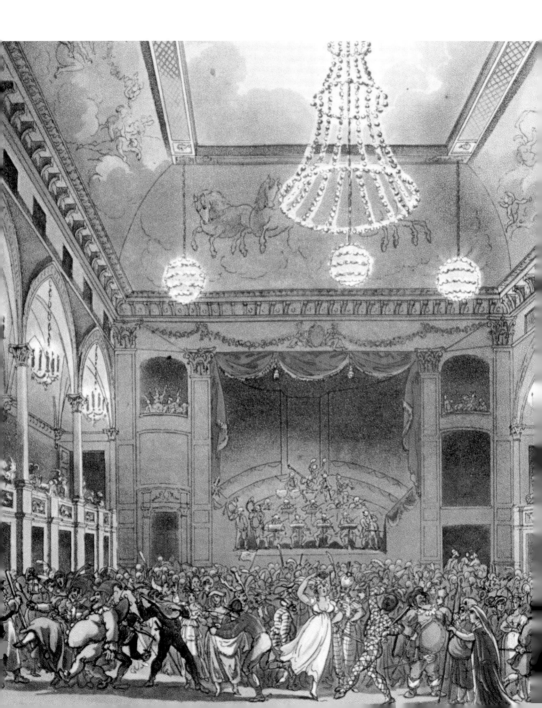

Above: Light entertainment: music in the pleasure gardens at Vauxhall. In the darkened shrubbery, on the other hand, there were sighs and screams.

Mean streets: a scene in present-day Soho. The Street Offences Act of 1959 drove the street-walkers away.

Left: Modern-day advertising: prostitutes' cards from phone boxes in central London.

Pepys's peccadilloes pale against the transgressions of one of the most notorious of all eighteenth century rakes, Colonel Francis Charteris, rapist, debaucher of young girls, cardsharp and Sally Salisbury's first lover when she was in her early teens. Charteris is shown in Plate 1 of Hogarth's print series *A Harlot's Progress*. A sweet young country girl newly arrived in town is propositioned by a bawd, easily recognised by contemporaries as the notorious Mother Needham. The colonel lurks nearby in a doorway with his cringing servant Jack Gourlay, who acted as his pander. The colonel was lucky to be alive to contemplate fresh sexual adventures. Shortly before Hogarth began his series early in 1730 Charteris was tried for the rape of his servant Anne Bond, having frightened her 'into Compliance with his filthy Desires' by holding his pistol to her head.

The court was told that Anne, who was out of work, was sitting by the door of her lodgings one day when a woman offered her a job as servant to Charteris. As soon as she took up her post he laid siege to her. At seven one morning 'the Colonel rang a Bell and bid the Clerk of the Kitchen call the Lancashire Bitch into the Dining Room.' Charteris locked the door, threw her onto the couch, gagged her with his nightcap and raped her. When she threatened to tell her friends he horse-whipped her and took away her clothes and money.

Charteris's rich and aristocratic friends packed into the court to hear him sentenced to death for rape. He was in Newgate less than a month, and received a royal pardon, probably negotiated by his cousin the Duke of Wharton, friend and protector of some of the great bawds of the age. He had been seen giving generous gifts to the Prime Minister, Robert Walpole. 'It was a bitter rebuff to popular notions of justice,' (Jenny Uglow, *Hogarth*, 1997). Charteris, who a made a fortune from South Sea stock and had great estates in Lancashire, was a hate figure for the poor. Known as the Rape-Master of Great Britain, he boasted of seducing more than a hundred women, and sent out servants to find 'none but such as were strong, lusty and fresh Country Wenches, of the first size, their B–tt–cks as hard as Cheshire Cheeses, that could make a Dint in a Wooden Chair, and work like a parish Engine at a Conflagration,' (Anonymous, *Some Authentic Memoirs of the Life of Colonel C–s, Rape-Master of Great Britain*, 1730).

Innocence and experience: in Plate 1 of A Harlot's Progress *a pretty country girl newly arrived in town is propositioned by the notorious bawd Mother Needham. Looking on is the rake Colonel Francis Chateris.*

Charteris's crimes were mind-boggling, and made entertaining reading in a flood of pamphlets. He was accused of rape, using loaded dice, fraud, bearing false witness, denying his bastard children and, not least, being an associate of Robert Walpole. He used his army rank, although he had been cashiered for embezzlement. His aristocratic connections got him out of several scrapes, as when he drew his sword on a constable in St James's Park, and when he raped a young virgin in the Scotch Ale-House in Pall Mall. He had to pay maintenance for the bastard child born to the girl. A Scots woman giving evidence against him for rape said: 'This is the huge raw beast that in guid faith got me with Bairn...I know him by his nastie Legg for he has wrapt it round my Arse mony a guid time!' (Burford, *Royal St James's*).

He owned brothels, financed by cheating at cards. He won £3,000 from the Duchess of Queensberry by placing her in front of a mirror in which he could see her cards. This got him banned from several clubs.

After a girl had been rescued from him by her sister, neighbours stormed Charteris's house with 'Stones, Brickbats, and other such vulgar Ammunition.' When he was released from Newgate following the Anne Bond case, he was set upon by a London crowd. (Uglow, *Hogarth*). He died in 1731, probably from venereal disease, and the mob threw 'dead dogs &c. into the grave' with him.

Unlike the type of the cynical aristocratic exploiter Charteris, Frederic Calvert, Baron Baltimore, perhaps earns our grudging sympathy because of his eccentricity. Baltimore was profoundly influenced by his travels. Upon his return to London, he used his immense fortune to build a fine house which he turned into a harem, on the lines of those he had seen at Constantinople. His seraglio consisted of 'five white and one black woman', whom he treated with great generosity. They were not permitted to go out unchaperoned, but otherwise could have anything they wanted. When he tired of them he loaded them with presents, even dowries, and sent them on their way. They were presided over by his wife, Lady Diane Egerton, who 'acted as the Mistress of her husband's harem... chaperoning the girls in their outdoor excursions'.

Naturally he became famous, or notorious, and songs and satires were written about him. Then he was accused of rape by a sixteen year-old he had kidnapped from her father's shop on Tower Hill. 'A criminal process was instituted in consequence of this accusation; but his lordship vindicated his innocence, and triumphed over the malice of his enemies. This affair, however, made a lively impression on his mind; he dismissed his mistresses, sold his house ... gave away the magnificent furniture, and in a short time left his native country' (von Archenholz). This true English eccentric died shortly afterwards in Naples in about 1778.

Perhaps the most debauched character of this period, and there are many to choose from, is William Douglas, fourth Duke of Queensberry, known variously as Lord Piccadilly or Old Q. Like Lord Baltimore he was immensely rich, and he had other passions besides sex: he gambled on a magnificent scale, he was a patron of the arts and the turf and he was a dandy. Old Q was a customer of the brothel-keeper Sarah Dubery. His housekeeper, Maria Moreton, wrote in her memoirs that he 'employed that skilful Procuress Mrs Dubery to procure his Sultanas ... candidates were paraded for inspection ... she seldom served him with a dish that he could not make at least one meal upon. If he approved, he rang a bell and Mrs D ... had to school the Novitiate in her duties ... ' Old Q's appetite may occasionally have been greater than his capacity, however: one girl disclosed that 'the Piccadilly Sultan left me as good a maid as he found me ... making a violent Fit of Coughing after an hour as an apology for his sudden retreat from the field of love'.

One of his mistresses was Kitty Fredericks, 'the very Thais of London'. She had originally been one of Charlotte Hayes's girls, and was passed on to Catherine Matthews when that bawd took over the Hayes establishment at 5 King's Place. Mrs Matthews became one of several panders employed by Old Q, and he acquired Kitty for £100 a year, 'a genteel house' and a carriage. Kitty became known as Duchess of Queensberry elect and Old Q's friends expected he would marry her. However, in 1779, when Old Q was in his mid-fifties, they quarrelled and parted. Kitty became one of the best-known and highest-paid courtesans of the epoch. Old Q never married.

Scandal sheet: an example of the 'Tête-a-Tête' series from the Town and Country Magazine. *This one features Old Q and his mistress the Contessa della Rena.*

Four years after the quarrel the *Rambler Magazine* carried a caricature of the bawd Mrs Windsor bargaining with Old Q for the services of three young whores – twenty-year-old Lucy; Polly, seventeen; and Priscilla, fifteen. Mrs Windsor wants £200 for Priscilla, claiming that 'old Mr Solomons' would pay even more. Old Q says: 'They are very young. Will you warrant them?' Mrs Windsor replies: 'Warrant, my Lord! I am astonished at you... They are chaste, virtuous girls... One has almost got her maidenhead!' In the end his lordship takes them all, in a kind of job lot.

Old Q presided over tremendous orgies at his houses in Richmond and at 138 Piccadilly, and it was said that his sexual powers, despite occasional failures like that mentioned above, seemed to increase with advancing years. Thackeray wrote of him in old age in *The Four Georges*: 'This wrinkled, paralysed, toothless old Don Juan died the same corrupt, unrepentant fellow he had been in the most fiery days of his youth. In a house in Piccadilly there is a low window where old Queensberry is said to have sat in order to peer at passing women with voluptuous eyes.'

Bawds, whores, bullies, fools and drunkards, fighting around under the Piazzas in Covent Garden surrounded by a number of daring pickpockets and frightened constables... Poor honest women who are waiting in their apartments for the coming home of their drunken husbands from night-cellars or bawdy-houses, are mending stockings and shirts, ironing linen, washing infants' apparel or performing other acts of good housewifery to pass the time until they return. Young maidens who have been awake two-thirds of the night, kicking and sprawling as they lie in bed, and praying for strong-backed husbands, no matter of what nation, religion or occupation.

Such persons as intend to act the characters of highwaymen the ensuing day, and have received intelligence the preceding night what road some particular gentlemen are to travel (who are known to be cowards and worth robbing) from the runners and sweepers of inns, are setting out on their expeditions, to reconnoitre the ground and find out a proper place for the attack. Poor people carrying their dead children nailed up in small deal boxes into the fields to bury them privately, and save the extravagant charge of parish dues...

Poor servant maids plagued in their bed-chambers with the pressing and wheedling persuasiveness of their lewd and infirm masters... News-collectors who are in bed, instead of at their prayers, are inventing stories of rapes, robberies, riots etc to fill up the newspapers for the ensuing week...

A knocking at pawnbrokers' doors by twelve-penny harlots to redeem some wearing apparel which they are obliged to put on, as they are being sent for to some bagnio on fresh duty. Great numbers of people of all nations, opinions, circumstances and sizes of understanding, going to the Bantering Booth on Windmill Hill, Upper Moorfields, to hear their beloved Apostle, Mr Wesley...

Poor devils of women, with empty bellies, naked backs, and heads intoxicated with Geneva, standing and gossiping with each other in the street, whose discourse always begins and ends with wishing each other the Compliments of the Season, it being Whit Sunday...

Handsome whores hurrying home from the bagnios in hack-coaches and chairs, to the houses of their keepers, that they may change their clothes and linen, and go upon fresh service. Kept mistresses are as lazy in their beds as lifeguardsmen and common soldiers are in their quarters. Beggars planting themselves about church doors, that with their forced cries and sham sores they may seize upon the parishioners going to Divine Service...

Vintners and publicans joyfully open their doors after the recess of business for two hours. Common servants in a great bustle in their dark, dirty kitchens, preparing dinner for their noisy, voracious and dainty masters. Measly pork, rusty bacon, stinking lamb, rotten mutton, stinking veal, and coddled cow, with yellow greens, sooty pottage, and greasy pudding, sold at the common cooks' shops about the skirts of the Town...

The friends of criminals under sentence of death in Newgate presenting money to turnkeys to get to the sight of them, in order to take their last farewell, and present them with white caps with black ribbons, prayer-books, nosegays and oranges, that they may make a decent appearance up Holborn, on the road to the other world...

Foolish husbands praising their wives before their faces, which only heightens their pride, and brings themselves under petticoat government. Poor undone dogs of husbands, who were foolish enough to spend all their money the preceding night, and not make a reserve by hiding some in the Family Bible, bottom of the chamber pot, or top of the bed's tester (where they may be sure wives never search) on their knees to borrow a sixpence of their termagant helpmates for the use of the afternoon...

Widows, whose husbands are to be buried in the evening, are dressing themselves in their weeds, and humming over tunes in a room by themselves, being pleased that they are their own mistresses...

Common whores and thieves, who have been out on their different occupations the preceding night, contriving as they lie in bed who they shall delude or rob the ensuing evening. The tap-rooms of the prisons are filling with the friends of prisoners

A Harlot's Progress: *Plate 2 of Hogarth's series shows the harlot upsetting a tea table so her lover can escape without being seen by her Jewish keeper.*

A Harlot's Progress: *In Plate 3 the harlot has become a common whore, robbing her clients. Unseen by her, Sir John Gonson, scourge of prostitutes, is coming to arrest her.*

who are come to see them, where they pay an extravagant price for pricked wine and muddy sour beer, since they cannot sell punch or spirituous liquors . . .

Well-dressed gentlemen and ladies of quality driven out of St James's Park, Lincoln's Inn Gardens, and Gray's Inn Walks by milliners, mantua-makers, sempstresses, stay-makers, French barbers, dancing masters, gentlemen's gentlemen, tailors' wives and butchers' daughters.

Night-walkers washing their smocks, caps, aprons, and hand-kerchiefs, against the evening, that they may appear clean in their walks.

The taverns about the Royal Exchange are filled with merchants, underwriters and principal tradesmen, who often-times do as much business on the Sunday evening as they do when they go upon the Exchange. A general ringing of bells on board the vessels in the river, in order to see the night's watch. The turnkeys of prisons locking all fast, that they may drink with the prisoners' friends . . .

As it is now twilight, reputable young fellows, as students in the law, merchants' clerks, non-commissioned officers, depend-ent nephews and grandsons, coasting commanders and mechanics' sons, who have been unhappily scarred in the wars of Venus, are repairing to their several quack doctors and surgeons' pupils, to get safe, easy and speedy cure for their several disorders . . .

Undertakers who have a body to bury from their own houses, which they have sold to be anatomised, are interring a coffin full of rubbish, and suffer a funeral service to be devoutly performed over it. Black eyes and broken heads exhibited pretty plentifully in the streets. A multiplicity of lies told by old men and travellers in public-houses, concerning the troubles, travels and adventures of their lives . . . Young highwaymen, venturing out upon the road, to attack such coaches, chaises and horsemen as they think are worth meddling with on their return to London . . .

The streets hardly wide enough for numbers of people who are reeling to their habitations. Sailors lately come from abroad, in close conversation with whores, punch and bottled ale, at the public-houses in Rotherhithe, Limehouse, Wapping and St Catherine's . . .

Some nurses and watchers in the hospitals getting together, when they think a poor patient is near making his exit, and taking the pillows from under their heads, that they may go quietly out of the world a few hours sooner than they otherwise would have done; in the meanwhile they search their pockets, carrying away what is valuable, and vouch for each other, that they found nothing but a tobacco-box, pocket-piece [lucky coin], and almanack, or some other trifling thing about them.

Link-boys who have just money sufficient to buy a torch taking their stands at Temple Bar, London Bridge, Lincoln's Inn Fields, Smithfield, the City Gates, and other public places, to light, knock down and rob people who are walking about their business. Mrs Mary Daggle-Ass and other ladies of her profession cursing and roaring at her wenches and drawers, to drown the dismal cries and groans of departing maidenheads. Destitute whores and runaway apprentices, who have neither lodging, money nor friends, carrying hay, etc, into empty houses to make their beds. The lamplighters of the several wards preparing to go out and give the lamps within their rounds a trimming. The slaves who do business for nightmen [removers of ordure etc] preparing their teams of horses, to come into the City and follow their occupation . . .

Street robbers and house-breakers patrolling about the streets, looking sharp after the watchmen, and considering who they may knock down and rob, or what houses they may break into . . .

The streets begin to swarm with whores and pickpockets. Smithfield in an uproar with drovers who are driving in oxen, sheep, lambs and hogs, for the ensuing market. Night-houses begin to fill with whores, thieves, drunkards, foolish tradesmen and lumberers. Attendance of 'I wish you a good night' bestowed by friends on each other, after spending the evening together. One-third of the inhabitants of London, Westminster and Southwark fast asleep, and almost penniless. The whole

body of the watch with their staves and lanthorns ready to cry the
hour, 'Past twelve o'clock´.

Finally back to Drury Lane. Perhaps best left to last is Swift's
loathsome depiction of an aged and heart-weary whore, 'A Beautiful
Young Nymph Going to Bed'. It is a work of marvellous invention,
but too true to be really funny:

> Corinna, pride of Drury Lane,
> For whom no shepherd sighs in vain;
> Never did Covent Garden boast
> So bright a battered, strolling toast...
> With gentlest touch, she next explores
> Her shankers, issues, running sores;
> Effects of many a sad disaster,
> And then to each applies a plaster.

Rascal Beadles

Thou rascal Beadle, hold thy bloody hand.
Why dost thou lash that Whore?...
Thou hotly lust'st to use her in that kind
For which thou whip'st her...

(William Shakespeare, *King Lear*)

The desire to inflict pain on women is strong in some men, particularly moralists. Shakespeare suggests one reason for this: he also points up the double standard that men, as the lawmakers, apply. Prostitutes are punished. Men, their customers, are not. A Royal Commission report of 1871 justified this by saying there was no comparison between women who sold sex for gain and men who were after all only giving in to a natural impulse.

The sixteenth-century Puritan writer Philip Stubbes tells of whores punished by being bound hand and foot and towed behind a rowing boat on the Thames. He considered this 'a soft punishment almost as a ducking' – he would have let them drown. He held prostitution to be the great social problem of his time.

Another terrible punishment was the branks, an iron mask with a vicious spike which was pushed into the mouth. This was a punishment for scolds and witches, but it was occasionally used for prostitutes. There is an engraving of a Mrs Anne Biddlestone wearing it in 1648. She was driven through the streets 'by an Officer, a Rope in his Hands at the other end fastened to an engine called The Branks like a Crown of Iron muzzled over her Head and

Face with a great Tongue of Iron forced into her Mouth which forc'd the Blood out . . .'

However, the normal punishment for whores and bawds was not so drastic. A series of ordinances set out how they were to be treated. In 1383 one on 'Men Found to be Whoremongers or Bawds' says that such an offender was to have his head and beard shaved save for a two-inch fringe on the scalp. He was then to be taken to the pillory accompanied by minstrels to drum up and excite a crowd. If caught a second time he would again get the pillory plus ten days' imprisonment. The punishment for a third offence was dire: the pillory, jail and expulsion from the city for ever. This banishment seems a very powerful sanction indeed, but from the numbers of frequent reoffenders it is clear that men and women simply returned to their old haunts as soon as possible.

The punishment for women was similar. A female bawd was taken in an open cart with a red and white awning to match her striped hood, accompanied by hired minstrels, to the thew, a special pillory for women; her hair would be cut. For further offences a spell in prison would be added, and then expulsion.

A 'common courtesan' would be taken from prison 'at the cart's arse' to the thew at Aldgate wearing her striped hood and carrying a white wand, accompanied by the minstrels. A 'Cause' – a piece of paper setting out her crime – would be read to the spectators, and then stuck on her head. She would be led through Cheapside to Newgate and thrown out of the gate to nearby Cock Lane, to 'take up her abode'. For the third offence she would additionally have her head shaved and be ejected from the city 'for ever'. It is difficult now to imagine the pain and shame of being led through streets full of jeering, laughing spectators, preceded by hired musicians, and that in a city and at a time when morality was loose.

There were other categories of sexual offenders, although the punishment was more or less the same. A priest found having sex with 'any woman' was taken to the prison called the Tun on Cornhill accompanied by minstrels. A third offence meant exile from the city. If an adulteress was found with a priest or a married man both would be taken to the Compter or prison. After that they would be arraigned before the mayor and aldermen, taken to Newgate where their heads would be shaved, then conveyed by cart with minstrels to the Tun, where they would remain 'at the discretion of the Mayor'. It is interesting that in theory both offenders were to be treated equally.

That was certainly not so when on 25 July 1385 Elizabeth Moring was taken before the mayor on charges of being a bawd. It was claimed that under the guise of carrying on the 'craft of broidery' she had employed several girls and women. This was a front for a kind of escort service, in which she sent out 'little Johanna' and others to various men including 'friars and chaplains'.

The court was told that on 4 May she had sent 'little Johanna' to an unnamed chaplain, with whom the girl stayed all night. When Johanna returned the next morning Mrs Moring asked her what she had been paid. Johanna said she had not been paid at all, and 'the said Elizabeth used words of reproof to her, and ordered her to go back to the chaplain again on the following night and steal whatever she could'.

Johanna spent the next night with the chaplain and in the morning stole a breviary, which Mrs Moring pawned for 8d. 'And many other times...this Elizabeth received the like base gains from the said Johanna and her other sewing women...she being herselfe common harlot and procuress...living abominably and damnably.' Mrs Moring was sent to prison but the chaplain, although clearly a regular customer of whores, was not punished or even named, despite having broken the law.

In 1550 a haberdasher named Middleton and his wife were arraigned for bawdry. Mrs Middleton was charged 'she for a common adulterix with one Nicholas Ballard, gentleman, both with her own body and also bawd to him for her own daughter also and a maid of ten or eleven yeares of age, her servant, which the said Ballard occupied all three carnally'.

The husband and wife were ordered to be carted with hoods and rods. Ballard was another matter: he was a gentleman, and therefore could not be treated like a commoner. However, the city authorities were determined to make an example of him. He pleaded guilty to rape and was given a short prison sentence and burned in the hand.

There was, as Bishop Latimer had said, much whoredom in London. In 1555, while the Catholic bigot Queen Mary I was on the throne, the harrying of bawds and whores reached new levels when she ordered cages, pillories and stocks to be set up in all the parishes in London. In November 1555 'the Ill-woman who keeps the Greyhound was carted about the City', and a gentleman, 'Master Manwarynge, with two whores from The Harry was carted to Aldgate for bawdry and whoredom'. The woman who kept The Bell in Grassechurche Street 'was carted as a bawd'. Her house was a long-established brothel.

In 1553, the first year of Mary's reign, another gentleman was in trouble for sexual impropriety. 'Sir Thomas Sothwood priest' was paraded through the streets in a cart for 'selling his wife'. Burford in *The Orrible Synne* says that this was one of the comparatively rare occasions on which a man was reported to have been carted for a sexual offence. By this date the ritual of carting seems to have changed. Now the mob ran before the cart banging metal bowls. In the worst cases the wretched whore or bawd was flogged at 'the cart's arse'.

In 1613 the brothel-keeper Mrs Crabbe was whipped and carted. In December of that year a prostitute named Joan Cole felt the full severity of the law: she was sentenced to be 'whipped and carted with Papers on her Head and with a Bellman ringing his Bell going before her, what time three other Turnbull Street whores must accompany her on this pilgrimage'. (Burford and Wotton, *Private Vices – Public Virtues*). Some whores had their noses slit as a permanent badge of shame.

Church courts could try certain cases involving sexual immorality, as well as some involving disorderly behaviour, slander and defamation. By and large, crimes which were the business of the secular courts, such as brothel-keeping and prostitution, were regarded as outside the jurisdiction of the church courts, but there seems to have been no hard and fast rule. The increasing influence of Puritans around the beginning of the seventeenth century led to a doubling of prosecutions for sexual impropriety in the church courts. However, these courts were seen as soft on sexual offenders and in 1646 they were temporarily suspended.

The Commonwealth brought important changes to the laws on prostitution. The pre-revolutionary Parliament had decreed that prostitution was no longer a felony, but a 'Nuisance if committed in public'. The penalty was a whipping and a brief term in a house of correction. Under the Commonwealth the secular courts were given greater powers against sexual offenders. Incest and adultery were made capital offences, fornication was punished by three months' imprisonment and brothel-keepers faced a combination of whipping, branding on the forehead and imprisonment. In 1660 the church courts were reinstated but they never regained their former influence, and gradually the secular courts took over the whole burden of policing morals.

Around 1700 new perils for whores were the recently formed Societies for the Reformation of Manners. These essentially consisted of Puritans who were deeply affronted by what they saw as the lewdness and profligacy of society after the Restoration, and by the failure of the authorities to grapple with the problem. Their sour disapproval extended to swearing, drinking and Sabbath-breaking.

Responsibility for public order lay with local watch committees, and was enforced by their constables, beadles, patrols and watchmen. There were other police forces, especially in the City, but it was the watch and its officers that usually interacted with prostitutes on the streets. Watchmen were supposed to patrol and keep order on a short 'beat' throughout the night. That could entail arresting disorderly whores and drunkards, raising a hue and cry against criminals and protecting the property of honest citizens. In practice they might prefer the relative warmth of their sentry boxes, and as they were often old and infirm it was easy to sleep away the dangerous watches of the night. Tipsy Regency revellers made a practice of pushing over the boxes with their sleeping occupants inside. Worse, there were many complaints that the watchmen were drinking on duty, failing to arrest or disperse crowds of prostitutes or even consorting with them. One of the constables of St Paul, Covent Garden, in the eighteenth century complained that watchmen spent the time between walking their beats chatting with whores at the coffee stands under the piazzas. Some watchmen refused to arrest prostitutes even when ordered to do so by the constables. When they did arrest one they might be set upon by her friends. And if they succeeded in getting the woman back to the parish watch house, they had to appear in court the next morning to press the charge. Sometimes the women sued for wrongful arrest. No wonder some of the poorly paid watchmen accepted bribes of cash, gin or tobacco from the women to let them go about their business, rather than get involved in all the trouble and risk of arresting them.

Some notoriously corrupt justices of the peace were virtually on the payroll of brothels and one Wapping magistrate rented space in his home to prostitutes. Among many such complaints, the Middlesex Bench was told in 1671 that constables and headboroughs were taking bribes from the brothels in Whetstone Park at the northern side of Lincoln's Inn Fields. The Tower Hamlets Reformation Society issued this broadside:

> Here 'tis the Impudent Harlots by their Antick Dresses, Painted faces and Whorish Insinuations allure and tempt our Sons and Servants to Debauchery, and consequently to embezel and steal from us, to maintain their strumpets. Here 'tis that Bodies are Poxt and Pockets are picked of considerable sums, the revenge of which Injuries have frequently occasioned Quarrellings, Fightings, Bloodshed, Clamours of Murther (and that some-times at midnight) pulling down of signs and parts of houses, breaking of windows, also other tumultuous Routs, Riots and Uproars...Here 'tis that many a House keeper is infected with a venomous Plague, which he communicates to his Honest and Innocent Wife...Here 'tis that Multitudes of Soldiers and Seamen get such bane that effeminates their spirits and soon rots their bodies.

> (Edward J Bristow, *Vice and Vigilance: Purity Movements in Britain Since 1700*)

The reformation societies had the backing of the royal couple, William and Mary. William had issued a *Proclamation for Preventing and Punishing Immorality and Profaneness* in 1698, in which he feared that 'the open and avowed practice of vice' might 'provoke God to withdraw his mercy and blessings from us, and instead thereof to inflict heavy and severe judgements'. With such high-level backing the societies spread across the country.

Thousands of secret informers, many of them small tradesmen such as James Jenkins and Bodenham Rewse from the Strand, were recruited to spy on prostitutes and others who infringed their rules. The informers were to take notice 'of all those, that for the time to come, shall impudently dare, in rebellion against the laws of God and man, to swear and curse, to profane the Lord's Day, or be guilty of the loathsome sin of drunkenness, also by searching out the lurking holes of bawds, whores, and other filthy miscreants, in order to their conviction and punishment according to law'.

Many of the victims of this crusade were the poor and miserable, the drunken labourer and the foul-mouthed working woman. As the anonymous author of *The Poor Man's Plea* pointed out, 'we don't find the rich drunkard carried before my Lord Mayor, nor a swearing lewd merchant punish'd...but if a poor man gets drunk, or swears an oath, he must to the stocks without remedy.'

The new morals police set about cleaning up the streets, to the great resentment of the general public. In 1699 the society reported that 500 disorderly houses had been suppressed:

> Some thousands of lewd persons have been imprisoned, fined and whipt; so that the Tower-End of the town, and many of our streets, have been purged of that pestilent generation of night walkers that used to infest them...forty or fifty of them have been sent in a week to Bridewell, where they have of late received such discipline, that a considerable number of them have chose rather to be transported to our plantations, to work there for an honest subsistence.

One society zealot, Samuel Cooke, arrested hundreds of prostitutes in the 1720s. Later the authorities were forced to admit that the warrants he was serving were illegal. By then many poor wretches had been tortured, including being whipped and having their noses slit. One of these sadistic punishments, stripping the woman to the waist and whipping her, was sanctioned by a sixteenth-century statute which was not repealed until 1817. It stipulated that she 'should be stripped naked from the middle upward and whipped till the body should be bloody'. This was a charter for sadists. The author Ned Ward visited the Bridewell by the Fleet behind Bride Lane and described such punishments in his *London Spy* (1698–1709):

> A grave gentleman whose awful looks bespoke him some honourable citizen, was mounted in the judgement seat, armed with a hammer... and a woman under the lash was in the next room, where folding doors were opened so that the whole court might see the punishment inflicted. At last went down the hammer and the scourging ceased... Another accusation being then delivered by a flat-cap [citizen] against a poor wretch, who had no friend to speak on her behalf, proclamation was made, viz.: 'All you who are willing E——th T——ll should have present punishment, pray hold up your hands.'

The audience having voted for instant punishment, the woman was stripped to the waist 'as if it were designed rather to feast the eyes of the spectators than to correct vice or correct manners' and lashed.

This display of public approbation for sadistic treatment of whores is misleading. There was widespread opposition to the methods of the odious Reformation Societies – particularly their use of informers – and hostile crowds sometimes intervened to stop prostitutes being arrested. In 1709 near Covent Garden a reformation society constable, John Dent, was killed by a group of soldiers as he tried to arrest a prostitute named Anne Dickens. The killers were later freed by a jury under the guidance of the Lord Chief Justice.[9]

The societies were determined to drive whores out of public places and the playhouses. In 1730, for instance, a whore and her client were arrested for fornicating in a shop window and a group of women were 'taken at 12 or 1 o'clock, exposing their nakedness in the open street to all passengers and using most abominable filthy expressions'.

After reaching a peak around the beginning of the eighteenth century, when there were twenty in London, the societies went into decline. 'Their prosecutions for all offences, including prostitution and bawdy-house keeping, fell away from a high point of 7,251 in 1722 to 734 in 1730. The last set of annual figures published by the Societies, for the year to 1738, totalled just 545 prosecutions' (Henderson, *Disorderly Women in Eighteenth-Century London*). They had failed to make much impact on the growth of whoredom: given the prevalent poverty this was not surprising. Their agitation did however provoke a debate which was to become a dominant topic for the Victorians: how to make the working class more moral.

The decline of the societies returned the responsibility for public morality to the inefficient and corrupt parish watches, which until the establishment of the Metropolitan Police in 1829 were responsible for public order. In 1822 intense public pressure to deal with disorderly street whores led to the Vagrancy Act, in which for the first time the term 'prostitutes' appeared as a definition:

all common Prostitutes or night Walkers wandering in the public Streets or public Highways, not giving a satisfactory account of themselves, shall be deemed idle and disorderly Persons; and it shall and may be lawful for any Justice of the Peace to commit such Offenders . . . to the House of Correction, there to be kept to hard Labour for any Time not exceeding one Calendar Month.

The onus on prostitutes to 'give a satisfactory account of themselves' may have come to be seen as unfair, for in 1824 a new Vagrancy Act was introduced replacing that stipulation with the definition, 'wandering and behaving in a riotous and indecent manner'. But in the opinion of some experts prostitution was not a crime, and persecution by the reformation societies was therefore itself illegal.

The penalties for keeping a disorderly house under a law of 1752 were not severe: a small fine, a spell in the pillory and a brief period in prison. 'An exception was Mary Bunce, who was fined £20 and given six months' imprisonment for running a disorderly house near the Hay Market'. (L Picard, *Dr Johnson's London*). The fact that she had another 21 such houses may have accounted for the relatively harsh punishment.

The authorities were generally reluctant to prosecute bawdy or disorderly houses. The difficulties were many and the prospects of success slim. If the owners pleaded guilty they often got off with a caution. They were more likely to disappear before the case came to trial. Even if found guilty they might be fined a shilling. Occasionally a brothel-keeper went to prison, but there was little to stop him, or more usually, her, from opening up somewhere else once freed.

The failure of the authorities to make much impact on the growing numbers of prostitutes and brothels led reformers to cast about for other solutions. It was suggested that the women should be deported to America. Large numbers were sent to the penal colonies in Australia, usually for theft. Several authors suggested the setting up of state-run brothels. The Reverend Martin Madan thought polygamy was the answer to what he saw as men's need for sexual variety. His suggestion got him sacked from his job of chaplain to the London Lock Hospital for venereal diseases. Other proposals were less radical and in some cases led to action. Sir John Fielding, one of the founders of the proto-police force the Bow Street Runners, proposed a public institution to 'preserve the deserted Girls of the Poor of this Metropolis; and also to reform those Prostitutes whom Necessity has drove into the Streets, and who are willing to return to Virtue and obtain an honest livelihood by severe industry'.

This was the first of several schemes for reforming fallen women through hard work. Fielding proposed a public laundry where the women would labour for a pittance. They would also learn cooking, knitting and cleaning. In 1758 Dr William Todd took up some of these recommendations when he founded the Magdalen Hospital near Goodman Fields in London. The regime was harsh: the women worked from 6 a.m. to 10 p.m. in summer and 7 a.m. to 9 p.m. in winter making clothes or small saleable items. Any spare time was devoted to religious instruction. The aim was to fit the women for domestic service, a career which was already turning young women into prostitutes in large numbers. Although only 2,217 women opted to be 'saved' by the Magdalen Hospital during the first forty years of its life, more homes for fallen women, run on the same lines, followed. In 1885 there were said to be 53 Church of England penitentiaries for the reform of prostitutes. The Roman Catholic Church also set up such reformatories.

The Evangelical Church of England was an important factor in the movement, with a more liberal approach. 'Evangelicals advocated an alternative system of reform and tried to establish a family home system rather than a penitential one'. (Paula Bartley, *Prostitution: Prevention and Reform in England, 1860–1914*). By 1908 the Evangelists' Reformatory and Refuge Union had 320 Magdalen Institutions. The Salvation Army opened the first English Salvation Army home in Whitechapel in 1884. The Church Army and the Jewish Ladies' Association also had homes, the latter setting up a home in Shepherd's Bush.

Individuals helped: the feminist and morals campaigner Josephine Butler would take ailing prostitutes to her own home, the wealthy philanthropist Angela Burdett-Coutts provided money for Charles Dickens to supervise Urania Cottage in Shepherd's Bush, and Adeline Duchess of Bedford ran an institution (Bartley, ibid.). Somehow Dickens found time from running a newspaper, writing major novels and stories and staging theatricals to visit prisons looking for likely candidates for Urania Cottage, and he wrote to Miss Burdett-Coutts: 'A most extraordinary and mysterious study it is, but interesting and touching in the extreme.'

Another enthusiastic reformer was the Prime Minister, William Gladstone. When told by his private secretary in 1886 that the climate of opinion had changed and that he must cease his activities among prostitutes, Gladstone commented that there was 'among some people a baseness and lack of charity which enables them to believe the worst. Because of this I will cease to visit clearing houses, brothels or places of assignation . . . and . . . promise never again to speak to women on the streets at night.' This should have been the end of a long series of encounters, during which he would sometimes accompany street walkers back to their rooms for long conversations. In July 1852, for example, he wrote in his diary in Italian of one such woman, Elizabeth

Collins: 'Half a most lovely statue, beautiful beyond measure.' Even after his 1886 promise he did not completely desist.

Prison was society's other way of dealing with recalcitrant whores. The Swiss commentator on London lowlife, César de Saussure, describes a visit to the Bridewell at Tothill Fields, Westminster:

> On one side of this room were the men, on the other the women, and between these two lines walked the inspector, or Captain Whip'em. This man had a surly, repulsive countenance; he held a long cane in his hand about the thickness of my little finger, and whenever one of these ladies was fatigued and ceased working he would rap them on the arms, and in no gentle fashion, I can assure you ... In the women's part we saw a fine, tall handsome and well-dressed creature. Her linen was of the finest and so was her lace, and she wore a magnificent silk dress brocaded with flowers. The captain took great heed of her; he made her arms quite red with the little raps he gave her with his cane. The girl received these attentions most haughtily and with great indifference. It was a most curious contrast, this handsome girl or woman in rich clothes, looking like a queen and having a mallet in her hand with which she was forced to beat out hemp, and that in such a way that she was covered with large drops of perspiration, all this being accompanied with raps from the cane. I confess that the sight made me quite unhappy. [This scene is almost uncannily reminiscent of Plate 4 of Hogarth's *A Harlot's Progress*.] I could not help thinking that such a handsome, proud, queenly woman should at least be spared the blows. We were told that she had been sent here the day before because she had stolen a gold watch from her lover, and that it was not her first visit, because she always stole everything she could lay her hands on. At the opposite end of the room we remarked a girl from fifteen to sixteen years of age, extremely beautiful; she seemed a mere child, and was touching to look at. (César de Saussure, *A Foreign View of England in the Reigns of George I and George II*, 1902)

A Harlot's Progress: *Plate 4 shows a harlot beating hemp in prison among diseased and imbecile whores, while being threatened by the overseer.*

A Harlot's Progress: *Plate 5 shows two pox doctors arguing about the efficacy of their cures as the harlot expires in a chair from syphilis.*

A Harlot's Progress: *Plate 6 is a splendid tableau of moral squalor round her coffin, from the groping parson to the girl admiring herself in the mirror.*

This girl told de Saussure and his friend she had eaten nothing for three days except dry bread. The two men paid for her release, and exhorted her to lead a better life. She promised to do so, but some months later de Saussure saw her at the theatre, occupying one of the principal boxes, 'dressed like a duchess and more beautiful than ever'.

Transportation was an obvious alternative to prison or even the gallows for whores who had been convicted of theft or coining, or one of the many other petty crimes which carried the death penalty. News of the horrors of the early voyages had filtered through, however, and some girls preferred a quick death to the lingering horrors of thirst, disease and depravity on the long voyage to New South Wales. In 1789 Sarah Cowden, 21, astonished the Old Bailey by preferring death to transportation. She insisted that she and another prisoner were innocent. 'I will die by the laws of my own country before ever I will go abroad for my life.' Three other women also refused transportation.

The recorder tried to bully the women into accepting. Distinguished visitors to the court, who included the Prince of Wales's secret wife Maria Fitzherbert, went down to the cells to reason with Sarah and the others. When they still refused to accept their sentence the recorder ordered them to be put in solitary confinement and fed on bread and water. After more than a month some of the women were broken. Sarah was the last to give in, and only after endless argument and persuasion.

Many of the transported women had been prostitutes. On board ship they were expected to give sex freely to members of the crew, some of whom, including the senior officers, took women convicts as 'wives' for the duration of the voyage. There were advantages in this arrangement for the women, particularly in those rare cases where the sailor made it a permanent arrangement after the women had been delivered to the penal settlement, perhaps coming back on the next voyage to marry them. For those women singled out by the officers the most obvious advantage was better food and accommodation. The other women had to spend much of the time below decks breathing foul air and assailed by the most noisome smells. In the tropics they all but suffocated. No wonder some preferred a quicker death.

Many women sentenced to death by hanging were held in Newgate Prison, on the site of the present Old Bailey. Newgate was a filthy death trap, with jail fever killing about thirty inmates each year. In 1719 Captain Alexander Smith wrote: 'Newgate is a dismal prison...a place of calamity...a habitation of misery, a confused chaos...a bottomless pit of violence, a Tower of Babel where all are speakers and no hearers.' Henry Fielding called Newgate 'a prototype of hell'. Physicians refused to enter, and the area round the prison was permeated by a dreadful stench. Prisoners without money were starved. Young girls traded their bodies for a crust. Older women gave sex for free, in the hope of getting pregnant and being able to 'plead their bellies' – pregnant women would not be hanged.

Women who murdered their husbands were burned at the stake. The last woman who suffered this punishment was Prudence Lee, executed in 1652. John Evelyn noted in his diary: 'Passing Smithfield I saw a miserable creature burning...the executioners setting her in a pitch barrel, bound her to the stake and placed the straw and faggots about her...The executioner then putting the fire to the straw, she cried out 'Lord Jesus have mercy on my soul' and when the fire was kindled was heard to shriek out terribly some five or six several times.' The Commonwealth abolished burning for murder in 1656, although it remained the punishment for adultery. After that the practice was to strangle the condemned woman on a low gibbet before covering her with faggots and setting them alight. But in 1726 the executioner bungled the killing of Katherine Hayes at Tyburn. Instead of first garotting Hayes, who had incited two men to murder and dismember her husband, he lit the faggots and was driven off by the flames before he could put her out of her agony. Two other women whose bodies were burnt at the stake for murder were Isabella Condon in 1779 and Margaret Sullivan in 1788. Both had been the victims of brutal sadists. Burning at the stake ended in 1789.

The laws relating to prostitution remained virtually unchanged until 1959, when the Street Offences Act was introduced. Until then the maximum fine for soliciting to the annoyance of passers-by or

Mother Clap's Profession

'Gusto' is a word often applied to the way men and women enjoyed mutual carnality in the seventeenth and eighteenth centuries. Homosexuals had to be more discreet. In 1570 Sir Thomas Gresham's Bourse, which later became the Royal Exchange, was opened and the area soon became the haunt of prostitutes and catamites, the latter attracting customers among the City's rich merchants. They had to be careful. Buggery was a capital offence, although juries were reluctant to convict. Only if 'penetration' was proved would the death penalty be imposed. Mostly the juries would decide that homosexual acts were common assaults, meriting a fine.

In May 1726 the *London Journal* wrote of twenty 'Sodomitical Clubs' where 'they make their execrable Bargains, and then with-draw into some dark Corners to perpetrate their odious Wicked-ness'. These 'clubs' included Mother Clap's in Holborn, where there were beds in every room with 'commonly thirty to forty Chaps every night – and even more – especially on Sunday Nights'. The Talbot Inn in the Strand was another haunt, as were even the 'Bog-Houses' of Lincoln's Inn.

A mollies' house opposite the Old Bailey had been in existence since 1559, the men addressing each other as 'Madam' or 'Ladyship', and in 1661 there was the Three Potters in Cripplegate Without. The Fountain in the Strand was a known haunt of homosexuals throughout the eighteenth century. There was a male brothel in Camomile Street, Bishopsgate – the manager was known

189

as the Countess of Camomile. The writer Ned Ward complained in the *London Spy* in 1700 about the antics of male prostitutes at the Fountain, a tavern in Russell Square. Dressed as women, they would enact mock childbirths using a doll, which would be 'Christened and the Holy Sacrament of Baptism impudently Prophan'd'. Ward later wrote about these members of the 'Mollies' Club': 'There is a curious band of fellows in the town who call themselves "Mollies" (effeminates, weaklings) who are so totally destitute of all masculine attributes that they prefer to behave as women. They adopt all the small vanities natural to the feminine sex to such an extent that they will try to speak, walk, chatter, shriek and scold as women do, aping them as well in other respects.'

There were 'mollies' in high places, of course. In February 1685 Henry Duke of Grafton killed the notorious Jack Talbot, younger brother of the Duke of Shrewsbury, in a duel. Grafton had objected to some remarks Talbot had made about Princess Anne and her husband. A contemporary satire described Talbot as:

> Thrice fortunate Boy
> Who can give double-Joy
> And every Turn be ready;
> With Pleasures in Store
> Behind and Before
> To delight both My Lord and My Lady.

There was a huge upsurge in sodomy around the beginning of the eighteenth century, and in 1707 a raid on a 'Sodomites' Club' in the City caused a great scandal. About forty men were arrested, including the respected Cheapside mercer Jacob Ecclestone, who later committed suicide in Newgate. Another respected City figure, the Cheapside draper William Grant, hanged himself there, and the curate of St Dunstan's-in-the-East, a Mr Jermain, cut his throat with his razor, as did another merchant, a Mr Bearden. Several others also committed suicide before the case came to trial. All these men frequented the alleys around the Royal Exchange. The favourite meeting place was Pope's Head Alley. In nearby Sweetings Alley the 'breeches-clad bawds' congregated.

In October 1764 the *Public Advertiser* reported that: 'A bugger aged sixty was put in the Cheapside Pillory... the Mob tore off his clothes, pelted him with Filth, whipt him almost to Death ... he was naked and covered with Dung... when the Hour was up he was carried almost unconscious back to Newgate.'

Some used the reaction against the upsurge in sodomy to blackmail innocents. In September 1724 a young man walking in the streets was accosted by a man who seized him and cried out, 'A sodomite! A sodomite!' The terrified youth was advised by a passing gentleman to give the blackmailer five or six guineas, but protested that he did not have the money. The two older men then followed him to the place where he worked, hoping to get money, but were driven off by one of the young man's colleagues, who drew his sword. The blackmailers ran away, 'leaving the boy prostrate with shock'. In January 1725 two men were found guilty of a similar attempt at blackmail, and were sentenced to 'two hours on Tower Hill Pillory, two hours on the Cheapside Pillory, a fine of Twenty pounds and six months in Newgate'.

Some men got off very lightly. In 1722, a year in which there was a spate of prosecutions, John Dicks picked up a young boy and took him to ale-houses where he got him drunk. He buggered the boy in the yard behind the Golden Ball in Fetter Lane. When a pot-boy who heard the commotion went to see what was going on Dicks attempted to bugger him as well, and the landlord caught him 'in the very act of buggery'. Dicks pleaded with the landlord not to report him, 'for if you swear against me you swear away my life'. Dicks was found guilty of attempted sodomy, fined twenty marks, stood in the Temple Bar pillory for an hour and was sent to Newgate for two years.

Women whores protested at all this unwanted competition:

> How Happy were the good old English Faces
> 'til Mounsieur from France taught PEGO a Dance
> to the tune of Old Sodom's Embraces.
> But now WE are quite out of Fashion.
> Poor whores may be NUNS, since MEN turn their GUNS
> And vent on each other their Passion.
> But now, we find to our Sorrow we are over-run
> By the Parks of the BUM
> and Peers of the Land of Gomorrah!

In 1726 the Societies for the Reformation of Manners succeeded in closing down more than twenty mollies' houses, including Mother Clap's. She was found guilty of keeping a 'sodomitical house' and put in the pillory at Smithfield. Three of her prostitutes were hanged.

The trial record shows that Mother Clap's house in Holborn was a regular meeting place for homosexuals. One of the witnesses for the prosecution was Samuel Stephens:

Stephens: On Sunday night, the 14th November last, I went to the prisoner's house in Field Lane, in Holborn, where I found between 40 and 50 men making love to one an other, as they called it. Sometimes they would sit in one another's laps, kissing in a lewd manner and using their hands indecently. Then they would get up, dance and make curtsies, and mimic the voices of women. 'O, Fie, Sir! – Pray, Sir – Dear, Sir, – Lord, how can you serve me so? – I swear I'll cry out. – You're a wicked devil, – and you've a bold face. – Eh, you dear little toad! Come, buss!' – Then they'd hug, and play, and toy, and go out by couples into another room on the same floor, to be married, as they called it. The door of that room was kept by — Eccleston, who used to stand pimp for 'em, to prevent anybody from disturbing them in their diversions. When they came out they used to brag, in plain terms, of what they had been doing. As for the prisoner, she was present all the time, except when she went out to fetch liquors. There was among them William Griffin, who has since been hanged for sodomy; and — Derwin, who had been carried before Sir George Mertins, for sodomitical practices with a link-boy...I went to the same house on two or three Sunday nights following, and found much the same practices as before. The company talked all manner of gross and vile obscenity in the prisoner's hearing, and she appeared to be wonderfully pleased with it.

One of the young catamites, Edward Courteney, told of the goings-on at another mollies' house, the Royal Oak in Pall Mall. He said that several rooms at the back of the tavern were used by homosexuals who acted as married couples. The landlord had 'put the bite on him' to go with a country gentleman who promised to pay him handsomely. He 'stayed all night but in the morning he gave me no more than a sixpence'.

A 'club of paederasts' used to meet in the Bunch of Grapes in Clare Market. When they appeared before Bow Street magistrates eighteen were wearing women's clothes. Although they were found Not Guilty for lack of evidence, they had to run the gauntlet of a large crowd which gathered outside the courtroom. Handcuffed together, they could do little to protect themselves from a storm of stones and filth hurled by these vindictive spectators.

In 1813 Robert Holloway published *The Phoenix of Sodom: or, the Vere Street Coterie* about the notorious male homosexual brothel at the White Swan in the street running north from Oxford Street. Holloway's book gives a description of the interior of the brothel:

> The fatal house in question was furnished in a style most appropriate to the purposes it was intended. Four beds were provided in one room: – another was fitted up for the ladies' dressing-room, with a toilette and every appendage of rouge, &c. &c.: a third room was called the Chapel, where marriages took place, sometimes between a female grenadier, six feet high, and a petit maitre not more than half the altitude of his beloved wife! These marriages were solemnised with all the mockery of bride maids and bride men; and the nuptials were frequently consummated by two, three or four couples, in the same room, and in the sight of each other! ... Men of rank and respectable situations in life might be seen wallowing either in or on the beds with wretches of the lowest description... Sunday was the general, and grand day of rendezvous! and to render their excuse the more entangled and doubtful, some of the parties came from a great distance ... to join the festivity and elegant amusements of grenadiers, footmen, waiters ... and all the Catamite Brood ...

In July 1810 officers from Bow Street, backed by a unit of troops, raided the premises and 23 people were arrested. Seven of them were sentenced to terms ranging from one to three years' imprisonment. They also had to endure a brief spell in the pillory. Here is a contemporary newspaper report of their ordeal, both in the pillory and travelling to and from it.

The miscreants were then brought out and placed in the caravan; Amos began a laugh, which induced his vile companions to reprove him, and they all sat upright apparently in a composed state, but having cast their eyes upwards, the sight of the spectators on the tops of the houses operated strongly on their fears, and they soon appeared to feel terror and dismay...

The mob, and particularly the women, had piled up balls of mud to afford the objects of their indignation a warm reception ...when the prisoners passed the old house which once belonged to the notorious Jonathan Wild they resembled beasts dipped in a stagnant pool. The shower of mud continued during their passage to the Haymarket. Before they reached half-way to the scene of their exposure they were not discernible as human beings...

At 1 o'clock four of them were exalted on the new pillory made purposely for their accommodation...their faces were completely disfigured by blows and mud; and before they mounted their persons appeared one heap of filth.

Upwards of fifty women were permitted to stand in a ring who assailed them incessantly with mud, dead cats, rotten eggs, potatoes and buckets of grub, offal and dung which were brought by a number of butchers' men from St James's Market. These criminals were very roughly handled; but as there were four of them they did not suffer so much as a less number might. When the hour was expired they were again put in the cart and conveyed to Coldbath Fields Prison...When they were taken from the pillory the butchers' men and the women who had been so active were plentifully regaled with gin and beer procured from a subscription made on the spot. In a few minutes the remaining two, Cook...and Amos...were desired to mount. Cook held his hands to his head and complained of the blows he had already received; and Amos made much the same complaint and showed a large brickbat which had struck him in the face.

Cook said nothing but Amos... declared in the most solemn manner that he was innocent; but it was vouchsafed from all quarters that he had been convicted before and in one minute they appeared a complete heap of mud and their faces were much more battered than those of the former four. Cook received several hits in his face and had a lump raised upon his eyebrow as large as an egg. Amos's two eyes were completely closed up; and when they were untied Cook appeared almost insensible, and it was necessary to help them both down and into the cart when they were conveyed to Newgate by the same road they had come and in their passage they continued to receive the same salutations the spectators had given them on their way out. As they passed the end of Panton Street, Strand, on their return a coachman stood up in his box and gave Cook five or six cuts with his whip. (*Morning Herald*, 28 September 1810)

The ferocity of the crowd is difficult to explain. The women who took such a prominent part – as women were to do when Oscar Wilde was tried later in the century – may have included many streetwalkers who resented the competition. Henriques in *Prostitution and Society*, vol. 3 suggests that 'highly placed male homosexuals may possibly have fomented the feelings of the mob' to conceal their own complicity.

In 1833 two Members of Parliament were found not guilty in separate trials. One of them, W J Bankes, had been accused of attempting to commit an unnatural crime in the grounds of Westminster Abbey. Charles Greville, clerk to the Privy Council, wrote in his diary: 'Nobody can read the trial without being satisfied of his guilt... The foreman said he left the court without a stain.' To which a wit added: 'On his shirt.'

For whatever reason, male homosexuality was less evident in the middle years of the nineteenth century. Whether this was because it had become more furtive or whether social pressures led to a drop in the number of practising homosexuals is unclear. There were certainly strong and even passionate friendships among men, as Tennyson's *In Memoriam* of 1850 bears witness. The Criminal Law Amendment Act of 1885 made almost any sexual contact between males a serious criminal offence, and also opened the way to blackmail. It was called a 'blackmailer's charter' at the time, and men who could face prison if convicted of what had hitherto been overlooked were now open to extortion.When the tide of Victorian morality was at the full, homosexuality was the crime that dared not speak its name. In 1871 two young men, Ernest Boulton and William Park, were arrested for dressing as women and mixing with prostitutes in the Burlington Arcade, at the Alhambra in Leicester Square and the Surrey Theatre south of the river. They were charged with inciting persons to commit an unnatural offence. From descriptions of their behaviour it seems clear to us today they were soliciting, but the judge suggested that they might have done it for a 'frolic' and the jury agreed, finding them not guilty.

For society, this state of innocence was not to last much longer. The trial of Oscar Wilde in 1895 forced the Victorians to confront the evidence for male homosexuality. There were revelations about a homosexual brothel in Little College Street, Westminster. The prosecutor spoke of 'these rooms, with their heavily draped windows, their candles burning on through the day, and their languorous atmosphere heavy with perfume'. After the trial W T Stead, then editing the *Review of Reviews*, commented: 'Should everyone found guilty of Oscar Wilde's crime be in prison, there would be a very surprising emigration from Eton, Harrow, Rugby and Winchester to the jails . . . '

The Wolfenden report of 1957 led to changes in the law which made homosexual acts between adult men legal if they took place in private. (Homosexual acts between women have never been illegal.) This ended the scandal of police officers hanging round public toilets in the hope of catching homosexuals in the act, or even enticing them. The toilets at Leicester Square and Falconberg Mews, Westminster, were among many others notorious for this police activity.

THE PLEASURE MAP OF CENTRAL LONDON IN THE VICTORIAN ERA.

1. There was a popular homosexual brothel in Fitzroy during the Oscar Wilde period.

2. Soho was for long the most crowded and cosmopolitan area of London. In the late nineteenth century prostitutes arrived in flocks and it became the centre of the vice and pornography trades.

3. Piccadilly Circus was at the heart of the main Victorian red-light zone. The casinos and night houses nearby included Kate Hamilton's Café Royal in Princess Street, Leicester Square, the lively Argyll Rooms by Windmill Street and Mott's.

4. The Haymarket, centre of perambulating prostitution both high and low. The French historian and statesman Hyppolite Taine wrote of the Haymarket and the Strand in the 1860s: 'Every hundred steps one jostles twenty harlots ... This is not debauchery which flaunts itself, but destitution – and such destitution!'

5. Burlington Arcade, off Piccadilly. Streetwalkers took shelter there in the winter, and some owners let them take customers to rooms behind the shops.

6. The famous courtesan 'Skittles' Walters lived in Chesterfield Street. For a time she was kept by Lord Hartington, leader of the Liberal Party, and she was the friend of the statesman Gladstone.

7. Drury Lane was a haunt of the cheaper prostitutes. Just to the south was Wych Street which was the centre of the pornography trade until it was swept away by the building of the Aldwych and Kingsway

8. Bow Street, where prostitution and respectability interacted. Walter, the memoirist who described his encounters with hundreds of prostitutes, describes his nights in an accommodation house there with Brighton Bessie. Whores thronged the Opera House, and their successors are still arraigned at Bow Street Court.

9. Fleet Street, where bohemianism met a wide range of sexual services. The Haunch of Venison in Bell Yard was described as 'the resort of all the abandoned women who reside in those places'. By the early twentieth century most of the girls had moved west

10. In Gracechurch Street, the Cross Keys offered rooms to couples for 4s., but for a stay of just a few hours it was necessary only to order wine. As the City became depopulated prostitution died out.

11. In Leman Street the Old Garrick tavern was a pick-up place for 'pretty black-eyed Jewesses'.

12. Vauxhall Gardens, the main pleasure gardens, which opened in the seventeenth century. They became more and more disreputable, and closed in 1859.

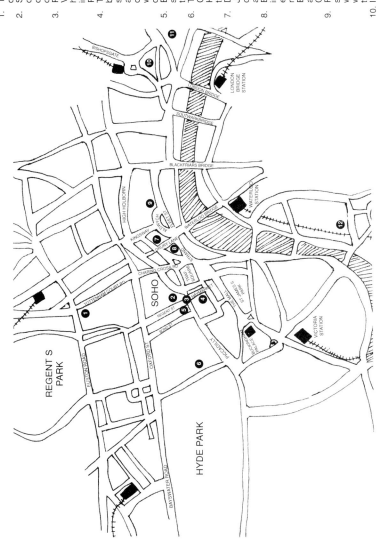

The Richest City in the World

Foreign visitors were shocked by the spectacle of young whores crowding the fashionable streets and public entertainments of nineteenth-century London. One estimate put the number of prostitutes in London in the 1830s at 80,000, many of them little more than children. (By contrast, in the 1950s there were believed to be about 5,000.) Mayhew's collaborator Bracebridge Hemyng agreed that there were 80,000 around the mid-century, and he was in a better position to judge than most. However, these are only guesses, and are almost certainly overestimates (see Appendix). Yet to contemporaries the throngs of whores were a scandal that seemed to be getting worse, and there is no doubt that vice was one of Victorian Britain's biggest industries.

To some it was the very blatancy of this vast illicit enterprise that was most offensive. Whores paraded in the most fashionable parts of the city, particularly inside and outside the main theatres, calling out, plucking at the coatsleeves of passing men and making lewd gestures and suggestions. Covent Garden, the Haymarket, Regent Street, Cremorne Gardens, Fleet Street, the front of Somerset House and St James's were bazaars of sexual opportunity. There were women for every taste and every pocket. Child prostitutes pestered single men. At night hideous hags haunted the parks, their diseased bodies disguised by rags and darkness. During the day Hyde Park saw successful high-class whores flaunting their wealth by driving among fashionable upper-class promenaders in expensive carriages. In the east, in the streets of Wapping and

*Law and disorder: a police officer moves on a coster boy while
ignoring the obvious sexual commerce nearby in the
New Cut, south of the river.*

Shadwell, raucous drunken sailors' tarts fought and shouted in the
streets. William Blake's lines

> But most through midnight streets I hear
> How the youthful harlot's curse
> Blasts the new-born infant's ear
> And blights with plague the marriage hearse

echoed a nightly reality for the respectable citizens of these areas.

Although Victorian moralists called it the road to ruin,
prostitution brought relative affluence to many young women and
riches to some. At the same time, a warning to the carefree young
women promenading in the same streets were the ghastly veterans
of harlotry, 'alcoholics, semi-imbeciles, female flotsam of all kinds,
soliciting an almost inconceivable interest in their dishevelled

bodies or offering to cooperate in the squalidest perversions for a few coppers' (Kellow Chesney, *The Victorian Underworld*).

Dr William Acton, a sympathetic observer, was one of the many writers who set the scene:

Who are those fair creatures, neither chaperons nor chaperoned: those 'somebodies whom nobody knows,' who elbow our wives and daughters in the parks and promenades and rendezvous of fashion? Who are those painted, dressy women flaunting along the streets and boldly accosting the passerby? Who those miserable creatures, ill-fed, ill-clothed, uncared for, from whose misery the eye recoils, cowering under dark arches and among bye-lanes? (Acton, *Prostitution Considered*)

Attempts were made to establish exactly how many prostitutes there were in London in the early nineteenth century. In 1817 the London Guardian Society, set up to preserve public morals and reform prostitutes, reported to the Parliamentary Committee on the State of the Police, established the previous year, the results of its survey of prostitutes in parts of the city. These were startling. In three parishes – St Botolph without Aldgate, St Leonard's, Shoreditch, and St Paul's, Shadwell, there were 360 brothels and 2,000 prostitutes in a population of 59,050. St Paul's, Shadwell, alone had 200 brothels and 1,000 prostitutes out of 9,855 inhabitants and 1,082 houses. Nearly a fifth of the houses in the parish were brothels.

In Stepney, four streets abutting on the Commercial Road had 65 brothels and 194 prostitutes. Southwark's parish of St George the Martyr had 370 prostitutes, and Lambeth, which housed many of the women who plied their trade in Vauxhall Gardens, had 1,176 brothels and 2,033 prostitutes. In the City, there were 22 brothels housing 150 prostitutes 'in the vicinity of New Court'. At Westminster Abbey the Almonry was a haunt of whores. These figures may be too low, as they are usually those women 'known to the police' and do not include women who were discreet.

Another area infested with brothels was the borough of Southwark. The Police Committee heard evidence that among the reasons were the area's theatres and circus, the three nearby bridges to the City and the fashionable parts of town, and the 'great numbers of small houses lately built in that parish, which are particularly suited for such occupants'.

In 1840 the French socialist and feminist Flora Tristan published *Promenades dans Londres*, an account of some visits to the capital between 1826 and 1839. In it she describes a visit to the western fringe of the Southwark area:

> There are so many prostitutes in London that one sees them everywhere at any time of day; all the streets are full of them, but at certain times they flock in from outlying districts in which most of them live, and mingle with the crowds in theatres and public places. It is rare for them to take men home; their landlords would object, and besides their lodgings are unfit. They take their 'captures' to the houses reserved for their trade . . .
>
> Between seven and eight o'clock one evening, accompanied by two friends armed with canes, I went to take a look at the new suburb which lies on either side of the long broad thoroughfare called Waterloo Road at the end of Waterloo Bridge. This neighbourhood is almost entirely inhabited by prostitutes and people who live off prostitution; it is courting danger to go there alone at night. It was a hot summer evening; in every window and doorway women were laughing and joking with their protectors. Half dressed, some of them *naked to the waist*, they were a revolting sight, and the criminal, cynical expressions of their companions filled me with apprehension. These men are for the most part very good looking – young, vigorous and well made – but their coarse and common air marks them as animals whose sole instinct is to satisfy their appetites . . .
>
> We went on our way and explored all the streets in the vicinity of Waterloo Road, then we sat upon the bridge to watch the women of the neighbourhood flock past, as they do every night between the hours of eight and nine, on their way to the West End, where they ply their trade all through the night and return home between eight and nine in the morning. They infest the

promenades and other places where people gather, such as the approaches to the Stock Exchange, the various public buildings and the theatres, which they invade as soon as entry is reduced to half price . . .

It is difficult today to imagine what it was like to walk the streets of London infested by these hordes of prostitutes. Even in the years before the passing of the Street Offences Act in 1959 the numbers of street prostitutes had declined greatly, and only a few areas, mostly in central London, were affected. In behaviour the women were restrained by comparison with their early nineteenth century counterparts. Then, the blatancy of the shameless and often drunken whores in the streets and theatres shocked visitors to the city. Erik Geijer, a Swede who arrived in London in 1809 commented:

The open and naked effrontery of the immoral transcends all description. They swarm around the streets of London at all hours of the day and night. They gather in crowds at the theatres which are regular market places for such wares, and the business is done in English fashion, coarsely and openly. The poor wretches do not know how to give their trade any prettier air than simple straightforward bargaining. To practise vice with decency, to ply a despicable trade with charm, to save appearances at all costs, this an English nature does not understand. (*Impressions of England 1809–10*)

In fact respectable English natures were outraged by the situation. In 1816 the inhabitants of the City petitioned the Lord Mayor and the Common Council to drive out the prostitutes, saying:

the principal streets of this City are every evening crowded with profligate women, who, by their riotous and obscene conduct, annoy or alarm the well-disposed inhabitants . . . The audacity with which these women accost passengers, and the horrid oaths and obscene language which they are accustomed to use, your Petitioners . . . cannot but consider an intolerable grievance: for no virtuous female, however protected, can pass through the streets in the evening without witnessing these disgusting scenes: and the utmost vigilance your Petitioners can use, is insufficient to preserve their sons and servants from frequent solicitation even at their own doors ...

The situation in the theatres was as bad as it had been in the eighteenth century. Fashionably dressed prostitutes roamed the bars and saloons, 'disturbing the performance, insulting the sober-minded and modest part of the audience, and exhibiting the most indecent appearance and gestures with perfect impunity, nay, apparently with encouragement from the profligate of the other sex' (*Address to the Guardian Society*, anonymous pamphlet, 1817). The women could be seen going from box to box, or flaunting themselves among the well-dressed patrons in the saloons, which were usually close to the boxes so that the playgoers could easily move from one to the other. Well-dressed whores with genteel manners – they could usually be distinguished from respectable women by their shorter skirts – mingled with single men. These were superior prostitutes, whose appearance could stand scrutiny in the harsh light of the saloons, unlike their raucous sisters in the streets outside. Nevertheless their conduct offended the writer of the *Address to the Guardian Society*:

When a young man meets there with handsome fine-looking girls ... he forgets the indecency of their appearance and the looseness and impropriety of their language and behaviour, if these do not attract him the more; and he gets interested and entangled with them, and is led astray; and this the more readily if he sees around him much older men of respectable appearance, without scruple talking and romping with them ...

Pierce Egan, the Regency writer of *Tom and Jerry, Life in London*, gives a fascinating account of the saloon at Covent Garden Theatre. Like all his works this book, famous and much admired and plagiarised for many years, is full of facetiousness and slang. He describes how the whores – he uses the euphemism Cyprians – surrounded men who visited the saloon unaccompanied by women:

Tom and Coz had scarcely reached the place for refreshments, when the *buz* began, and they were surrounded by numbers of the gay *Cyprians*, who nightly visit the place ... The '*Fair* MARIA', dressed in a blue riding habit, seated on a chair in the corner, near the recess; and the '*pretty* ELLEN', standing behind her, are throwing out '*lures*', in order to attract the notice of the Corinthian and Jerry. The 'Old Guy' on the top of the stairs, with his spectacles on ... is gently tapping, in an amorous way, the white soft arm of 'lusty *black-eyed* JANE': and inviting her to partake of a glass of wine, to which she consents in a most '*business'-like* manner. Indeed, 'Black-eyed Jane' has often publicly remarked, that it is immaterial to her whether it is a DUKE or his *Groom*, so that she receives her compliment. Several Jewesses may also be recognised promenading up and down the Saloon. In the motley group are several Coves of Cases [brothel keepers] and procuresses, keeping a most vigilant eye that none of their 'decked-out girls' [whores who had been provided with their finery by a brothel] brush off with the property entrusted to them for the night; and other persons of the same occupation may be seen closely WATCHING the females belonging to their establishments, that they are not idle, as to the purposes for which those unfortunate girls are sent into the SALOON ...

We owe much of our knowledge of the lives of mid-nineteenth-century prostitutes to Henry Mayhew and Bracebridge Hemyng. Hemyng interviewed many prostitutes for *London Labour and the London Poor*. One of them, who called herself 'Swindling Sal', was a powerfully built working-class woman of about 27 who associated with criminals, particularly a burglar called Joe the Magsman, who was clearly one of her lovers. Hemyng interviewed her in a public house, and recorded her vigorous turn of phrase: 'She changed places, she never stuck to one long; she never had no things to be sold up, and as she was handy with her mauleys [fists], she got on pretty well. It took a considerable big man, she could tell me, to kick her out of a house, and then when he done it she always give him something for himself, by way of remembering her. Oh! they had a sweet recollection of her, some on 'em.'

This impression of truculence is strengthened by her reference to 'rows' she had been involved in. 'Been quodded [imprisoned] no end of times. She knew every beak as sat on the cheer as well as she knew Joe the Magsman, who, she might say, wor a very perticaler friend of her'n.'

Like many prostitutes, Sal had been a servant but hated the life. She chose to work in the sex trade instead, as she told Hemyng:

> I was a servant gal away down in Birmingham. I got tired of workin' and slavin' to make a living, and getting a —— bad one at that; what o' five pun' a year and yer grub, I'd sooner starve, I would. After a bit I went to Coventry...and took up with soldiers as was quartered there. I soon got tired of them. Soldiers is good...to walk with and that, but they don't pay; cos why they ain't got no money; so I says to myself, I'll go to Lunnon and I did. I soon found my level there.

Her 'level' was that of a fairly successful street prostitute. She told Hemyng what she earned.

> Well, I'll tell yer, one week with another, I makes nearer on four pounds not three – sometimes five. I 'ave done eight and ten. Now Joe, as you 'eered me speak on, he does it 'ansome, he does: I mean, you know, when he's in luck. He give me a fiver once after cracking a crib, and a nice spree me an' Lushing Loo 'ad over it. Sometimes I get three shillings, half a crown, five shillings, or ten occasionally, according to the sort of man.

She was called Swindling Sal because of her habit of 'chousing'; absconding without paying her rent. Sal told Hemyng that 'she never paid any rent, hadn't done so for years and never meant to'. The landlords were 'mostly Christ-killers, and chousing a Jew was no sin, leastways none as she cared about committing'.

Her friend 'Lushing Loo' had a more genteel appearance than Swindling Sal, and was neatly if cheaply dressed. At first she seemed too depressed to speak, and Hemyng gave her half a crown which she spent on brandy. After she had drunk it she became tipsy and began to answer his questions. 'My heart's broken...I wish I was dead; I wish I was laid in my coffin. It won't be long...I've just driven another nail in. Lushing Loo as they call me, will be no loss to society...'

Her story was similar to that of some other 'fallen women'. She had been seduced by a cousin when very young and this had been her 'ruin'. When Hemyng asked why she did not enter a refuge she replied: 'I don't want to live. I shall soon get DT [delerium tremens], and then I'll kill myself in a fit of madness.'

As the century wore on the focus of the trade changed, moving west to follow the exodus of wealthy clients from the City, whose population was falling rapidly. Redevelopment had an inevitable effect. As the better-off residents moved out of Stepney and the run-down area was colonised by warehouses and offices prostitution dwindled, as it did in Lambeth. The Strand and Charing Cross were now the eastern end of the main prostitute belt, although the depopulation of the City would soon affect the Strand too. In 1881 a police witness gave the following evidence to a Select Committee of the House of Lords:

> the state of affairs which exists in this capital is such that from four o'clock, or one may say from three o'clock in the afternoon, it is impossible for any respectable woman to walk from the top of the Haymarket to Wellington Street, Strand. From three or four o'clock in the afternoon Villiers Street and Charing Cross Station and the Strand are crowded with prostitutes, who are openly soliciting prostitution in broad daylight.
>
> At half-past twelve at night a calculation was made a short time ago that there were 500 prostitutes between Piccadilly Circus and the bottom of Waterloo Place.

Some of the importunate wretches who walked the streets were children. A German traveller wrote: 'Every ten yards one is beset, even by children of twelve years old, who by the manner of their address save one the trouble of asking whether they know what they want. They attach themselves to you like limpets...Often they seize hold of you after a fashion of which I can give you the best notion by the fact that I say nothing about it.'

The Russian author Dostoevsky noticed in the Haymarket how 'mothers brought their little daughters to make them ply the same trade'. He left a heart-rending description of one exploited child. The little girl was:

> not older than six, all in rags, dirty, barefoot and hollow cheeked; she had been severely beaten and her body, which showed through the rags, was covered with bruises...Nobody was paying any attention to her...the look of such distress, such hopeless despair on her face...She kept on shaking her tousled head as if arguing about something, gesticulated and spread her little hands and then suddenly clasped them together and pressed them to her little bare breast.

One wants to believe she had been taken there by a prostitute to give her a dubious air of respectability, rather than for sex.

Although there were many brothels, most prostitutes were street-walkers. The Haymarket was known as 'Hell Corner'. The French historian and statesman Hyppolite Taine recorded a stroll down the Haymarket and the Strand in the 1860s: 'Every hundred steps one jostles twenty harlots; some of them ask for a glass of gin; others say, "Sir, it is to pay my lodging." This is not debauchery which flaunts itself, but destitution – and such destitution! The deplorable procession in the shades of the monumental streets is sickening; it seems to me a march of the dead. That is a plague-spot – the real plague spot of English society.'

A prostitute told Bracebridge Hemyng of her daily routine. She rose and dined about four in the afternoon and went on the streets for an hour or two 'if I want money'. Afterwards she would go to the Holborn Casino, 'and if anyone likes me I take him home with me'. If she was unsuccessful she would go to various cafes in the Haymarket, and try her luck there. If she was again unsuccessful she would go to the 'cigar divans', but that was almost the last resort: 'You don't as a rule find any good men at the divans.' These divans were places men went late at night to buy and smoke cigars, drink and pick up whores.

Sin city: the Haymarket, heart of London's vice industry, at midnight around 1860. Short skirts were a giveaway.

The places where whores went for pick-ups were many and varied. Casinos – large dancehalls – were popular. The Holborn Casino was an enormous dancehall, 'glittering with a myriad prisms', where young middle-class men could pick up working-class whores who 'dressed up flash'. The men were 'medical students, apprentice lawyers, young ships' officers, clerks, well-off tradesmen' (Chesney, *Victorian Underworld*).

The most luxurious of the dancehalls was the Portland Rooms, known as Mott's, where the most expensive courtesans sought customers between midnight and four or five in the morning. Gentlemen not wearing dress coats and white waistcoats were refused admission. Shaw's lively memoir of the mid-century capital, *London in the Sixties*, sets the scene:

> The ladies who frequented Mott's, moreover, were not the tawdry make-believes who haunt the modern 'Palaces' but actresses of note, who if not Magdalens [prostitutes] sympathised with them; girls of education and refinement who had

succumbed to the blandishments of youthful lordlings, fair women here and there who had not yet developed into peeresses and progenitors of future legislators. Among them were 'Skittles' [the courtesan], celebrated for her ponies, and sweet Nelly Fowler, the undisputed Queen of beauty in those long-ago days. This beautiful girl had a natural perfume so delicate, so universally admitted, that love-sick swains paid large sums for the privilege of having their handkerchiefs placed under the Godess's pillow, and sweet Nelly pervaded – in spirit if not in the flesh – half the clubs and drawing rooms of England.

The most celebrated of the cafes, or night houses, in the 1850s and 1860s was the Cafe Royal in Princess Street, Leicester Square, known after the woman who ran it as Kate Hamilton's. It was approached down a long passage and carefully guarded to keep out the lowest and poorest prostitutes. Kate weighed twenty stone 'with a countenance that had weathered countless convivial nights'. The author of *London in the Sixties* describes her as 'shaking with laughter like a giant blancmange' as she sat all night with her favourites drinking champagne. Her bodice was always cut low, and she herself must have cut a tremendous figure ensconced on a platform above the fray, her powerful voice keeping order. High-class night houses such as Kate's[10] made their money by selling food and drink at outrageous prices – champagne and moselle at twelve shillings a bottle.

Mayhew's *London Labour and the London Poor* says that Kate was so selective – only men prepared and able to spend five or six pounds, or even more, were admitted – that 'these supper rooms are frequented by a better set of men and women than perhaps any other in London'. These were people who would 'shrink' from appearing in the Haymarket cafés, or the supper rooms of the surrounding streets, 'nor would they go to any other casino than Mott's'.

Not even Kate's was immune to raids by the police, although generous bribes probably ensured no harm came of them. *London in the Sixties* describes what happened when a raiding party was spotted:

Before the fall: Kate Hamilton as a demure young woman. In her heyday as proprietor of the Cafe Royal off Leicester Square she became hideous and swollen from drink.

An alarm gave immediate notice of the approach of the police. Finding oneself within the 'salon' during one of these periodical raids was not without interest. Carpets were turned up in the twinkling of an eye, boards were raised and glasses and bottles – empty or full – were thrust promiscuously in; everyone assumed a sweet and virtuous air and talked in subdued tones, whilst a bevy of police, headed by an inspector, marched solemnly in and having completed the farce, marched solemnly out. What the subsidy attached to this duty, and when and how paid, it is needless to inquire.

The lively Argyll Rooms by Windmill Street was one of the most famous of the Haymarket's places of entertainment. It had a dance floor and gallery, and on one occasion Lord Hastings, known as something of a sportsman, emptied a sack of rats among the dancers. This is how the author of *London in the Sixties* depicts the scene, although he places it at Mott's: 'To describe what followed is impossible. Two hundred men and women and two hundred sewer rats compressed within the

Night life: a bloated Kate Hamilton presides over the revels at her Cafe Royal in the 1860s. Such houses made vast profits on food and drinks.

compass of forty feet by thirty, and in a darkness as profound as any that was ever experienced in Egypt.' Hastings was a man of noted generosity: 'Six cases of champagne invariably formed the first order' as he treated all and sundry.

The Argyll was regarded as a pick-up place for prostitutes. Dr Acton, that zealous social commentator and expert on prostitution, said of the Argyll: 'The women are of course all prostitutes. They are for the most part pretty, and quietly though expensively dressed, while delicate complexions, unaccompanied by the pallor of ill-health, are neither few nor far between. This appearance is doubtless due in part to the artistic manner of the make-up by powder and cosmetics, on the employment of which extreme care is bestowed.'

Although for a long time the authorities tolerated the Argyll because they felt it was better to have its prostitutes in one place rather than dispersed in the streets, it fell victim to the rising tide of Victorian morality and closed in 1878.

The author of *London in the Sixties* writes of the Haymarket he had known in his youth that it 'literally blazed with light' from such temples as the Blue Posts, Barnes's, the Burmese and Barron's Oyster Rooms. 'The decorous Panton Street of today was another very sink of iniquity. Night houses abounded, and Rose Burton's and Jack Percival's were sandwiched between hot baths of questionable respectability and abominations of every kind.' Barron's Oyster Rooms was ancient and creaking. One night after the building gave a particularly ominous groan the customers fled into the street. Old Barron watched from the pavement as the house began to subside, then remembered his cash box and ran back in. The house collapsed and his body was found with the cash box clasped in his arms.

All these places, and many more, had one thing in common: respectable women did not go there. Men could and did eat in supper rooms and drink in night houses without seeking female company, but the fact remained that prostitution kept the houses in business.

Brothels and Flash Houses

Prostitutes who did not simply take their customers to a nearby alley for brief sex against a wall needed somewhere to entertain them. This was not a problem for the high-class courtesans, who would have houses of their own, perhaps as far away as Fulham or St John's Wood. All other prostitutes found their lives and their working practices dominated by this problem.

Girls who worked in brothels had a degree of security, as long as they did not succumb to disease or drink. Women on the game aged quickly and might lose their looks by their late twenties, so their careers were usually short. The women – occasionally men – who ran brothels were expert at keeping most of the clients' cash for themselves, so the prostitutes were unlikely to accumulate the kind of nest-egg that would attract a husband. For that a girl had to operate on her own, boldly advertising her charms by her presence in the theatres, night houses, casinos, or even the most fashionable stores of the West End.

The rooms these successful whores took their clients to were often in lodging houses which were in effect brothels, in that all the rooms would be rented by prostitutes. These lodging-house brothels were found all over London, and varied enormously in the rents they charged the whores. In 1857 Acton describes how a kind of communal life in the kitchens of these houses had a corrupting effect on the girls:

> her company is sought for novelty's sake when she is a new-comer, and her absence or reserve is considered insulting when

she is fairly settled in; so if she had any previous idea of keeping herself to herself, it is very soon dissipated... They are usually during the day, unless called upon by their followers, or employed in dressing, to be found dishevelled, dirty, slipshod and dressing-gowned in this kitchen, where the mistress keeps her table-d'hote. Stupid from beer, or fractious from gin, they swear and chatter brainless stuff all day, about men and millinery, their own schemes and adventures, and the faults of others of the sisterhood... As a heap of rubbish will ferment, so surely will a number of unvirtuous women deteriorate, whatever their antecedents or good qualities previous to their being herded under the semi-tyranny of a lodging-house-keeper of this kind. In such a household, all the projections of decency, modesty, propriety and conscience must, to preserve harmony and republican equality, be planed down, and the woman hammered out, not by the practice of her own profession or the company of men, but by her association with her own sex and class, to the dead level of harlotry. (Acton, *Prostitution Considered*)

The brothel-keepers were notoriously mean towards their whore-lodgers, but they had justified fears of the girls 'chousing', or absconding without paying their debts. This was particularly so in the case of 'dress lodgers', girls who were lent fashionable clothes to wear as they sought customers. In return the girl had to take the customers back to her room, and pay most of her takings to the brothel owner, which meant she would never save enough to buy her own smart clothes. Dress lodgers were naturally tempted to disappear with the clothes, or to take their customers to another house without their landlady knowing.

James Greenwood tells in *The Seven Curses of London* (1869) the story of a 'really handsome' girl who was tricked by a woman brothel-keeper into a form of slavery. The girl had taken a room in the brothel, for which she paid 9s. a week, but refused to work for the bawd. One night when she returned she found a 'detective' waiting for her. He accused her of stealing a diamond shirt pin from a customer, and claimed he had found it in her room. He said he was arresting her, and the terrified girl pleaded with the bawd to intercede on her behalf. The bawd and the detective went into another room, and the bawd returned to say that he had agreed to accept £10 to cover up the 'crime'. The girl had no money, and the bawd agreed to lend her it in return for all her clothes and belongings and a signed paper saying the girl still owed £5. Later the girl discovered that the 'detective' was a bully from another brothel.

'That's how I came to be a dress lodger. She didn't wait long before she opened her mind to me. She told me that very night: "You've got a new landlady now, my fine madam," said she; "you've got to work for your living now; to work for me, d'ye understand? You can't work – can't earn a penny without you dress spicy, and every rag you've got on is mine; and if you say one wry word I'll have them off and bundle you out." 'So what could I do or say?' continued the poor wretch, tears streaming down her really handsome face. 'I've been a dress lodger ever since, not being able to get a shilling for myself, for she takes away all I get, and besides is always threatening to strip me and turn me out, and to sue me for the five pounds I owe her.'

The brothel-keepers sometimes sent servants to keep an eye on the dress lodgers. Mayhew's colleague Hemyng came across a whore named Lizzie in the Strand who was regularly followed by an old woman in a dirty cotton dress. After being plied with gin this old woman agreed to tell him her story.

She had been a prostitute and was now a servant in a brothel. One of her duties was to watch Lizzie as she sought customers. Lizzie was not a top-rate whore, her dress was too garish for that. She usually attracted men who worked in shops, commercial travellers, impecunious medical students. Occasionally she picked up a clergyman from nearby Exeter Hall. Some nights the two of them tramped the streets in vain. Nevertheless she had good times, and that particular night, the old woman said, Lizzie had three clients in as many hours and had earned 45s. 'for herself'. Seamstresses at the time might be paid as little as 3s. a week.

Another option, and one chosen by many prostitutes, was the 'accommodation house'. These establishments hired rooms for just a few minutes or for several hours. Food and drink might be available, according to the status of the house. There were many advantages for prostitutes in using accommodation houses. They could keep their working and home lives separate, vital if they wanted to keep up a facade of respectability, which many married prostitutes did. Although they had to pay for the room it was cheaper than living in a lodging-house brothel. A room in a slum might cost a shilling, a more discreet and luxurious house in the centre of the city a guinea or two. The average was about five shillings. The owner of a successful establishment in the Haymarket retired to a villa in Camberwell and called it Dollar House after all the 'dollars' (5s.) she earned by letting her rooms again and again throughout each day.

Accommodation houses abounded in many parts of London. The important vice area around the Haymarket and Leicester Square had its share, and there was a string of such premises all the way from Bond Street to beyond Covent Garden. In the heart of fashionable London the man of pleasure could be sure he was not far from a quiet and relatively inexpensive refuge for dalliance. The poorer areas and the slums also had a variety of accommodation houses. There were large houses in the slums of St Giles and Seven Dials, one of which had 32 bedrooms. Soho and the slums north of Leicester Square offered cheap rooms for assignations.

Some accommodation-house owners also ran an introduction service, and advertised the whores' attractions in directories such as *The Man of Pleasure's Pocket Book* of the 1850s:

> JAN FOWLER. Tall, slender, of graceful form and carriage; light hair, with a surprisingly fair and transparent complexion, a full blue eye fringed with beautiful silken lashes, through which her luscious orbs dart a thousand killing shafts.

'Walter', the Victorian diarist who left a record of his encounters with 1,200 women (see pages 255–265) described how a prostitute called Brighton Bessie took him to an accommodation house in

Bow Street. It was dearer than the usual house of its type but had the advantage that couples were not interrupted by the landlord asking them to hurry up. Walter described it as a large building nearly opposite the Opera House. It had large and small rooms, well or poorly furnished according to price. 'In it there must have been twenty rooms, and there were more sighs of pleasure in that house nightly than in any other house in London, I should think.' In winter there were large fires in the rooms, and wine and liquor 'of fair quality' was available. The beds, 'large enough for three', always had clean linen. 'It was one of the most quiet, comfortable accommodation-shops I ever was in, and with Brighton Bessie I passed there many voluptuous evenings.'

In competition with the accommodation houses were cigar divans, chop houses, coffee rooms and particularly, shops. The latter included some exclusive West End establishments, and some of the elegant fronts in the Burlington Arcade were known among the cognoscenti to have rooms where a man and woman, entering the shop separately, might discreetly retire. Sometimes the girls behind the counter were available.

Obviously such shops held dangers of blackmail. The acknowledged mistress of this art was Rachael Leverson, known as Madame Rachael, who ran a kind of beauty salon called the Temple of Beauty in New Bond Street. Despite styling herself 'Madame Rachael', Rachael Leverson was an illiterate working-class woman who hailed from Lancashire. She is described in *London in the Sixties* as a 'bony and forbidding looking female with the voice of a Deal boatman and the physique of a grenadier'. She had tried fortune-telling, selling old clothes and fish before going into the beauty business, and at first even that didn't go well. In 1862 she was sent to a debtor's prison, but the following year she was out and running the 'handsomely appointed' shop in New Bond Street, with the slogan 'Beautiful for Ever' over the door. *London in the Sixties* says: 'Old men desirous of enamelling their bald old pates, ponderous females with scratch wigs and asthma, and girls pretty and ugly with defects capable of improvement hustled and tussled to pay the fee of the wonderful enchantress who guaranteed to restore youth to old age

and make one and all "beautiful for ever".' She advertised her wares
in a brochure with that title, price half a crown:

> In the interior of the Sahara, or the Great Desert, is a magnetic
> rock, from which water distils sparingly in the form of dew,
> which is possessed of an extraordinary property. Whether a
> latent electricity is imparted by magnetism, or an additional
> quantity of oxygen enters its composition, it is not easy to say.
> But it appears to have the property of increasing the vital
> energies, as it restores the colour of grey hair apparently by
> renewing the circulation in its capillary tubes, the cessation of
> which causes greyness: and it gives the appearance of youth to
> *persons of considerable antiquity*. This water is brought to
> Morocco on *swift dromedaries* for the use of the Court, and its
> virtues are much extolled by their physicians. It might be called
> the antipodes of the Lythean Styx of ancient times.

This masterly come-on was for Magnetic Rock Dew Water at two
guineas a bottle. There was something called the Bridal Toilet Cabinet
at up to 200 guineas, or the Royal Bridal Toilet Cabinet, which cost
1,000 guineas. Her crude blackmail was even more extortionate. Next
to her shop were Madame Rachael's Arabian Baths, which doubled as
a beauty parlour and house of assignation. Here clients, guilty or
innocent, were in danger of being compromised or robbed.

The wife of a City broker who had indulged in some expensive
beauty treatments found, when she emerged from the celebrated
Arabian Baths, that her diamond rings and earrings had vanished.
When she complained Madame Rachael dropped her pretentions to
gentility and told her 'not to give herself airs'. She had been followed
to her home, and if she caused trouble her husband would be told that
she was at the Arabian Baths to meet a lover. The woman had the
courage to tell her husband, and the couple took legal advice. Their
lawyer told them that if they took action Madame Rachael would use
the legal process to destroy the woman's character. The couple did
not proceed.

Madame Rachael was making a good living from her rackets,
with a house in Maddox Street in Mayfair, a coach and pair and a

box at the opera, for which she paid £400 for a season. Then she cheated a foolish widow named Mary Tucker Borradaile of her entire £5,000 capital. Mrs Borradaile, who had been married to an Indian Army officer, agreed to pay £1,700 for beauty treatments 'to repair the ravages of time and the tropics'. On one occasion when she was in the Arabian Baths she caught a glimpse of a middle-aged bachelor, who turned out to be Lord Henry Ranelagh. Lord Henry also caught a glimpse of her in the bath, and was captivated. He was determined to marry her, and Madame Rachael was to be the go-between. For the moment they would communicate by letter, as he expected objections from his family to him marrying somebody of lower social status.

Poor Mrs Borradaile was taken in, and soon she had parted with all her money to the fake 'Lord Ranelagh', who said he was temporarily short of cash. Her infatuation must have been total, for his love letters were written in different hands, and sometimes bore the wrong signature. Here is one of them:

> Mary, my heart's love. Is it your wish to drive me mad? Granny [Madame Rachael] has my instructions. Do as she tells you. Four letters, and not one reply. What is the meaning of this delay at the eleventh hour? Granny lent me the money. You shall pay her, my own sweet one ... Your sister and her husband have behaved very badly towards you if you knew all ... I receive letters every day, telling me that you only laugh at, and show, my letters. Mary beloved one of my heart, do not trifle with me; I love once, I love for ever. Leave all to me. I guard your honour with my life. With fond and devoted love, I am your devoted William.

Mrs Borradaile had been told that Lord Ranelagh's name was Henry, not William, but apparently she still did not suspect that she was being tricked.

When the money was all gone, Mrs Borradaile was left with only a pension of £300 a year. Madame Rachael decided to have that too, got her to sign a bond and, when Mrs Borradaile refused to sign the pension over to her, had her committed to prison. It was her undoing. Mrs Borradaile's relatives intervened. Although silly and vain, she now had the courage of desperation, and she sued Madame Rachael in the Court of Queen's Bench, a trial that was overtaken by a prosecution for fraud in the Central Criminal Court in September 1868.

William Ballantine, the barrister who prosecuted, described Mrs Borradaile as 'a skeleton encased apparently in plaster of Paris, painted white and pink, and surmounted with a juvenile wig'. She was the butt of much crude humour – one newspaper described her as a 'senescent Sappho' – and she was laughed at in court. The ludicrous letters made a bad impression, and the defence made it seem that Mrs Borradaile was simply a silly old woman seeking to gratify desires that should have died down long ago. The first jury could not reach a decision, but a month later a second trial ended with Madame Rachael being sent to penal servitude for five years.

She was released in 1872 and set up in the fashion business again, near her old premises. Six years later a young woman accused her of stealing necklaces she had left as security for beauty treatments, and she was sent to jail again, where she died. She had two lawyer sons who were said to make a practice of sailing close to the wind. Ballantine, the prosecutor, claimed Madame Rachael's victims were people 'who would sooner submit to felony and fraud than that their names should be exposed to the public'.

Brothels were sometimes owned by eminently respectable citizens. In 1817 evidence given to the Police committee implicated a Mr Dancer in brothel-keeping. To the astonishment of the committee members, he was also clerk to the Bedford Chapel in Charlotte Street: a pillar of the community. The parish beadle was questioned:

> Are there many houses of ill-fame in St Giles? – A great number...
>
> There is one in particular belonging to Mr Dancer, in New Street... He has three or four houses in New Street. How long has this man kept houses of ill-fame? – A good while, as long as I have been in the situation of beadle...

Do the parish officers know that this man keeps houses of ill-fame? – I have heard it mentioned, that it has been mentioned to some of the officers.

It may be that in this area of festering tenements, brothels, low lodging houses, thieves' kitchens and disorderly public houses nobody thought twice about Dancer's situation. 'Dancer's houses provided a base for both prostitution and crime. In many instances the police traced criminals to them where the latter were found in bed with whores. Dancer also operated at the lowest level of all – he let rooms to women who survived on prostitution and parish relief' (Henriques, *Prostitution and Society*, vol. 3).

The committee heard evidence of the wives of respectable men keeping brothels. A Mr Cummins of Bloomsbury obviously preferred to pursue a respectable career and leave his wife to run the brothels, something she did very successfully.

the houses of Mr Cummins are not conducted in general as houses of that sort are; they are generally very secure; there is no robbery in them, I understand. They are supposed to contain much accommodation? – Yes, no doubt of it.

From one hundred to one hundred and fifty beds? – I cannot speak to the number.

Are they weekly or nightly lodgers? – Nightly I believe.

Or hourly? – Yes, some of them, I apprehend.

Did you ever hear that eighteenpence or two shillings was the price? – I do not know.

Have you reason to believe that persons of both sexes go to Cummins' houses? – I have reason to believe so, certainly.

The hearing was told that Mrs Cummins had a well-furnished suburban house in Camden Town and was also reputed to be 'a person of considerable property'.

The committee was also told of the Union Hotel in Dean Street, Soho, which was owned by a sheriff's officer. Although it was clearly a brothel, it was so discreetly conducted that the authorities could not act against it. Milk Alley nearby was then 'a kind of parade ground' for prostitutes, who would take their clients to the Union Hotel or other similar premises in the neighbourhood. 'There were of course other districts where the precise opposite occurred. For example a brothel near St Martin's-le-Grand in the city; "...there were continually girls standing at the door enticing young people in, and at all times of the night fighting and quarrelling, giving charge, and sometimes men taken out..." In this particular instance the evidence of people in the surrounding houses was so overwhelming that an indictment succeeded.' (Henriques, ibid.). The brothel-keeper was pregnant and so escaped the pillory, but she was sentenced to three months in prison.

St Giles, known as the 'Holy Land', was a hideous and lawless slum, later cut through by New Oxford Street. Its criminal roots reached back to the seventeenth century. The celebrated whore Sally Salisbury was born there in 1692, and Charles Dickens and Henry Mayhew both wrote eloquently about it. It was the most feared and deplorable of all the rookeries, or criminal ghettoes, and was said to have had for Dickens 'a profound attraction of repulsion'. St Giles extended roughly from Great Russell Street south to Long Acre, with Drury Lane and Charing Cross Road as its eastern and western boundaries. There were other rookeries that were bigger and more dangerous, but St Giles was surrounded by some of the city's most fashionable and prosperous areas. It was connected to the important promenades of Leicester Square and the Haymarket by alleys and dives.

The area had long been one of London's citadels of vice and crime. As far back as 1751 over a quarter of its 2,000 houses were gin shops, and it had 82 lodging houses which harboured prostitutes and receivers. Hogarth used it as the setting for his print *Gin Lane*. Its impenetrability and the fact that it had a large Irish population made it seem even more alien. By 1851 it had 54,000 inhabitants, about one-fifth of them Irish, living on average about twelve to a house, and as well as being known as the 'Holy Land' the area was called 'Little Dublin'.

Inspector Hunt of the Metropolitan Police gave Henry Mayhew a description of St Giles in the 1840s, before much of it was demolished to make way for New Oxford Street. The streets of decayed buildings, some dating from the seventeenth century, were so narrow that in places a man had to turn sideways to get between the houses. On the corner of Church Street and Lawrence Street was an infamous brothel where the rooms were rented by prostitutes. As Inspector Hunt explained, robbery rather than sex was the business that went on there. The prostitutes would pick up drunken men in the streets around the Strand or nearby Drury Lane or even as far west as Regent Street and take them back to the brothel. 'When they had plundered the poor dupe he was ejected without ceremony by the others who resided in the room; often without a coat or hat, sometimes without his trousers, and occasionally left on the staircase as naked as he was born.' The girls might be as drunk as their customers. Inspector Hunt said: 'In this house the grossest scenes of profligacy were transacted.' When the house was pulled down it was found to be connected by a series of secret escape routes to other houses in the rookery.

These escape routes were a feature of the buildings in St Giles. They linked the houses in one street 'by roof, yard and cellar' to those in another, and made it almost impossible for the police to arrest a fugitive there.

William Logan worked in the area as a city missionary in 1838. He described (in *The Great Social Evil*, 1871) a visit to a house where there were eight to ten 'miserable' young women:

> The mistress of this vile den was one of the most forbidding creatures a person could look on – a sort of demon in human form, such as has been described to the life by Sir Walter Scott. One of the girls, about sixteen years of age, of fascinating appearance 'like a stricken deer', occupied a seat by herself. It was evident she was nearing her journey's end. A few kind earnest words were addressed to her about the importance of coming without delay to Christ for pardon. More than thirty years have passed since that interview, but I have a vivid recollection of the somewhat hopeful, yet dejected look of that pale, comely countenance, as it seemed to say, 'Is it possible that there is mercy for a poor wanderer such as I?'. . . This case was the first which specially drew my attention to the subject of prostitution.

Logan goes on to tell of a visit to a tenement in the same area. His account captures the nightmarish atmosphere in the brothel tenements and the precautions the inhabitants took against surprise.

> I entered a dark passage, and ascended a few steps to what might be called the second landing ... there was no stair to be found. I groped about in the dark, but as far as the right arm could reach, I felt nothing. There seemed to be a plank stretching across the chasm at my feet, and on this I ventured, but after advancing a little, being unable to feel anything like a wall, I thought it most prudent to retrace my steps. I did so as cautiously as possible, and was about to descend when I heard the sound of human voices ... I therefore got down on my hands and knees and moved along very cautiously and slowly till I reached the other end of the plank ... I fancied that the people above me heard my movements, for the sound of voices as of persons talking in a kind of whisper reached me. Arriving at the top of the stair I knocked at the door, which was opened, and I observed at a glance that the house was a third class brothel in which I found several young men and women. One of the young men said, with a self-condemned look, 'I am not sir, where I ought to be, and shall be glad to accept one of your tracts.' After a short and somewhat hopeful interview, I retraced my steps, getting along the narrow plank in the same way as before, and on reaching the first stair felt inexpressibly grateful to recognise a few rays of heaven's light, which enabled me to descend safely.

One of the scandals of the age were the 'flash houses', low lodging houses or brothels, perhaps associated with public houses, where boys mixed with mature thieves and prostitutes, and girls of their own age, who were often their mistresses. A nine-year-old boy named Burnet, who had a long criminal record and had been sentenced to hang but reprieved, had a mistress aged thirteen. Some of the flash houses were exclusively for the young. In one of them, in St Giles, according to the reformer William Crawford 'four hundred beds are made up every night; a boy who was in the habit of visiting this house confessed that he had slept there upwards of thirty times with girls of his own age, and he particularly named five: this boy was fourteen years of age, the girls were to be met with at the flash houses to which he resorted'.

The sexual precocity of young criminals was often commented upon. A former Newgate prisoner wrote that most boys there who were over twelve years old, and some even younger, had mistresses who visited them in prison by pretending to be their sisters. In 1836 the Prison Inspectors for the Home District said that some of the girls were only twelve or thirteen years old. Sixteen years later the Select Committee on Juvenile Offenders heard that many young criminals lived with prostitutes, and that they had been known to have venereal diseases at the age of twelve. A London judge told the committee about girls aged fourteen or fifteen who could not remember when they first had intercourse. This sexual precocity was noted by Henry Mayhew, who remarked of the street children 'their most remarkable characteristic ... is their extraordinary licentiousness'. This led him to think that the onset of puberty came much earlier than was commonly believed. Couples as young as thirteen could live openly together in respectable working-class districts and have children. For those who could be bothered, there was a church in Bethnal Green where fourteen-year-olds could be married for sevenpence.

The Select Committee on the Police 1816-18 was told of brothels especially for children. The prostitutes were mainly under fourteen, and some only eleven or twelve. The customers were also youngsters. Another witness named a girl then aged sixteen who had been working as a prostitute in her father's brothel for the past five or six years.

The promiscuity of the lodging houses was shocking to the Victorians, with their fetish for female modesty. The beds were verminous and inmates of both sexes often lay on them entirely naked. A girl recalled:

There were very wicked carryings on. The boys, if any differ-ence, was the worst. We lay packed on a full night, a dozen boys and girls squeedged into one bed ... I can't go into all the particulars, but whatever could take place in words or acts between boys and girls did take place, and in the midst of the others...Some boys and girls slept without any clothes, and would dance about the room in that way. I have seen them and, wicked as I was, I felt ashamed...

Henry Grey Bennet, MP, chairman of the 1816 committee, insisted that something had to be done to suppress the flash houses. Although some police officers had denied that they even existed, and others said that they should not be closed down because they were useful sources of information, Bennet responded:

I say then, that there are above two hundred regular flash-houses in the metropolis, all known to the police officers, which they frequent, many of them open all night; that the landlords in numerous instances receive stolen goods, and are what are technically called fences; that this fact is known also to the officers, who, for obvious reasons, connive at the existence of these houses; that many of the houses are frequented by boys and girls of the ages of ten to fourteen and fifteen, who are exclusively admitted, who pass the night in gambling and debauchery, and who there sell and divide the plunder of the day, or who sally forth from these houses to rob in the streets.

Bennet disclosed the open secret that the police took bribes for keeping the activities of the flash houses secret from the magistrates, and named some of the more notorious houses. These included the Black Horse in Tottenham Court Road, haunt of thieves such as Huffey White and Conkey Beau. The landlord, Blackman, 'has been considered a thief for fifteen years...there is not a regular flash-house in London that is not known to the officers of the police, from the Rose in Rose Street, Long Acre, kept by Kelly, which he kept long with impunity, to the Bear, opposite to Bow-Street office, the infamous character of which is notorious, and which unites the trades of brothel and public-house.'

The flash houses were central to the whole criminal enterprise. Thieves and their prostitute associates used them to eat and sleep, to plan robberies, to exchange information, to recruit new gang members, to dispose of or acquire stolen goods. In 1851 the Common Lodging House Act was passed in an attempt to control them. Police were given powers to inspect and close them if they failed to reach an elementary standard of decency and cleanliness. Hundreds were closed, and in the remainder put their prices up to meet the costs of the new standards. Some of the poor were thus made homeless because they could not afford to pay.

A prostitute who became pregnant faced almost insuperable difficulties if she wanted to keep the child and continue to ply her trade. Or she might simply want to get rid of it. The only practical solution in either case was to farm out her baby. Baby farming of illegitimate children was common – Acton reckoned that there were more than 30,000 children in the hands of baby farmers. Some looked after their charges well. Others were simply homicidal. Among them were some who charged a single payment for looking after unwanted children, and thus had an interest in their early demise. The most sensational case of murderous child minders was that of two sisters, Sarah Ellis and Margaret Walters, the 'Brixton Baby Farmers' of the 1870s. The bodies of several babies were found lying on the streets of Lambeth and police visited Ellis's lodgings, where they found five babies dying from malnutrition and opium poisoning. 'Waters, the less culpable of the sisters, was hanged, but Ellis, who was charged only with fraud, escaped with 18 months' hard labour' (Stephen Inwood, *A History of London*).

A typical newspaper advertisement by a baby farmer read:

NURSE CHILD WANTED, OR TO ADOPT. – The Advertiser, A Widow with a little family of her own, and a moderate allowance from her late husband's friends, would be glad to receive the charge of a young child. Age no object. If sickly would receive a parent's care. Terms, Fifteen shillings a month; or would adopt entirely if under two months for the small sum of Twelve pounds.

At times the prostitutes seemed about to overwhelm the legal system by sheer weight of numbers. The magistrate Allen Laing, appalled by the hordes of women being brought into his Hatton Garden office, was reported to have ordered the constables to 'drive all such women into the City', which was of course outside the jurisdiction of the Metropolitan Police. In the evenings the constables escorted the prostitutes they had picked up to the boundary of the City at Temple Bar, which then stood in Fleet Street/Strand. The City authorities objected strongly, and their constables and watchmen resisted the attempts by the Metropolitan officers to dump the street girls on them. For several nights this 'whimsical war' raged, with crowds gathering and members of the public joining in. After order was restored Laing, who was castigated by Dickens, was removed from office. He denied giving the order.

Condemned by Poverty

It was difficult for the children of the poor to be virtuous. Leah Davis had thirteen daughters, 'all either prostitutes or brothel-keepers'. Maria Scroggins, a fifteen-year-old stay-maker, was on her way home one evening when she was 'decoyed to a brothel kept by Rosetta Davis, alias Abrahams, and turned upon the streets'. Another fifteen-year-old was sold into prostitution in an east London brothel by her stepmother.

Mayhew interviewed a sixteen-year-old streetwalker. Hers is the old story of a poor, illiterate child hopelessly astray in a hostile world.

> A good-looking girl of sixteen gave me the following awful statement. Her hands were swollen with cold. 'I am an orphan. When I was ten I was sent to service as a maid of all work, in a small tradesman's family. It was a hard place, and my mistress used me very cruelly, beating me often. I stood my mistress's ill-treatment for about six months...at last I ran away. I got to Mrs —'s, a low lodging house.

Although she was only twelve she became the mistress of a young thief, who gave her a venereal disease. He was arrested for picking pockets, and jailed for six months.

> I was sorry, for he was kind to me; though I was made ill through him; so I broke some windows in St Paul's Churchyard

231

to get into prison to get cured. I had a month in the Compter [prison] and came out well. I was scolded very much in the Compter, on account of the state I was in, being so young. I had 2s 6d given to me when I came out, and was forced to go into the streets for a living.

I continued walking the streets for three years, sometimes making a good deal of money, sometimes none, feasting one day and starving the next. The bigger girls could persuade me to do anything they liked with my money. I was never happy all the time, but I could get no character and could not get out of the life. I lodged all this time at a lodging house in Kent Street. They were all thieves and bad girls. I have known between three and four dozen boys and girls sleep in one room. The beds were filthy and full of vermin...At three years' end I stole a piece of beef from a butcher. I did it to get into prison. I was sick of the life I was leading, and didn't know how to get out of it. I had a month for stealing. ...I have since been leading the same life as I told you of for three years, and lodging at the same houses, and seeing the same goings-on. I hate such a life now more than ever. I am willing to do any work that I can in washing and cleaning...

This poor girl was illiterate. A prostitute who wrote to *The Times* in January 1858 was well-educated and had worked as a governess. Objecting to the moral crusade being carried on against prostitutes, she wrote:

Appoint commissioners who are fitted for the office, intelligent, respectable and responsible gentlemen, and make it worth their while to devote themselves entirely to the reduction of the scandal complained of. Empower these officials to have us taken up and punished for riot or impropriety of any kind. But let not the 'pelting petty officer', the ignorant constable of a few shillings a week, and it may be an unfeeling and unthinking brute, interfere with us as he will. Recollect it was man who made us what we are. It is a man who pays for the finery, the rouge and the gin...it is a man who, when we apply ourselves to industry and honesty, employs us upon starvation wages; and if a man had his way, and women's nature were not superior to his, there would be no virtue extant. Say, then, is it for man to persecute even the most profligate among us?

Pray, Sir, think of this, and tell those gentlemen whose speeches I read to act upon it. They may be husbands and fathers . . . and I allow for their parental solicitude. But if they be Christians they will imitate one who said, 'Go and sin no more', and not 'move on', 'anywhere, anywhere, out of the world'.

Another prostitute, interviewed by Hemyng, lived in a closed, stay-in brothel. She was in her early twenties, the daughter of an East End carpenter. She told how she had met the woman who ran the brothel in the street one day, and accepted her invitation to tea. She was kidnapped and taken to a house south of the Thames, where she was kept for some months and abused until she became compliant to the demands of her captors. She was then taken to a house in a better district and, well-fed and dressed, became reconciled to the life of a prostitute. She had regular clients, but got little of the money and would have run away if she could, but on her few excursions from the brothel she was well guarded. If this reads a bit like a penny dreadful, there is no doubt that the women – and men – who kept brothels and acted as prostitutes' pimps were capable of great viciousness.

Many women were condemned to prostitution by wages that were below subsistence level. In the 1880s the pioneer sexologist Havelock Ellis met a widow of 32 with two children:

She was earning eighteen shillings a week in an umbrella factory in the East End: she occasionally took to the street near one of the big railway stations. A comfortable and matronly person, who looked quite ordinary except that her skirts were shorter than normally worn. If talked to she would remark that she was 'waiting for a lady friend', talk in an affected way about the weather and parenthetically introduce her offer. She will either lead a man into one of the silent neighbouring lanes filled with warehouses, or will take him home with her. She will take what she can get . . . sometimes £1, more often only

working-class virgins. Most working-class girls lost their virginity to members of their own class by their early teens. The diarist 'Walter' lamented:

> Few of the tens of thousands of whores in London have given their virginities to gentlemen, or to young men, or to old men, or to men at all: their own low-class lads had them before anyone else ... that is the truth of the matter, though greatly to be regretted, for street boys cannot appreciate the treasure they destroy. A virginity taken by a street boy of sixteen is like a pearl cast before swine.

Brothel owners resorted to subterfuges. Before paying, customers would demand a certificate signed by a doctor and a midwife to prove that the girl was virgo intacta. Apart from fake certificates, brothels had many ways of fooling the customer. 'Canny young whores ... knew lots of ways in which to fake the rupturing of the hymen – for instance the use of strategically placed bags of pigeon's blood, combined with the tightening of the vagina (various astringent potions were used for this purpose) – or a young whore would simply have sex during her period' (Roberts, *Whores in History*).

The evidence of child prostitution in Victorian London was all around. Girls from twelve to fifteen years old paraded up and down between Piccadilly Circus and Waterloo Place, says Henriques in *Prostitution and Society*, vol. 3, and there was even a market where children could be bought for any purpose. W T Stead asked an experienced police officer if it would be possible to buy a genuine young virgin. '"Certainly" he replied without a moment's hesitation. "But", I continued, "are these maids willing or unwilling parties to the transaction – that is, are they really maiden, not merely in being each a *virgo intacta* in the physical sense, but as being chaste girls who are not consenting parties to their seduction?" He looked surprised at my question ... "Of course they are rarely willing, and as a rule they do not know what they are coming for."'

In his 6 July 1885 issue of the *Pall Mall Gazette*, W T Stead, the editor, quoted a former brothel-keeper:

Did they begin willingly? Some; others had no choice. How had they no choice? Be cause they never knew anything about it till the gentleman was in their bedroom, and then it was too late. I or my girls would entice fresh girls in, and persuade them to stay out too late till they were locked out, and then a pinch of snuff in their beer would keep them snug until the gentleman had his way.

This man admitted picking up a girl of thirteen on the pretext that he would employ her as a maid. Instead he took her to his brothel. 'A gentleman paid me £13 for the first of her, soon after she came to town. She was asleep when he did it – sound asleep. To tell the truth, she was drugged. It is often done.'

Other unwilling girls would be taken to soundproofed rooms and raped. Many would scream and fight, so they were held down by the brothel-keeper or strapped to the bed. The resistance and screaming of their victims was part of the attraction for clients. 'To some men, however, the shriek of torture is the essence of their delight, and they would not silence by a single note the cry of agony over which they gloat' (Henriques, ibid.). Stead wrote in the article quoted above:

To oblige a wealthy customer...an eminently respectable lady undertook that whenever the girl was fourteen or fifteen years of age she would be strapped down hand and foot to the four posts of the bedstead, so that all resistance except that of unavailing screaming would be impossible...Strapping down for violation used to be a common occurence in Half Moon Street.

Howard Vincent, director of the Criminal Investigation Department of the Metropolitan Police, told a parliamentary select committee in 1881:

There are houses in London, in many parts of London, where there are people who will procure children for the purposes of immorality and prostitution, without any difficulty whatsoever above the age of 13, children without number at 14, 15 and 16 years of age. Superintendent Dunlap will tell you that juvenile prostitution is rampant at this moment, and that in the streets about the Haymarket, Waterloo Place and Piccadilly, from nightfall there are children of 14, 15 and 16 years of age, going about openly soliciting prostitution...this prostitution actually takes place with the knowledge and connivance of the mother and to the profit of the household...These procuresses...have an understanding with the mother of the girl that she shall come to that house at a certain hour, and the mother perfectly well knows for what purpose she goes there, and it is with her knowledge and connivance, and with her consent that the girl goes...

With so few young virgins available in London the procurers sought girls from the country or from abroad. Advertisements in provincial newspapers would offer jobs in domestic service. When the girls arrived in the capital they would be taken to a house and introduced to a kind mistress, who would give them alcohol and gradually make them aware of what really went on inside. There was little the girls could do: the local police would have been bribed and it was useless appealing to them for help. Stead cited a brothel in the East End which paid the Metropolitan Police the huge sum of £500 a year for protection. So the wretched girls had to make the most of their situation. Here, from a tract called *Miseries of Prostitution* dated 1844, is a letter from a procurer offering a client a young girl who is 'fresh', that is a virgin.

Sir, When I was at your office, to bring you a letter from Miss Villiers, I promised to let you know when I knew of any lady – *fresh*. I can recommend you a very pretty fair young girl, just come from the country, and I think you will like her much; and if it is convenient to you to meet her tomorrow at – Lichfield Street, at the bottom of St Martin's Lane, at eight o'clock, she shall be there waiting for you. If it is not convenient, will you have the kindness to send me a note by post, and inform me when it will suit your convenience.

Flora Tristan, who wrote that memorable description of prostitutes flocking over Waterloo Bridge to the West End one evening, quotes a document produced by the Society for the Prevention of Juvenile Prostitution in 1838. It concerns a brothel specialising in young girls, mostly foreign, which had been prosecuted by the Society. The madam, a Frenchwoman named Marie Aubrey, had fled abroad.

The house in question was situated in Seymour Place, Bryanston Square. It was an establishment of great notoriety, visited by some of the most distinguished foreigners and others...The house consisted of twelve or fourteen rooms, besides those appropriated to domestic use, each of which was genteelly and fashionably furnished...a service of solid silver plate was ordinarily in use when visitors required it...At the time when the prosecution was instituted, there were about twelve or fourteen young females in the house, mostly from France and Italy...Marie Aubrey had lived at the house a number of years, and had amassed a fortune...Upon receiving a fresh importation of females, it was the practice of this woman to send a circular, stating the circumstance, to the parties who were in the habit of visiting the establishment... There are a number of houses of this description at the West End now under the cognizance of the Society...

Your Committee desire to lay before this meeting the means adopted by the agents of these houses. As soon as they arrive on the Continent they obtain information respecting those families who have daughters and who are desirous of placing them in respectable situations; they then introduce themselves, and by fair promise induce the parents to allow the stranger to accompany [the girl] to London, with the understanding that they are to be engaged as tambour workers, or in some other genteel occupation... While they remain in the house they were first taken to, the money is duly forwarded, and the parents are thus unconsciously receiving the means of support from the prostitution of their own children; if they remove, letters are sent to the parents to apprize them that their daughters have left the employ of their former mistress, and the money is accordingly stopped.

Irish girls coming to England in search of work were a favourite target of the procurers. They would be met on the wharf at Liverpool after they left the ship by a stranger who offered to take them to a cheap hotel – really a brothel. Once there their money would be taken away for board and lodging and they would be gradually introduced to the real business of the house. Some lucky girls might evade the traps at Liverpool and make it to London. 'There an extremely effective device was utilised. A woman dressed as a Sister of Mercy would approach them saying she had been sent from a convent to meet them, and take care of them. Introduced to the brothel the system worked as in the other methods – drink, no money, and the life of luxury awaiting them' (Henriques, *Prostitution and Society*, vol. 3).

Procuresses also prowled the streets of London looking for suitable girls. They would approach the young women offering to help with shopping, accommodation or directions. Inevitably they would end up in a brothel. The Society for the Protection of Young Females stated:

> It has been proved that upwards of four hundred individuals procure a living by trepanning [trapping] females from eleven to fifteen years of age, for the purposes of Prostitution ... when an innocent child appears in the streets without a protector, she is insidiously watched by one of these merciless wretches and decoyed, under some plausible pretext, to the abode of infamy and degradation ... She is stripped of the apparel with which parental care, or friendly solicitude has clothed her, and then decked with the gaudy trappings of her shame, she is com-pelled to walk the streets; ... should she attempt to escape from the clutches of her seducers she is threatened with instant punishment, and is often barbarously treated.

Stead revealed an even more revolting means of supplying the market with virgins. He quotes a brothel-keeper:

> Another very simple mode of supplying maids is by breeding them. Many women who are on the streets have female

children. They are worth keeping. When they get to be twelve
or thirteen they become merchantable. For a very likely 'mark'
of this kind you may get as much as £20 or £40. I sent my own
daughter on the streets from my own brothel. I know a couple
of very fine little girls who will be sold before very long. They
are bred and trained for the life. They must take the first steps
some time, and it is bad business not to make as much out of
that as possible. Drunken parents often sell their children to
brothel-keepers. In one street in Dalston you might buy a
dozen...

Some of the young girls who pestered male pedestrians in the
streets by plucking at their sleeves and making obscene suggestions
were under age, but by no means virgins. As we have seen, many
were sent on to the streets by their families, and were expected to
return with their night's takings. They were the product of the over-
crowding, degradation and vice of the rookeries and slums. 'One
may read of a man convicted of outraging a small child begotten by
himself on his own daughter' (Chesney, *Victorian Underworld*).

The police were powerless to stop men taking advantage of girls
over the age of consent, or the girls from prostituting themselves. An
1881 report to a Lords committee contained this evidence from a
police superintendent about a visit to a house in Windmill Street:

I went in with my chief inspector, and in each of the rooms in
that house I found an elderly gentleman in bed with two of
these children. They knew perfectly well that I could not touch
them in the house; and they laughed and joked me, and I could
not get any direct answer whatever. I questioned them, in the
presence of the brothel keeper, as to what they were paid, and
so on. They were to receive six shillings each from the gentleman, two of them; and the gentlemen had paid six shillings
each for the room. It was four shillings if there was only one
girl, but six shillings if there were two girls for the room.

The Pangs of Desire

The English have long been recognised as peculiarly addicted to whipping. An early insight into the origins of *le vice anglais* came in Thomas Shadwell's 1676 play *The Virtuoso* where one character explains his addiction to the habit: 'I was so us'd to't at Westminster School I could never leave it off since.' London, the world capital for flagellation, had its own special brothels. Mother Burgess's in Covent Garden was well enough known to be named in *The Paphian Grove*:

> With Breeches down, there let some lusty Ladd,
> (To desp'rate Sickness desperate Cures are had!)
> With honest Birch excoriate your Hide
> And flog the Cupid from your scourged Bankside!

So popular were flagellation houses in the nineteenth-century that one madam, Mrs Theresa Berkely, was reputed to have made £10,000 in eight years. The book *Venus School Mistress*, published in 1830 with a preface by another madam, Mary Wilson, and devoted wholly to flagellation, gives an account of Mrs Berkely and her establishment at 28 Charlotte Street. In her preface Mary Wilson says that she is giving up her own whipping establishment in St Pancras, and suggests that her patrons should try the delights of Mrs Berkely's.

> She is a clever, pleasing, and trustworthy woman, in the prime
> of life, and perfectly mistress of her business. She is an

excellent ontologist, and therefore quite au fait in treating the aberrations of the human mind. Her museum of natural and artificial curiosities and her collection of 'Illustrations de arcanis Veneris et amoris' are by far the most extensive to be found in any similar institution.

The book in its description of Mrs Berkely suggests perhaps surprisingly that whores must be lustful to succeed:

She possessed the first grand requisite of a courtizan, viz., lewdness; for without a woman is positively lecherous she cannot long keep up the affectation of it, and it will soon be perceived that she only moves her hands or her buttocks to the tune of pounds, shillings and pence. She could assume great urbanity and good humour; she could study every lech, whim, caprice and desire of her customer, and had the disposition to gratify them, if her avarice were rewarded in return.

Venus School Mistress lists Mrs Berkely's extraordinary equipment in detail and with not a little humour:

Her instruments of torture were more numerous than those of any other governess. Her supply of birch was extensive, and kept in water so that it was always green and pliant; she had shafts with a dozen whip thongs on each of them; a dozen different sizes of thin bending canes; leather straps like coach trades; battledoors, made of thick sole-leather, with inch-nails run through to docket and curry-comb tough hides rendered callous by many years' flagellation. Holly brushes, furze brushes, a prickly evergreen called butcher's brush; and during the summer, glass and china vases, filled with a constant supply of green nettles, with which she often restored the dead to life. Thus, at her shop, whoever went with plenty of money could be birched, whipped, fustigated, scourged, needle-pricked, half-hung, holly-brushed, furze-brushed, butcher-brushed, stinging-nettled, curry-combed, phlebotomised and tortured...

For those who preferred to scourge rather than be scourged, Mrs Berkely was prepared to act the role of victim in return for a large fee, as long as the beating was not too violent. For sadists who wanted to inflict serious pain she kept a number of strong women to play victim.

Mrs Berkely's greatest claim to the considerable fame she acquired in these circles was the Berkely Horse. This was invented in 1828 for her to flog her clients on. *Venus School Mistress* says:

It is capable of being opened to a considerable extent, so as to bring the body to any angle that might be desirable. There is a print in Mrs Berkely's memoirs, representing a man upon it quite naked. A woman is sitting in a chair exactly under it, with her bosom, belly and bush exposed she is manualizing his embolon, while Mrs Berkely is birching his posteriors ... When the new flogging machine was invented the designer told her that it would bring her into notice, and go by her name after her death; and it did cause her to be talked about, and brought her a great deal of business ... Mrs Berkely also had in her second floor, a hook and pulley attached to the ceiling by which she could draw a man up by the hands ...

Mrs Berkely died in 1836 and her brother, who had been a missionary in Australia for thirty years, returned to claim her fortune as his inheritance. When he learned how she had earned it he renounced his claim and returned to Australia. Mrs Berkely's executor, a Dr Vance, refused to administer the estate and the wages of sin became the property of the Crown. The Berkely Horse was given to the Royal Society of Arts.

Another famous whipping establishment was Mrs Colet's in Covent Garden, established about 1766, among whose clients was the Prince Regent. 'It is not known whether the Royal Wrist wielded the whip or whether the Royal Buttocks submitted to it!' Nickie Roberts writes in *Whores in History*: 'Such was the fever for scourging during this period that Chace Pine [a roué of the period] devised a machine which could whip forty persons at a time.' Other women who kept whipping establishments included Mrs Colet's niece Mrs Mitchell, whose place of business was first in Waterloo Road and later in Kennington. Mrs James of Carlisle Street, Soho, made enough money to retire to 'jewelled splendour' in Notting Hill, says Henriques in *Prostitution and Society*, vol. 2.

Mary Wilson, proprietor of the Eleusinian Institution, also specialised in flagellation. This interesting woman, who translated and published European erotic novels, wrote extensively about men's addiction to flagellation, and in *Venus School Mistress* classified the different types drawn to this form of masochism:

1. Those who like to receive a fustigation, more or less severe from the hands of a fine woman, who is sufficiently robust to wield the rod with vigour and effect.
2. Those who desire to administer birch discipline on the white and plump buttocks of a female.
3. Those who neither wish to be passive recipients nor active administrators of birch discipline, but derive sufficient excitement as mere spectators of the sport.

Miss Wilson makes it clear that the taste for flagellation is not confined to the elderly debauchee or worn-out roué.

Many persons not sufficiently acquainted with human nature, and the ways of the world, are apt to imagine that the *lech* for Flagellation must be confined either to the aged, or those who are exhausted through too great devotion to venery: but such is not the fact, for there are quite as many young men and men in the prime and vigour of life, who are influenced by this passion as there are amongst the aged and the debilitated.

It is very true that there are innumerable old generals, admirals, colonels and captains, as well as bishops, judges, barristers, lords, commoners and physicians, who periodically go to be whipped, merely because it warms their blood, and keeps up a little agreeable excitement in their systems long after the power of enjoying the opposite sex has failed them; but it is equally true, that hundreds of young men through having been educated at institutions where the masters are fond of administering birch discipline, and recollecting certain sensations produced by it, have imbibed a passion for it, and have longed to receive the same chastisement from the hands of a fine woman . . .

Miss Wilson goes on to say that the expert flagellant or governess would have learned her skills from some older practitioner of the art. 'It is not merely keeping a rod, and being willing to flog, that would cause a woman to be visited by the worshippers of birch.' She mentions some of the teachers, including 'the late Mrs Jones, of Hertford Street and London Street, Fitzroy Square; such was the late Mrs Berkely, such is Betty Burgess of York Square, and such is Mrs Pryce, of Burton Crescent'. It is clear that this 'lech', as she called it, was much in demand.

One of Mrs Berkely's most famous successors was Sarah Potter, alias Stewart. At various times she had establishments, including brothels specialising in flagellation, in Castle Street off Leicester Square, Wardour Street, Albion Terrace off the King's Road, Howland Street off Tottenham Court Road, the Old Kent Road and eventually, before her death in 1873, in Lavinia Grove, King's Cross. She was arrested in 1873 and a pamphlet gave the following account of her business:

> under the auspices of the Society for the Protection of Females, seizure was made at the then notorious 'Academy' of Sarah Potter, alias Stewart, in Wardour Street, and a rare collection of Flagellation appurtenances taken to the Westminster Police Court when the general public for the first time became aware that young females were decoyed into Stewart's School of Flogging, to undergo the ordeal of the birch from old and young Flagellists, for the benefit of the woman Stewart. These curious specimens of her stock-in-trade consisted of a folding ladder, with straps, birch rods, furze brooms and secret implements, for the use of male and female.
>
> Her method of conducting business was to get hold of young girls, board, lodge and clothe them, and in return they were obliged to administer to the lusts of the patrons of the boarding-house. They were flogged in different ways. Sometimes strapped

to the ladder, at others they were flogged round the room – at times they were laid on the bed. Every device or variation which perverted ingenuity could devise was resorted to to give variety to the orgies, in return for which the mistress of the house was paid sums varying from £5 to £15. The profits of this school enabled Stewart to keep a country house and a fancy man, to the great scandal of the community.

The case against Mrs Potter/Stewart was brought by a girl of 'about fifteen', Agnes Thompson, at the instigation of the Society for the Protection of Females and Young Women. Agnes said that a year previously she had gone with a man to a house where he had 'effected her ruin'. Since then she had worked for Mrs Potter at the Albion Terrace address. She said: 'I was flogged by gentlemen with birch rods. I was beaten on my naked flesh.' She described an occasion when she was whipped by a man called 'Sealskin' and another known as 'The Count'. During this ordeal she had been tied to the ladder which was produced in court.

Two other girls, Catherine Kennedy, who was seventeen, and Alice Smith, described in a report in *Lloyd's Weekly London Gazette* as 'a young woman of considerable personal attractions', told of similar floggings. Smith said she was not paid for her services. Mrs Potter was found guilty and sent to prison. She cannot have been altogether a bad mistress, for Agnes Thompson returned to her when she was released and worked for her for some time. Mrs Potter died in 1873 'and is commemorated by an imposing tombstone in Kensal Green Cemetery' (Thomas, *The Victorian Underworld*).

Addicts of flagellation could seek solace outside the specialised establishments. In *Disorderly Women in Eighteenth-Century London*, Henderson tells of a trial at the Old Bailey in 1718 in which a prostitute named Amy Warrington was accused of stealing two guineas from Bernard Kemble. Warrington, from St-Giles-in-the-Fields, and two other prostitutes were paid 10s. by Kemble for a thrashing, during which Warrington broke a broom over his back. She was acquitted, the court deciding that Kemble was 'an old clumsy Fellow' who 'deserved to be whipped for picking up Whores'.

*

Flogging in schools has often been blamed for the Englishman's addiction to flagellation, but girls were also whipped. The London magazine *Society* had a long correspondence on the subject. 'Your correspondents often ask whether corporal punishment is still in force in the better class girls' schools. I can assure you that it does still exist…Others of our better class girls' schools use the old-fashioned canes, sticks and scourges, sometimes on the upper and sometimes on the lower parts of the body.' (Henriques, *Prostitution and Society*, vol. 3). This magazine also carried correspondence on the merits of chastisement in marriage. 'With my whole heart I endorse the opinion of your correspondent with regard to the reciprocal punishment of man and wife; family discords of many sorts can easily be avoided thereby…There is a unique attraction in whipping one's wife or being whipped by her hand. I hope a time will come when all quarrels will be settled by the hand.'

The Englishwoman's Domestic Magazine, founded by the husband of the famous cookery writer Mrs Beeton, carried letters on the subject of whipping young girls, and also a strangely ambiguous series on the sensual pleasure produced by tight-lacing. Female correspondents generally seemed to find that it created a 'delightful sensation':

> My nieces…respectively sixteen and seventeen years old…
> have a governess who is very severe with them in the matter of
> tight-lacing and insists, through my orders, on the utmost
> compression that they can bear…the elder…is always
> anxious to help her maid and governess in their efforts with the
> staylace, and delights in the half-pleasure, half-pain, of the
> intense pressure.

Gentlemen too savoured similar pleasures: 'the sensation of being tightly laced in an elegant, well-made, tight-fitting pair of corsets is superb' was the opinion of one male reader. The popularity of this correspondence resulted in the publication of a book – *The Corset and the Crinoline*.

The fact that girl apprentices in trades such as bonnet-making and millinery were whipped and that the public whipping of women was not abolished until 1817 leads Henriques to conclude that 'a definite tradition of flagellation existed in Britain over a long period, and this tradition helps to explain the addiction which characterised so many of the prostitutes' clients in the nineteenth century.'

There was a distant echo of the correspondence in the *Englishwoman's Domestic Magazine* in 1939 when *Picture Post* ran a series of letters on the wisdom or otherwise of caning teenage girls. It began with a letter saying it was a mistake for women cyclists to wear shorts. A woman then wrote to say it would give her great pleasure to 'apply a good pliable cane to the seats of some of those tight-fitting shorts'. It transpired that girls were being flogged for staying out late, speaking without permission, posing nude for photographs. Paul Ferris writes that many of the letters read like fantasies, and it must be said that the Victorian letters quoted above may have been invented by a clever journalist. It would be by no means the first time a lively correspondence was provoked and then kept going with 'planted' letters. The practice continues in the national newspapers today.

'Walter': The Secret Life

Who were the clients of prostitutes? Few Victorian men have left us detailed reminiscences of their sexual lives, although a great many, forced by low wages to remain bachelors into their late twenties or early thirties, were the clients of streetwalkers and brothels. Others, middle- or upper-class married men, had good reason to keep their affairs secret. 'Walter', the diarist who left an account of his encounters with about 1,200 women, mostly prostitutes, has filled in many of the gaps in our knowledge. His diary, published as *My Secret Life*, consists of eleven volumes and gives a truly unique portrait of the Victorian underworld of vice.

Walter has never been identified, although the bibliographer of pornographic writing Henry Spencer Ashbee has been considered as a possibility. Ashbee was head of an international oil company and had homes in London, Paris and Kent. He used his wealth to amass an unrivalled collection of erotica, which he left to the British Museum. Ashbee also compiled the *Index Librorum Prohibitorum*, the first major English bibliography of erotic and pornographic writing. As his dates – 1834–1900 – do not match what little we know of Walter, it seems that Ashbee was more likely to have been the person who arranged for the publication of the diaries. This is how Charles Carrington, a Paris-based publisher of English-language erotica, described how they came to be published:

About the year 1888, a well-known publisher and bookseller of Amsterdam, whose speciality was literature of an incandescent kind, was summoned to London by one of his customers, a rich old Englishman, who desired to have privately printed for his own enjoyment an enormous MS., containing in the fullest detail all the secret venereal thoughts of his existence. He defrayed all costs of printing, on condition that no more than six copies should be struck off. A few years afterwards, this eccentric amateur shuffled off the mortal coil, and a few copies of the extraordinary work made a timid appearance on the market, being quoted at the high figure of £100. It is evident that many more than the half-dozen copies stipulated must have been printed – let us say about twenty-five or so ...

The diaries themselves suggest that the author was born about 1820. He was educated at a public school and worked for a time at the War Office. The death of his father seems to have plunged the family into reduced circumstances, but he later inherited a fortune and somehow always found funds for his forays into the *demi-monde*. His attitude to the working-class girls he picked up was probably typical of a certain kind of middle-class Victorian gentlemen: he could be callous to the point of treating them as sub-human. Thus when he 'bought' a little girl from a woman in Vauxhall Gardens he remarked on her anxious look, and after he had finished, he says, 'She did not holler at all really.' On another occasion he had sex with a pregnant fourteen-year-old, and asked her what she was going to do about the baby. 'Go to the workhouse if they won't keep me,' said the weeping girl. Yet Walter's summing up of this episode is: 'It was an exciting termination to the day.' As we shall see, he eventually came to a compassionate and affectionate view of the women who had given him so much pleasure.

Some of his first successes were with the family's servants; one of them, Charlotte, had his child, which she passed off as her husband's. Later he went on whoring expeditions with his cousin Fred, 'a very devil from his cradle'. It was with Fred that he had his first encounter with a prostitute.

'She is a whore,' said Fred, 'and will let us feel her if we pay her.'
'You go and ask her.' 'No, you.' 'I don't like.' 'How much

money have you got?' We ascertained what we had, and after a
little hesitation, walked on, passed her, and turned round and
stopped. 'What are you staring at, kiddy?' said the woman. I was
timid and walked away, Fred stopped with her. 'Wattie, come
here,' he said in a half-whisper. I walked back. 'How much have
you got?' the woman said. We both gave her money. 'You'll let
us both feel?' said Fred. 'Why of course, have you felt a woman
before?' Both of us said we had, feeling bolder. 'Was it a woman
about here?' 'No.' 'Did you both feel the same woman?' 'No.'
'Give me another shilling then, and you shall both feel my cunt
well, I've such a lot of hair on it.' We gave what we had, and off
she walked without letting us. 'I'll tell your mothers if you come
after me,' she cried out. We were sold; I was once sold again in
a similar manner afterwards, when by myself.

There were other disappointments. Sometimes Walter was
disgusted by the women he picked up, either by their looks or their
vulgarity. One of the first whores he had sex with turned out to be
very ugly when he finally got a good look at her in a well-lit room.
'She was so plain that all desire left me.' Another such encounter
was in Granby Street, Waterloo Road. This was an area Flora Tristan
visited, and she described half-naked women sitting at the windows
soliciting. Walter used to walk there for the pleasure of looking at
the women. One night one of the whores pulled him into her home.

A woman standing at a door seized my hand, asking me in and
at the same time pulling me quite violently into the little
passage. I had barely seen her, and upon her saying 'Come and
have me' replied that I had scarcely any money. 'Never mind,'
said she, 'we will have it for all that.' She shut the door, closed
rapidly the other wooden shutters, which all the ground-floor
windows had in that street, and began to kiss and feel me. I
then saw that she was half-drunk. Quickly she pulled me
towards the bed, threw her self on it.

'I can't do it,' I said in fright, for her manner was so lewd,
and became so ferocious, that it quite upset me. 'What! a fine
young man like you can't do it,' said she. 'No' (and as an

apology) 'I often can't do it.' 'I will *give* you a pleasure,' said she, 'I can if anyone can,' and although it disgusted me, she dropped on her knees saying 'a man can always do it one way or another.' That over she rose and said, 'You will come to me again, won't you? I will always do that to you, and anything else you like.' I gave her a shilling and promised, but never felt so sick and disgusted with a woman before. Everything about the woman was repulsive. I avoided the street for some months, which was a great loss to me, for I often used to go through it to gloat on the charms of the women as they lolled out of the windows.

Occasionally he would have an affair with a prostitute. One of these was a Frenchwoman, Camille, whom he met in Waterloo Place when she was about 25 and he 21. He describes her as 'a fine, clear-complexioned woman'. She was 'exclusively supported by gentle-men at the West End'. She told him about lesbianism and hetero-sexual sodomy – he tried the latter – and introduced him to other women of the town, whom he had in various multiples. Walter had an eye for detail as sharp as Mayhew or Dickens, and his account of his first visit to her apartment is full of period interest:

The room was nicely furnished, out of it was a nice large bedroom and a smaller one . . . Four wax candles were lighted, down she sat, so did I, and we looked at each other. I could say nothing.

'Shall I undress?' said she at length. 'Yes' I replied, and she began. Never had I seen a woman take off such fine linen before, never such legs in handsome silk stockings and beautiful boots. I had had the cleanest, nicest women, but they were servants, with the dress and manner of servants. This woman seemed elegance itself compared to them. A fine pair of arms were disclosed, a big pair of breasts flashed out, a glimpse of a fine thigh was shown, and as her things dropped off, and she stooped to pick them up, with her face towards me, her laced chemise dropped, opened, and I saw darkness at the end of the vista between her two breasts.

The whole affair was unlike anything I had seen or dreamed of; a quiet, businesslike, yet voluptuous air was about it, which confused me; it affected my senses deliciously in one way, but all the horrors about gay [prostitute] women were conjured up in my imagination at the same time. I was intensively nervous.

She, seeing me so quiet, sat herself on my knee and began unbuttoning my trousers. I declined it . . . She kissed and fondled me, but it was useless . . . [She said] 'Come to the bed.' She got off my knee, went to the bed, laid down on one side, one leg on, one dropping down to the floor, drew up her chemise above her navel and lay with beautiful large limbs clad in stainless stockings and boots . . . I had never seen such a luscious sight, nor any woman put herself unasked into such a seductive attitude.

'Come,' she said. I obeyed and went to the side of the bed. What movement! what manner! I had till then never known what a high-class, well practised professional could do. How well they understand the nature and wants of the man; hers was the manner of quiet woman, so like bawdy nature in a lady that I was in the seventh heaven.

I had scarcely finished when curiosity took possession of me. She yielded in the way a French woman does to all a man wishes, almost anticipating them.

Promising to see her again, I left. One does not get silk stockings, laced chemises, four wax lights and three goes for a pound now, if the rooms be well furnished or not.

Walter had a marvellous ear for the speech of the young street-walkers he picked up. It is worth quoting at length his account of a fifteen-year-old he called Yellow-Haired Kitty, with whom he began a relationship several years after he stopped seeing Camille. He met her in the Strand one hot June day. She was looking in a shop window with a younger girl. Walter described them as looking like 'the children of decent mechanics'. He offered them money, and heard Yellow-Haired Kitty saying to the younger girl, who was reluctant: 'You are a foole. You are a foole. Oh! you foole. Come he wants us. You *foole.*'

One day in bed with Kitty he asked her whether she was 'gay', which then meant a prostitute.

'I ain't gay,' said she astonished. 'Yes you are.' 'No I ain't.'
'You let men fuck you, don't you?' 'Yes, but I ain't gay.' 'What
do you call gay?' 'Why the gals who come out regular of a
night dressed up, and gets their living by it.' I was amused.
'Don't you?' 'No, mother keeps me.' 'What is your father?'
'Got none, he's dead three months back – mother works and
keeps us. She is a charwoman and goes out on odd jobs.'
'Don't you work?' 'Not now,' said she in a confused way.
'mother does not want me to, I takes care of the others.' 'What
others?' 'The young ones.' 'How many?' 'Two – one's a boy,
and one's a gal.' 'How old?' 'Sister's about six, and brother's
nearly eight – but why do you ask me all this for?' 'Only for
amusement. Then you are in mourning for your father?' 'Yes,
it's shabby, ain't it. I wish I could have nice clothes, I've got
nice boots – ain't they?' cocking up one leg, 'a lady gived 'em
me when father died – are my best.'

    'Are you often in the Strand?' 'When I gets out I likes walking
in it, and looking at the shops. I do if Mother's out for the day.'
'Does she know you are out?' The girl had been lying on her
back with her head full towards me, and giggling said in a
confidential sort of way, 'Bless you, no – she'd beat me if she
knew – when she be out, I locks them [the other children] up, and
takes the key, and then I goes back to them – I've got the key in
my pocket, and shall be home before Mother – she is out the
whole day.'

This is the authentic voice of the Victorian street prostitute. Kitty
has already decided, despite her protest that she is not 'gay', that she
will be a whore: it is the only way she can get the clothes and the
luxuries she craves. Those luxuries include food. She and Walter
discussed what she did with the money she earned:

I buy things to eat, I can't eat what Mother gives us, she is poor
and works very hard, she'd give us more but she can't; so I
buys food, and gives the others what Mother gives me, they
don't know better – if Mother's there I eat some, sometimes we

have only gruel and salt; if we 'ave a fire we toast the bread, but I can't eat it if I'm not dreadfully hungry.' 'What do you like?' 'Pies and sausage-rolls,' said the girl, smacking her lips and laughing, 'Oh! my eye, ain't they prime – oh!' 'That's what you went gay for?' 'I'm not gay,' said she sulkily. 'Well, what [do] you let men fuck you for? Sausage-rolls?' 'Yes. Meat-pies and pastries too.'

Eventually, as with all of Walter's affairs, that with Kitty tailed off. He returned from abroad to find her better dressed and prosperous. She had become the mistress of a man to whom she promised to be faithful for the rest of her life. However, she slept with Walter one last time.

The odds were against young working-class girls like Kitty staying chaste. Walter tells of a girl of fifteen he had sex with in her home while her mother was in the next room. The mother told him: 'We are so poor, we are almost starved, we are – what was I to do for a living? I've lost nearly all since my husband's left me, and I can't afford to keep a big gal like that; if she will go wrong I can't help it. I could not keep her in and the chaps were allus arter her – she must live, and she's better at home doing that, than doing it away from me.'

Many London whores worked with criminals to extort or steal, often with violence, from their clients. Walter must have been aware of the dangers, although he does not mention them. Perhaps the fact that he was not a heavy drinker – the women's victims were usually drunk – saved him. But one night in the Strand he met a young woman who took him to a house in a court near Drury Lane Theatre where an ugly scene followed. Walter begins as usual by describing the girl's charms:

there was an exceedingly well-dressed and very short-petticoated (they all wore them then) girl of about seventeen years of age; her legs especially pleased me, they were so plump and neat, and her feet so well shod. After my offer had been accepted we went to a house...She stripped and I plugged her, and recollect now my enjoyment of her.

When the time came to leave Walter paid her the ten shillings they had agreed, but she claimed he had promised her £5. 'Look at this room, look at my dress – do you expect me to let a man come here with me for ten shillings?' She called him a bugger, and opening the door called out: 'Mrs Smith, Mrs Smith, come up, here's a bilk, come up quickly.' An old woman, described by Walter as 'shortish, thick, hook-nosed, tawny-coloured, evil-looking,' appeared and berated him.

> Was I a gent? She was sure I was, why not pay properly then?
> – a beautiful girl like that – just out – look at her shape and her
> face – she had written to a dozen gents who knew her house,
> and they had all come to see this beauty – all had given her five
> pounds, some ten pounds, and they were delighted with her –
> and much of the same talk. The girl began to whimper, saying
> she had never been so insulted in her life before.

The scam had obviously been well rehearsed. Walter said he had not got £5: the ugly old bawd demanded his watch, which she said she would pawn for the money. Walter, who had hidden his watch, countered that he had no watch either. The bawd shouted for a man called Bill and he replied from below in a loud voice 'Hallo'. Walter threw up the window and shouted 'Police! – police! – murder! – murder! – police! – police!' He saw a policeman under the window, but the officer ignored his cries and walked away, and Walter feared that he had been bribed to turn a blind eye to the goings-on in the brothels on his beat. However the two women were alarmed by the commotion and the ugly bawd said, 'Go if you want, who is keeping you? This is a respectable house, this is.' But she demanded £3, then £2. When they refused to open the door Walter seized a poker and smashed the window, then struck and broke a chair. They begged him to go, and he edged cautiously down the stairs, dropping the poker on the mat as he left. 'My blood was roused, I would have smashed woman or man who stood in my way, and eyeing the girl said, "Look at me well, if you meet me in the Strand again cut away at once, get out of my sight, or I'll give you in charge [have you arrested] for annoying me or robbing me, you bloody bitch, look out for yourself."'

A fortnight later he saw her again in the Strand, and followed her. He watched as she solicited various men. Not recognising him she tried to pick him up, but stepping into the lamplight so she could see him properly he said: 'Look at me, you damned whore, you attempted to rob me the other night, go out of the Strand or I'll tell the next policeman you have picked my pocket.' The girl fled with her old bawd running after her, cursing. He saw her again some weeks later, chatting with a group of prostitutes. Walter approached them and said: 'That bitch attempted to rob me the other night...' "It's a lie" said she, but again turned round and ran up a side street as fast as she could. I don't recollect seeing her afterwards.'

Some years later a man died in a fight in the house where the whore had taken him. The owner was transported. Walter commented, 'I don't know if it was the same man who was called Bill, but suspect that it was, and that many a visitor had been bullied out of his money in that house.'

On the evidence of the diaries Walter had scant interest in anything except sex. Occasionally he mentions reading a book or going to the theatre. Utterly self-absorbed, he appears to have none of the intellectual concerns of his class: the great advances in technology and science passed him by. He went to the pleasure gardens. He describes hiding in the shrubbery at Vauxhall Gardens listening to women pissing and chatting in the darkness. 'I have heard a couple of hundred do so on one evening, and much of what they said. Such a mixture of dull and crisp baudiness I never heard in short sentences elsewhere...it amused me very much.' Nevertheless the narrow field in which he specialised for more than forty years, his own sexuality and that of women in general, gave him valuable insights:

To their class I owe a debt of gratitude, and say again what I think I have said elsewhere: that they have been my refuge in sorrow, an unfailing relief in all my miseries, have saved me from drinking, gambling, and perhaps worse. I shall never throw stones at them, nor speak harshly to them. They are much what society has made them, and society uses them, spurns, damns, and crushes them even whilst frequenting them and enjoying them. In short, it shamefully ill-treats them in most Christian countries, and more so in protestant England than in any others that I know.

Walter's view of women's sexuality is refreshingly different to that of the morals campaigners. One of those, Dr Acton, wrote that 'the majority of women (happily for them) are not very much troubled with sexual feeling of any kind'. On the contrary, said Walter, 'women who give themselves up to sexual pleasure have infinitely more enjoyment of life for a time than virtuous women have.' Of course, Walter may have known little of the lives of virtuous women. Nor did he accept the view that most whores were ridden by guilt and longed to reform. 'Some say that harlots are sick of their business, and hate the erotic whims and fanciers to whom they minister. Such is not my experience.'

Scattered through the diaries are observations on his peculiar way of life. He admits that he had wasted much money on women, but does not regret it. 'That which women had I do not regret, they have been the greatest joy in my life, and are so to every true man, from infancy to old age. Copulation is the highest pleasure, both to the body and mind, and is worth all human pleasures put together. A woman sleeping or waking is a paradise to a man, if he be happy with her, and he cannot spend his money on anything better, or as good.' Yet he was unhappily married, and wrote bitterly of his wife. 'I had an unquiet home, and a woman there whom I hated in bed and at board.'

No other writer gives us such a sense of the reality of the underworld of vice as Walter. It is a gaslit world of foggy winter evenings, seen through the windows of the gin palace, a lurid world of transient pleasure and lingering regret. At times even Walter is world-weary: 'Fucking is a commonplace thing, the prince and the beggar do it the same way, it is only the incidents connected with it that are exciting. Voluptuous, reckless, youth and beauty together make the vulgar, shoving, arse-wagging business poetical for a while, but it is animalism.'

Walter was probably in his sixties when the diary ends. He hints at some new sense of obligation – perhaps a new marriage, for he had been a widower for many years.

I break with the past, my amatory career is over, my secret life finished. My philosophy remains the same. My deeds leave me no regrct – with the exception perhaps of a very few – Would that I were young enough to continue in the same course – that all might happen to me over again – But age forbids, duty forbids, affection forbids – Eros adieu.

The Age of Reform

> We see hundreds of little children with their naked feet in the snow, and we pity them, for we know they are hungry... You talk about sending blackcoats [missionaries] among the Indians; now we have no such poor children among us... now we think it would be better for your teachers all to stay at home, and go to work right here in your own streets. (Party of Ojibway Indians who visited London in the 1840s)

Prostitution in Victorian London differed from that of the previous century in that it was even more wretched, more public and more widespread. It took place against a background of great inequality. Poverty was all around, and to the more enlightened of the reformers, that poverty was largely responsible for the prevalence of vice.

In 1829, the year the Metropolitan Police Force was founded, pressure for reform was exerted on many fronts: Parliament, the penal code, the Church, the judiciary, factory conditions, poor laws and child welfare. These were national problems, some of them magnified in London, and besides, the capital had specific problems of its own. The city was now seen as the most prosperous in the world, and yet the problems of poverty, health, vice and crime seemed to be getting worse.

Charles Greville, diarist and clerk to the Privy Council, wrote in 1829 in his *Memoirs*: 'I am afraid there is more vice, more misery and penury in this country than any other, and at the same time greater wealth... The contrasts are too striking, and such an unnatural, artificial and unjust state of things neither can, nor ought to be, permanent. I am convinced that before many years elapse these things will produce some great convulsion'.

Pamphlets appeared on the streets warning of a decline in churchgoing, the increase in Sabbath-breaking, the 100,000 London women who had slain their babies, the surge in savage crimes, the flood of pornography and the 80,000 prostitutes, among other ills, but the most pressing problems were poverty and disease. The poor were at greater risk from a range of killer diseases – smallpox, measles, whooping cough, diphtheria, scarlet fever – than the affluent. Roy Porter in *London, A Social History* explains that they had borne the brunt of the cholera epidemics of 1832 and 1848–9. The following letter appeared in *The Times* on 5 July 1849 above 54 signatures:

> May we beg and beseech your proteckshion and power. We are Sur, as it may be, living in a Wilderniss, as far as the rest of London knows anything of us, or as rich and great people care about. We live in muck and filthe. We aint got no privez, no dust bins, no drains, no water splies, and no drain or suer in the whole place. The Suer Company, in Greek Street, Soho Square, all great, rich and powerfool men, take no notice watsomedever of our complaints. The Stenche of a Gully-hole is disgustin. We al of us suffer, and numbers are ill, and if the Colera comes Lord help us.

Part of the problem was the explosive growth of the population. In 1801, when the first national census was taken, London's population was 958,863 – about a tenth of all the people in England and Wales, and almost double that of 1700. A century later the population of Greater London was 6,586,000, a fifth of all the people in England and Wales, and about the same as the combined populations of Europe's four greatest cities, Paris, Vienna, Berlin and St Petersburg.

After 1851, when birthplaces were first recorded in the census, it was possible to establish the origins of migrants to London. Most of them were British: the next largest group in most years were the Irish, although their numbers fluctuated.

It has been calculated that there were about 156,000 Irish, or 6.6 per cent of the population, in London in 1851. Resentment towards the Irish was strong, particularly among the working class. They had long memories of the Irish being used as cheap labour. In the 1880s this hostility was transferred to the Jews, who had begun to arrive from Tsarist Russia and Poland in large numbers. By 1905, when legislation was stemming the influx, London's Jewish population was about 140,000.

Naturally Jewish areas had Jewish prostitutes. Elizabeth Gould or Gold opened what Burford, in *Private Vices, Public Virtues*, conjectures was 'a (more or less) Jewish brothel' and in 1745 she had an impressive establishment in Russell Street. 'She had the backing of the wealthy Jewish Notary Public Moses Moravia...' Burford says that by the second third of the eighteenth century the younger generation of refugee Sephardic Jews from the Iberian Peninsula 'were completely anglicized' and had become generous patrons of whores. In August 1742 a Jewish bawd named Rose Marks was convicted of keeping a brothel in Duke's Place, St James's, an area of high-class bordellos. According to Burford, she was ordered to find a security for good behaviour of £2,000, although we don't know the reason for this extraordinary sum.

In the late nineteenth century the majority of poor Jews settled in east London, particularly Stepney. By 1901 the area had 54,000 immigrants; 'it was easy for the London public to develop exaggerated fears of an "alien" invasion of the East End. There was no doubt that the streets of Spitalfields and Whitechapel... were transformed almost into a foreign Yiddish-speaking town in the space of fifteen or twenty years.' (Inwood, *A History of London*).

Popular hostility grew. The Jack the Ripper murders, widely rumoured to have been carried out by a Jew, led to minor disturbances. Racist propagandists blamed the Jews for the area's social problems. The Jewish Board of Guardians, set up in 1859, organised the repatriation of 31,000 Jews between 1881 and 1906 for fear of a backlash against their old-established Anglo-Jewish community.

One contemporary writer who took a contrary view of the effect of Jewish immigration was C Russell, who wrote in 1900 that there were 'certain districts of Whitechapel which – before they were over-run by the foreigners – were haunted by roughs and criminals of the worst description... These are now exceptionally quiet and orderly.'

many localities that are hidden in London, wholly unknown, even by name, to the great mass of its inhabitants'.

Mayhew introduces us to worlds and people whose lives were unimaginable to the well-to-do shoppers thronging the fashionable thoroughfares just yards away. There are the three orphaned Irish children whose stubborn streak of independence stops them seeking charity. The older girl, now fifteen, had looked after her brother and sister since her mother died when she was eight. The girls sold flowers, and usually made sixpence a day. Their brother earned threepence or fourpence a day as a coster's boy. They tried always to have a shilling in reserve for stock. The older girl said:

> If it's bad weather, so bad that we can't sell flowers at all, and so if we've had to spend our stock money on a bit of bread, she [their landlady] lends us 1s., if she has one, or she borrows one of a neighbour, if she hasn't, or if the neighbour hasn't it, she borrows it at a dolly-shop [an illegal pawnshop]. There's 2d. a week to pay for 1s. at a dolly, and perhaps an old rug left for it; if it's very hard weather, the rug must be taken [home] at night time, or we are starved with the cold. It sometimes has to be put into the dolly again next morning, and there's 2d. to pay for it for the day. We've had a frock in for 6d., and that's a penny a week, and the same for a day. We never pawned anything; we have nothing they would take in at the [licensed] pawnshop. We live on bread and tea and some times a fresh herring of a night.

She had put the three of them through school: the girls could read and their brother could write.

Then there were the scavengers: 'toshers' who trawled the sewers for bones and ropes and scrap, and 'dredgers' who like Gaffer Hexam in Dickens' *Our Mutual Friend* trawled the river and on a good day might recover a corpse in their nets. Like Gaffer they would go through the pockets, and there was further bounty at the inquest. 'There's 5s. 6d. inquest money at Rotherhithe, and on'y a shilling at Deptford,' said one dredger. 'I can't make out how this is but that's all they give.'

The toshers delved up to their armpits in sewage, which in some of London's ancient drains had grown to a depth of five feet, trying

THE BEADLE OF THE BURLINGTON.—"SOMETIMES A SOVEREIGN, AND SOMETIMES LESS."

Blind eye: two fashionable Victorian prostitutes bribe an officer to look the other way as they enter Burlington Arcade in Piccadilly. Some of the shops had rooms where the girls could take their clients.

to recover old ropes, bones and scrap metal. Mayhew interviewed a tosher, a Birmingham man who had run away from home as a child and had worked for twenty years in the mud and sewage of Cuckold's Point on the south bank of the Thames. Sometimes he found coins, and once a silver jug as big as a quart pot. There were dangers of disease and gas, but what the toshers feared were the sewer rats, which they believed could overpower a lone man and pick his bones clean. 'The rats is wery dangerous, that's sartin,' he insisted, 'but we always go three or four on us together, and the varmint's too wide awake to take us then, for they know they'd git off second best.'

The destruction of the old criminal rookeries began with municipal improvements in the middle of the nineteenth century. Those of St Giles and Clerkenwell, ancient citadels of vice and crime, were partly obliterated in the 1840s and 1850s with the building of New Oxford Street, Queen Victoria Street and Farringdon Road. Victoria Street penetrated the Pye Street rookery in the shadow of Westminster Abbey in the 1850s, and Commercial Street was cut through Whitechapel and Spitalfields. The ruthless destruction gathered pace later in the century with Shaftesbury Avenue, Charing Cross Road, Queen Victoria Street, Clerkenwell Road and Holborn Viaduct being driven through working-class areas. Between 1830 and 1880 an estimated 100,000 people were evicted by the new roads. The Nichol, where the gangster Arthur Harding was born in 1886, went in the late nineteenth-century slum clearances. In the 1890s it was replaced by the Boundary Street Estate, the first of the London County Council developments.

In Holborn and the Strand about 6,000 tenants from thirty filthy courts and alleys between Bell Yard and Clement's Lane were evicted in the late 1860s to make way for the Law Courts, and thousands more were cleared out for the construction of Holborn Viaduct. Where did the poor who lived in these areas go? Superintendent G W Cornish of Scotland Yard believed the crimes associated with these areas were dispersed across London, but mostly the poor crowded into neighbouring areas such as Spitalfields, making conditions there even worse. Church Lane, one of the streets that survived the building of New Oxford Street through northern St Giles in 1844–7, was invaded by refugees from the demolished slums. The 28 houses in Church Lane had a population of 655 in 1841: by 1847 it had risen to 1,095. These ousted Holy-landers were soon reinforced by a flood of Irish refugees fleeing famine in their homeland.

Slum clearance was inevitable, given the urgent need for new roads, railways and docks, but it was also seen as a cheap and easy method of getting rid of 'congregations of vice and misery'. It suited the authorities, and it suited the developers, who found slum land relatively cheap and slum dwellers easy to get rid of. The depopulation of slum areas around the City pushed the centre of gravity of whoredom further west.

After the 1850s crime, as measured by arrests, fell off sharply. Drunkenness, the most common cause of arrest in London, also declined. Charles Booth wrote in *Life and Labour of the People in London*: 'Such scenes of open depravity as occurred in years gone by do not happen now. There is greater intelligence, even though it be largely devoted to betting, and wider interests prevail, even if they be too much absorbed in pleasure seeking.'

The spread of middle-class morality – Victorian values – had an effect. Morals campaigns made prostitution by their wives and daughters less acceptable to the working classes, and universal education raised aspirations. But we must remember that for all classes the turbulent eighteenth century was not long past. The respectable classes too were capable of barbarous behaviour. In December 1850 George Sloane, attorney and director of the Church of England Assurance Association, with a house in Pump Court, Temple, was with his wife accused of cruelty by their servant Jane Wilbred. The following is from a newspaper report of the case:

Mr Sloane often beat me; sometimes in the morning early and sometimes in the day time. Mrs Sloane used to beat me because I wore my shift sleeves over my arms and shoulders in the morning [to keep warm]; and when I cried Mr Sloane used to beat me for crying. Mr Sloane called me round to the bedside one morning and beat me on the hands with a shoe. My mistress would not let me wear my shift on my shoulders and neck in the morning ... she used to beat me on the back with a shoe. She would not let me wear anything on my neck, or any part of my body above the waist; so that, from the waist upwards, I was obliged to go about the house exposed, in the presence of Mr Sloane ... (Sensation)

The girl's plight had come to light when she was admitted to a charity hospital covered with bruises and 'in a most frightful state of emaciation and debility'. There were 'marks of vermin' all over her body, and she weighed only 59½lb. She told the court:

There was no watercloset of any kind in the chambers belonging to Mr Sloane. There was only one chamber utensil for the use of Mrs Sloane, Miss Devaux and myself, which was kept in a pan under the kitchen table. I was only allowed to use it once a day. I sometimes used it at night, and when she found it out in the morning she told me she would make me eat the contents. (Great sensation) I was generally locked in my bedroom all night, so that I could not use the chamber utensil. When she told me she would make me eat the contents she used to try and do so. (Prolonged hissing) She had made me eat it more than once, and when I struggled to prevent her, and it dropped on the floor, she picked it up and put it in my mouth. (Sensation). When I have not been able to get to the chamber utensil at all during the day I have dirtied the floor, but I could not help it. My mistress on one occasion got a piece of turnip and cut a hole in it and filled it with some of the dirt, and forced it down my throat by means of a large iron tablespoon. (Great sensation) Mr Sloane was not present when she at first attempted it, but he was when she succeeded in pushing it down my throat. He stood behind me, so as to keep me close in front of my mistress while she put it into my mouth. (Sensation) He beat me on that occasion with a shoe because I refused to do as my mistress wanted, and he beat me again after it ...

After the hearing an angry mob was waiting when the Sloanes emerged from the court. They stoned them and chased them home. The Sloancs wcrc latcr found guilty and sentenced to two years' hard labour. 'It was generally believed that the depth and breadth of the news coverage of the trial had incited the public to retributory action, and, no doubt, had influenced the judge' (Thomas Boyle, *Black Swine in the Sewers of Hampstead*, 1990).

The East End was a place of mystery and menace to respectable Londoners before the Jack the Ripper murders of 1888. There were fears of dark forces, of immorality and disease and hopeless poverty, Chinese drug dens and ungovernable workers. Two years before, a vast mob of unemployed dockers and building workers who had been attending a rally in Trafalgar Square went on the rampage through Mayfair and St James's. The mob, perhaps 20,000 strong, struck terror into the very heart of fashionable London, plundering shops in Piccadilly and Oxford Street. The riot soon died down, but for two days there were rumours that the destitute were massing to sack the West End again.

Writers and social investigators were beginning to awaken the Victorian conscience about the problems of the East End. In 1870 Dickens had made a real opium den in Bluegate Fields, Shadwell, the focus of his unfinished *The Mystery of Edwin Drood*; Gustave Doré made an engraving of the same den two years later for *London: A Pilgrimage*. Walter Besant's East End novel *All Sorts and Conditions of Men* of 1882 was followed by those of Arthur Morrison and Israel Zangwill, among others. The year after the Ripper killings the first part of Charles Booth's seventeen-volume investigation of London poverty and vice, *Life and Labour of the People in London*, was published. Its title was *East London*. In this atmosphere of heightened awareness and anxiety, the Ripper murders were sensational. All the victims had their throats slashed and their bodies were mutilated in a way that suggested the killer had knowledge of surgery.

The killings began in August. Six wretchedly poor women, all but one of them prostitutes, were murdered within 500 yards of Whitechapel High Street, 'where the wealth of the City met the poverty and mystery of the East End'. The first to die, on 7 August, was Martha Turner, 35. She was stabbed again and again at George Yard Buildings off Whitechapel Road. The next victim was Mary Ann Nicholls, 42, who was found lying on the pavement of Buck's Row (now Durward Street). She had been staying in a room in Flower and Dean Street, long notorious for its prostitutes. She is said to have told the lodging-house keeper: 'Don't let my doss, I'll soon be back with the money. See what a fine new bonnet I've got,' although this remark has also been attributed to another of the Ripper's victims.

A week later Annie Chapman was killed half a mile away in Hanbury Street. She had been married to a veterinary surgeon but her drinking ruined the marriage. Her death, and the press attention the murders now received, started a panic. The murderer struck twice on the night of 30 September, first butchering Elizabeth Stride in the back yard of a working men's club in Berner Street. She had claimed she turned to drink and prostitution after her entire family died when the pleasure steamer *Princess Alice* sank in the Thames. Early next morning the horribly mutilated body of Catherine Eddowes, 43, was found in Mitre Square.

There was a break of five weeks before the last murder. On 9 November Mary Kelly, took the Ripper back to her squalid room in Miller's Court, off Dorset Street (now Duval Street). Kelly, a widow, lived there alone. The rent collector found parts of her body strewn about the room.

The killer sent taunting letters to the police. More than 600 plain-clothes officers were drafted in, without success. Public confidence in the police fell. The Police Commissioner, Sir Charles Warren, resigned, not before he had been chased across Tooting Common by the bloodhounds he was training to help him catch the Ripper.

Among the groups suspected – they included doctors, butchers and foreigners – were the Jews. There were minor disturbances and popular hostility against Jews might have turned into something much more serious had not a policeman had the sense to erase a chalked message, believed to have been left by the Ripper, implicating the 'Jewes' in the fifth killing.

It was pointed out that National Vigilance Association campaigns leading to the closure of brothels and the dispersal of prostitutes had forced destitute whores in the most dangerous parts of the city to trade sex in dark alleys and the most squalid doss houses.

Victorian Values

A puritan backlash against the dissolute manners and morals of the Georgians began in the 1830s when the last royal representative of that era, King William IV, was still on the throne. The rakish man of affairs, the cynical upper-class libertine did not vanish overnight. But as the moral climate changed hedonism became less self-confident. Men felt it prudent to pay at least lip service to the new standards being set by the middle classes. These standards were reinforced by the court, newspapers, poets, novelists, tractarians, and a host of religious and social reformers. One of the aims of this revolution in manners was to make the poor moral.

At first it made little headway. As Trevor Fisher writes in *Prostitution and the Victorians*:

> it was unable to mobilise enough political mass to outweigh the intransigence of the male political elite. Its supporters were too easily dismissed as ineffective do-gooders or politically marginal individuals. It attracted no major political figures, no major journalists, and no charismatic public campaigners, capable of winning mass support. The contrast with the movement after 1870, led by James Stansfeld and Josephine Butler and attracting the support of W T Stead and the *Pall Mall Gazette* at the critical moment, is very marked.

One of the problems was the taboo on discussion of prostitution. Although among politicians, medical experts, morals campaigners, feminists and scientists there was a lively debate on all aspects of the profession, particularly syphilis, this debate did not extend to polite society. Middle-class men operated the double standard: their homes were citadels of moral probity where the topic was simply unmentionable, yet some of the men were among the prostitutes' best customers.

Another problem was the *laissez-faire* ethos of the establishment. The sex industry was like any other, with free sellers and buyers, and however much society might be exercised by the sight of street-walkers flaunting themselves in the most fashionable promenades of the capital, few people in positions of power wanted to interfere with free-market economics. This was particularly evident in 1844 when the Bishop of Exeter's Brothels Suppression Bill was defeated by a government led by the Duke of Wellington.

The situation was further confused by the passing of the Contagious Diseases Acts of 1864, 1866 and 1869. Pressure for some form of control, which would amount to legalisation, of prostitution had been growing for some time. The government was concerned about the effects of venereal disease on the efficiency of the army and navy. The disasters of the Crimean War brought further calls for reform, the High Command using the prevalence of venereal disease as a convenient excuse. In May 1857 a government commission was set up to 'inquire into the sanitary condition of the British Army'. The following February the medical journal *The Lancet* commented on the effects of venereal diseases on the armed forces. It claimed 'unchecked prostitution' was 'inflicting increasing evils, the full extent of which has hitherto been unrecognised'. The journal went on to give some interesting statistics:

from 1830 to 1847 the number of soldiers annually diseased varied from 181 to 206 per 1,000 men, or in other words... about one-fifth of the whole effective force in this country are yearly in hospital with venereal disease for a period of twenty-two days.

If the course of the diseased '*femme publique*'... be borne in mind, it is scarcely necessary to point out how glaring an instance of wasteful inconsistency the above figure represents

...If, in the pursuit of her miserable avocation, she infect only three soldiers, they are forthwith submitted to skilful treatment at the national charge...Had proper hospital room been provided for the woman, her treatment and cure would have scarcely cost a tithe of the sum which is...lost to the State through her being at large. The result of the physical evil on the latter class of persons even more forcibly shows the necessity for state interference...(Fisher, *Prostitution and the Victorians*)

The *Saturday Review* also pressed the case for legalisation, but at first could not bring itself to speak openly of venereal disease. In June 1862 it wrote: 'It is impossible to follow this subject up. It will suggest itself to everyone thoughts which we dare not clothe in words.' By September of the following year the debate had moved on sufficiently for the paper to be explicit:

The mischief done to the State and the nation by diseases which arise from sexual vice is incalculable. It has been computed (chiefly from hospital statistics) that two hundred women are newly infected every day in London, who have no other means of obtaining food and shelter than by communicating the diseases thus contracted. But even more startling... are the results of a recent official investigation as to the extent of the evil in the army and navy. We gather from the returns of a committee appointed to report on this subject that these loathsome diseases are six times more prevalent among British than among French and Belgian soldiers – the numbers each year being 70 for France against 442 for England, in every 1,000 men...As is the health condition of the soldiers, so also is that of the marines and sailors. There is the same enormous extent of disease contracted, disabling the men from active service whilst under treatment. The egregious folly of permitting things to remain as they are is well exemplified by the condition of the crew of the great fighting iron-plated ship, the *Warrior*. This vessel was built at fabulous cost, and was filled with picked men. She was employed on the Home Station, and during a year the daily loss of service from the causes referred to averaged upwards of 22 men, not less than 220 cases being treated out of a force of 711 men. These figures need no comment.

These studies spurred on the passing of the Contagious Diseases Acts, which empowered the authorities to detain prostitutes near barracks and dockyards and examine them to see if they were infected. This first move to regulate prostitution, which might have been expected to encourage the morals campaigners, instead goaded them to a furious resistance to this infringement of women's civil liberties. Moralists and proto-feminists were incensed that prostitutes were being regulated and punished while their clients went free. Another objection was that the acts, by regulating prostitution, accepted that it was legal.

Under the 1869 act police morals squads were set up with powers to stop and detain women they deemed to be 'common prostitutes'. Such women could then be ordered by a magistrate to have an internal medical examination. If infected they would be detained until well. If they refused the inspection they could also be confined in a hospital for examination and treatment. After that they were subject to regular fortnightly examinations. In those towns where the act applied morals squads were told to keep a close watch on places where prostitutes were known to live and work – pubs, beershops, music halls, fairs, private lodgings and common lodging houses. The police powers were arbitrary in the extreme. Any woman they chose to label a prostitute was then registered as such. (The situation is the same today). One police briefing stated: 'In all military centres nearly every woman of the lower...classes who may happen to possess personal attractions is of a loose character.' A campaign of entrapment began, with disguised police pretending to be clients and also acting on anonymous tip-offs. Women were dragged through the streets to be examined, a humiliating and dangerous procedure, given the state of medical hygiene.

All accompanied by the usual double standards. 'It did seem hard', said one imprisoned woman, 'that the Magistrate of the bench . . . had paid me several shillings a day or two before, to go with him' (Judith R Walkowitz, *Prostitution and Victorian Society*).

THE DAYS' DOINGS.

An Illustrated Journal of Romantic Events, Reports, Sporting & Theatrical News at Home & Abroad.

VOL. II.—No. 48.]   PUBLISHED AT No. 300, STRAND, LONDON, W.C.—SATURDAY, JUNE 24, 1871.   [PRICE THREEPENCE.

AWKWARD CONTRE-TEMPS IN REGENT STREET DURING THE HEIGHT OF THE SEASON.
"That Girl seems to know you, George!"

Scenting trouble: the wife says to her husband of the pretty flower girl
who accosts them in Regent Street, 'That girl
seems to know you, George.'

The morals campaigners had an outstanding leader in Josephine Butler. 'Beautiful and histrionic . . . [Butler] was adored by men and women alike. A charismatic leader and a gifted speaker, she was able to capture the popular imagination and inspire personal loyalty that bordered on idolatry' (Walkowitz, ibid.). Butler was an ardent Christian who wanted to abolish prostitution, but she was also a feminist. 'The Women's Manifesto', published in the *Daily News* on 1 January 1870, stated:

> We . . . enter our solemn protest against these Acts . . . Because, as far as women are concerned, they remove every guarantee of personal security which the law has established and held sacred . . . Because it is unjust to punish the sex who are the victims of vice, and leave unpunished the sex who are the main cause, both of the vice and its dreaded consequence: and we consider the liability to arrest, forced medical treatment, and (where this is resisted) imprisonment with hard labour, to which these Acts subject women, are punishments of the most degrading kind . . . Because . . . the path of evil is made more easy to our sons, and the whole of the youth of England; inasmuch as a moral restraint is withdrawn the moment the state recognises, and provides convenience for, the practice of a vice which it thereby declares to be necessary and venial.

Butler wrote in her autobiography, *Personal Reminiscences of a Great Crusade*, that 'among the two thousand signatures which [the manifesto] obtained in a short time were those of Florence Nightingale, Harriet Martineau, Mary Carpenter, the sisters and other relatives of the late John Bright, all the leading ladies of the Society of Friends, and many well known in the literary and philanthropic world'.

Women from Butler's Ladies National Association went into the working-class areas of towns where the Contagious Diseases Acts were in operation and incited whores to rebel against forced registration and examination. Mrs Butler led from the front, as the following extract from a history of the movement for repeal by one of the campaigners, Benjamin Scott, makes clear:

Mrs Butler and Professor Stuart, with others, went down to Colchester to join the fray. Their campaign was commenced by the holding of earnest prayer meetings, whereat they gained strength and courage. Then they went into the streets. They distributed thousands of handbills containing Sir Henry Storks' views on prostitution, and a statement made by him to the House of Commons Committee that 'Not only prostitutes, but also SOLDIERS' WIVES OUGHT TO BE EXAMINED!'

The blood of the Liberal partisans was up. They attacked the hotel in which Mrs Butler and her friends were staying, and when Dr Baxter Langley began to hold a meeting they went mad and created a riot...Dr Langley tried to hold a meeting in the theatre, but he and Professor Stuart were...driven from the platform and chased to their hotel, which they reached, Langley covered with flour and dirt from head to foot, his clothes torn, his face bleeding, and Stuart wounded in the arm by a heavy blow...the followers of Storks may have justified this playfulness as one of the amenities of political warfare, but there was no sort of justification for the next thing they did. They posted on the wall an exact description of Mrs Butler's dress in order that she might be recognised and mobbed...Her friends never addressed her by name in the streets lest some listener should rally the ever-present mob to attack her...On one occasion, after repeated flights from different houses, a room was taken for her in a Tory hotel, under the name of Grey. There she had gone to bed, and was falling asleep when she heard a knock on the door of her room, followed by the shout of the proprietor, 'Madam, I am sorry to find you are Mrs Butler; please get up and dress at once and leave the house. The mob are round the house, breaking the windows. They threaten to set fire to it if you don't leave at once...' Then he harangued the mob while Mrs Butler was dressing, and, led by one of the servant girls, ran along a little back street as fast as she could go, until she found shelter...

Faced with this strange new power, a women's movement, the government eventually caved in. An MP told Butler: 'We know how to manage any other opposition in the House or in the country, but this is very awkward for us – this revolt of women. It is quite a new thing: what are we to do with such an opposition as this?' After years of agitation the repealers won in the House of Commons. On 20 April 1883 the acts were suspended. They were later repealed.

There were several reasons for middle-class fear and loathing of the whore. She was the carrier of a disease that destroyed middle-class homes. In fact some whores recognised that they had too much to lose to be careless about sexual diseases, and would examine clients before agreeing to sex. Nickie Roberts in her polemical book *Whores in History* presses this point, but there is no doubt that prostitution was responsible to some extent for the prevalence of venereal diseases.

The whore was a threat in another and, to us with our notions of Victorian respectablity, surprising way. In March 1868 the *Saturday Review* carried an article about the manners and morals of modern young women entitled 'The Girl of the Period'. It said the daughters of the middle classes were aping the habits and fashions of the *demi-monde*: they had become bold and flirtatious, in effect '"a loud and rampant modernisation" whom no man could respect' (Lynda Nead, 'The Girl of the Period'). The anonymous author of the article describes 'the appearance and style of this new type of woman: she dyed her hair and wore cosmetics; her clothes were vulgar and extravagant, with calf-length skirts and outrageous bonnets. In fact she she appeared to have abandoned modesty and purity entirely and to have become little better than a prostitute' (Nead, ibid.). As Nead says, 'the real fear behind the vitriol was that distinctions between the pure and the fallen, the virtuous and the vicious, were breaking down. Good girls and bad girls now looked like each other and were even behaving like each other.' The article excited a lively debate with by no means everyone on the side of the author of 'The Girl of the Period'. 'Many sprang to the defence of Victorian girlhood and denied the accusations made in the article. Others suggested that the author must be an ugly old woman, whose jealousy of pretty young girls had fuelled her venomous prose' (Nead, ibid.).

When the name of the author of the article was revealed it suggested the moral tensions in Victorian society. Eliza Lynn Linton (1822–98) was a journalist and author. She had left her Lake District home at the age of 23 to become a writer, married, left her husband and stepchildren and made a successful career. A girl of the period indeed.

Another cause for resentment against whores was the high wages prostitutes earned. They could get in a day what a working-class woman would earn in a week or even a month. The diarist 'Walter' has given us invaluable information about prices. A sovereign – 20s. – would 'get any woman and ten shillings as nice a one as was needed. For five or ten shillings he could get 'quite nice' girls, some of whom had their own rooms. sometimes he would take a girl to a room in an accommodation house, for which he would pay half a crown. There were times when, short of money, he would pay by giving the whore his silk handkerchief. As we have seen, Swindling Sal would earn about £4 a week, a very good wage for a working-class woman. If she was careful and saved, she would soon have enough to attract a husband, perhaps a tradesman who needed capital to finance his business. Sal's major expense would be clothes: prostitutes had to dress well – there were many complaints from moralists that they dressed far 'above their station' – and a 'handsome silk dress' would cost anything from £5 to £10. For £1 a week she could rent 'two good furnished rooms near Pall Mall'.

Of course, most prostitutes spent the money as fast as they got it. Bracebridge Hemyng was told by a whore: 'I get enough money to live on comfortably, but then I am extravagant, and spend a great deal of money on eating and drinking...I have the most expensive things sometimes, and when I can, I live in a sumptuous manner.' The German Prince Pückler Muskau wrote to his wife during a visit to the capital in 1826:

> The Ambassador of —— accompanied me to the theatre and told me...many not uninteresting details concerning this or that beauty as she swept by...'See that rather overblown beauty,' he went on. 'Ten years ago she was living on a scale of luxury which few of my colleagues could emulate. Far from laying by part of her riches from those days, she had a real

passion for throwing everything out of the window, and today she will be grateful if you help her with a shilling.' (Fisher, *Prostitution and the Victorians*)

The Victorian taboo on the discussion of sex continued into the twentieth century. G M Young's highly regarded *Early Victorian England, 1830–1865*, published in 1934, has no references to vice, prostitution, syphilis or brothels, even though the period covered by the two volumes was one in which vice was rampant and flagrant in the capital. Edward Smithies says in *Crime in Wartime*, that even in the thirties and forties that subject was by and large shunned, 'and academics felt obliged to apologise when they introduced it into works of scholarship'.

Hello Sailor

The seamen who with their girls made the neighbourhoods of the taverns of Shadwell and other riverside areas hideous to the local residents were mostly from the merchant fleet. The Royal Navy solved the problem of sexual deprivation by turning its ships into floating brothels. Because some men had been press-ganged and could be expected to abscond they were kept on board ship while vessels were in port in London. Men thus deprived of women's company for long periods could become mutinous, so women were allowed to stay overnight. Prince William Henry, captain of the *Andromeda* and later King William IV, recorded that an order he had given that strangers should be off the ship by a certain time 'is by no means meant to restrain the officers and men from having either black or white women on board through the night, so long as discipline is unhurt by the indulgence . . . ' (M Lewis, *A Social History of the Navy*, 1960). One captain who refused to allow women on board signalled to his admiral that he feared a mutiny. The latter signalled back, 'Send 200 women from the X to the Y.' (Lewis, ibid.). In *Prostitution and Society*, vol. 3, Henriques relates how another captain, Richard Keats, had forms printed to be filled in with lists of the whores on board, who they slept with and how they conducted themselves.

A pamphlet of the 1880s alludes to the practice of allowing prostitutes on board navy ships:

No leave to go on shore from the day the ship was in commission until paid off. No wages until paid off, but occasional

prize money. The ship filled with prostitutes at every port, by permission of the C. O. Not many years ago (it was since 1840) the Captain of a frigate at a West Indian port (Barbados) gave an order to the First Lieutenant that every man and boy was to have a black woman on board, and the order was carried out...
(Henry Baynham, *Before the Mast*, 1971)

When the *Lady Juliana* sailed for Australia in 1789 with 237 women convicts who had been sentenced to transportation, a variety of men took advantage of the situation. Members of the crew, including officers, took 'wives' among the women, and in ports the crew acted as pimps to help the women sell sex to the crews of other ships. Sian Rees, in *The Floating Brothel*, tells how in another transportation ship seamen broke through a bulkhead to be with the women. The surgeon general of that fleet wrote that 'neither shame ... nor the fear of punishment could deter [the women] from making their way through the bulkheads to the apartments assigned the seamen.'

Mayhew says in *London Labour and the London Poor* that dockside areas were 'infested with nests of brothels'; in Shadwell taverns that wished to attract sailors had to provide both women and music. One of the most notorious was Paddy's Goose in High Street, Shadwell, 'the owner of which is reputed to make money in more ways than one'. Here he makes an interesting observation: 'Brothel-keeping is a favourite mode of investing money in this neighbourhood. Some few years ago a man called James was prosecuted for having altogether thirty brothels; and although he was convicted, the nuisance was by no means in the slightest degree abated, as the informer, by name Brooks, has them all himself at the present time.' Paddy's Goose was known for its rough entertainment and horseplay. The writer Thomas Archer recalled being invited by a friendly young whore to smell her nosegay. He declined, but a young sailor was tempted, and was squirted with pepper when he put his nose to the flowers.

The landlord of Paddy's Goose had ingratiated himself with the authorities during the Crimean War. The government wanted to recruit sailors to man the fleet, and the landlord sailed among the ships in the river in a small steamer with a band playing, drumming up recruits. Mayhew says: 'All this rendered him popular with the Admiralty authorities, and made his house extensively known to the sailors, and those connected with them.'

Sailors' tarts were a distinct class in several ways. They earned less and dressed poorly. Men who had been without a woman for months did not want an expensively dressed whore or even a very pretty one. They wanted a buxom wench who was high-spirited and could be expected to share the rough comforts of the brothels and bars and dance halls along the Ratcliffe Highway. As their ships headed home the sailors would sing:

> And when we get to London docks,
> There we shall see the cunt in flocks!
> One to another they will say
> 'O welcome Jack with his three-years pay!
> For he is homeward bou-ou-ound,
> For he is homeward bound!'

Waiting for them in the streets of Wapping or Shadwell or along the Ratcliffe Highway were throngs of boisterous young women, dressed in bright low-cut dresses short enough to reveal pink or white stockinged calves – we know from the diarist 'Walter' what effect a glimpse of calf or even ankle could have on a man in those buttoned-up days. The girls were usually bare-headed according to Chesney in *The Victorian Underworld*, and wore ornamental hairnets, ribbons and sham flowers. Their boots were coloured morocco with shiny brass heels. They moved about in groups, calling to each other in their drink-coarsened voices.

The evening might begin in one of the dance halls attached to public houses. After a few drinks the men and women would whirl about the dance floor or sing along to the music provided by a small orchestra. One by one the couples would leave the dance floor for a room in a nearby brothel or lodging house. There would follow much post-coital boozing, and if the sailor liked the tart he would probably expect her to stay with him, perhaps even for his whole time ashore. Some sailors returned to the same women each time they came back to port.

Sailor's girl: Black Sarah, one of the Ratcliffe Highway tarts who waited for seamen to arrive home on leave.

London in the Sixties recalls a party of middle-class men going sightseeing around the Ratcliffe Highway:

One of the most popular pastimes of the long-ago Sixties was going the rounds of the dens of infamy in the East End, and the rookeries that then abutted upon the Gray's Inn Road. In this latter quarter, indeed, there was then one narrow tortuous passage that in broad daylight was literally impassable, and to escape with one's life or one's shirt was as much as the most sanguine could expect.

The Ratcliffe Highway, now St George's Street East, alongside the Docks, was a place where crime stalked unmolested, and to thread its deadly length was a foolhardy act that might quail the stoutest heart. Every square yard was occupied by motley groups: drunken sailors of every nationality in long sea-boots and deadly knives at every girdle; drunken women with

Burning desire: sailors sack and burn the Star tavern in the Strand after three of their colleagues were robbed there by prostitutes in league with the proprietor in 1748.

views' he said that if the government refused to prosecute 'I simply decline to go on with the case'. Pressure mounted on the government. There were massive demonstrations of support for Stead's campaign: on 30 July a petition signed by nearly 400,000 supporters was borne to Parliament accompanied by hundreds of Salvation Army officers.

On 10 July, in the last of his articles, Stead wrote of young women being despatched as 'white slaves' to Continental brothels just weeks earlier. In the wake of this latest sensation on 7 August the Criminal Law Amendment Act was finally carried in the Commons by 179 votes to 71. It raised the age of consent to sixteen and incidentally criminalised acts of indecency between men. It also outlawed brothels, throwing many more prostitutes on to the streets.

But what about the adolescent girls Stead said were being sent to the Continent as 'white slaves'? To what extent white slavery really existed is unclear. Nickie Roberts says in *Whores in History* that it was largely a Victorian fantasy, a misunderstanding of a two-way commerce in prostitutes who were mostly willing migrants – English girls to brothels in France and Belgium and Continentals to London. There was a widespread belief, however, fostered by the social purity campaigners and lurid novels and plays, that there was an organised and vicious international traffic in women. In these tales girls would be drugged and abducted, to wake up captive and terrified in a foreign brothel. Whatever the truth about white slavery, Josephine Butler wrote in the puritan paper *The Shield* on 1 May 1880:

In certain of the infamous houses in Brussels there are immured little children, English girls of from ten to fourteen years of age, who have been stolen, kidnapped, betrayed, carried off from English country villages by every artifice, and sold to these human shambles. The presence of these children is unknown to the ordinary visitors; it is secretly known only to the wealthy men who are able to pay large sums of money for the sacrifice of these innocents.

In 1880 Alfred Dyer, founder of the London Committee for the Exposure and Suppression of the Traffic in English Girls for the Purposes of Continental Prostitution, published a pamphlet claiming English girls were being abducted by the score, and forced to work in the licensed brothels of Brussels. A Parliamentary committee was set up and discovered some migration of young women between Britain and the Continent. The British embassy in Brussels, which had helped about two hundred women return home in the 1870s, knew about this. They also knew that 'the overwhelming majority of the young women who were recruited for the *maisons closes* of Brussels and Antwerp had already been prostitutes in Britain and had migrated voluntarily' (Roberts, *Whores in History*).

Nevertheless Josephine Butler turned to Stead for help in the fight against the 'white slavers'. Stead saw the possibility of creating an even greater sensation and serving the moral purposes dear to his heart. He proposed to buy a young girl from her parents and take her to Paris to demonstrate how the trade worked.

Stead first went to see the Archbishop of Canterbury, one of his supporters. The Archbishop warned him of the risks he was running. Josephine Butler was now allied to the Salvation Army, and with the aid of the Army's Bramwell Booth, Stead bought thirteen-year-old Eliza Armstrong from her drunken mother for £5.

On 3 June 1885 he took the child to a London brothel where her virginity was confirmed by a midwife. Next Stead took her to a low boarding house where he entered her bedroom in disguise, pretending to be a 'client', perhaps as an added touch of authenticity. The girl was terrified and Stead left the room. Finally he sent her to safety in Paris in the company of a Swiss Salvationist.

Stead had given the Establishment the excuse they needed. He had committed a criminal offence in taking Eliza out of the possession of her parents while she was under the age of sixteen, and the examination in the brothel was indecent assault. He was charged in October 1885, together with Bramwell Booth and others who had helped. Stead was sentenced to three months' imprisonment. The judge said that the 'Maiden Tribute' articles had deluged the country with filth. Their publication 'has been – and I don't hesitate to say ever will be – a disgrace to journalism.' In prison Stead was given privileged treatment. For years afterwards he celebrated the anniversary of his imprisonment by wearing his old prison uniform. The woman who had reluctantly helped him procure the child, Rebecca Jarrett, got six months and had a much more unpleasant time in jail. She was a reformed prostitute and alcoholic, and the aftermath of Stead's stunt almost drove her back to drink.

For some time Benjamin Scott, Chamberlain of the City of London and chairman of the London Committee for the Exposure and Suppression of the Traffic of English Girls for the Purposes of Continental Prostitution, had been trying to prosecute Stead's old enemy Mary Jeffries, who had been identified as a white slaver. There was a story that she had a 'white-slave house' by the river at Kew, and that drugged girls were sent abroad in closed coffins with air-holes in the lids. A charge which had real substance, that she kept brothels for the nobility, was regarded by the assistant commissioner at Scotland Yard as 'highly improper': he refused to prosecute. Instead on 16 April 1885 she was charged with keeping a disorderly house.

Mary Jeffries, once described as the wickedest woman of the century, had started her career as a prostitute at the exclusive establishment of Madame Berthe in the 1840s. 'Berthe's had been operating since the 1820s under different owners, and had built up an almost exclusively aristocratic clientele. But it had refused to move with the times – it merely provided straightforward commercial sex with no concessions to the growing appetite for "perversion"' (Henriques, *Prostitution and Society*, vol. 3). Mrs Jeffries, who wanted to cater for all forms of perversion, saw the possibilities and with finance provided by wealthy clients opened an establishment in Church Street in Chelsea which catered to the latest tastes in sexual matters. She got the formula right and soon she was running four houses in Church Street – nos. 125, 127, 129 and 155 – as well as her flagellation house in Hampstead, and other brothels.

When the case against her was heard in May 1885 Mrs Jeffries arrived at court in a carriage provided by a member of the House of Lords. She was fined £200 and ordered to find another £200 as surety. A titled Guards officer stood the latter sum for her, and before the day was over she was back in business.

When Stead stood trial Jeffries was seen handing out rotten fruit for crowds outside the courthouse to throw at him. As Thomas observes in *The Victorian Underworld*, she had her own troubles. Many of her clients in the Guards had been sent to Egypt to defend it against invasion by the army of the Mahdi. She was reported as saying: 'Business is very bad. I have been very slack since the Guards went to Egypt.'

Some light is thrown on the question of white slavery by the statement of a girl taken to Holland with a friend in 1876 by a man named Klyberg. The girl, whose name is given as Fanny, said that she was eighteen and living with her mother in Chelsea when she met her friend Jennie one evening with a woman who called herself Mrs Dunner. Bizarrely, Mrs Dunner asked if she could see Fanny's teeth. Then she asked her if she was 'all right', meaning did she have VD. Finally Mrs Dunner asked if she would like to go abroad, as an 'actress'. The association between the theatre and whoring was still strong, and Fanny must have known what Mrs Dunner was suggesting. After Fanny had fetched some clothes from home they all went to Klyberg's dwelling in Soho, where the girls had supper with Klyberg and his wife. During the meal Klyberg asked if they had been told what they were going abroad for. When Fanny replied that they were to be actresses, Klyberg replied: 'Quite right.' His wife questioned the girls about their families, and discovered that they both had older sisters. The girls stayed the night, and next morning were taken to Somerset House, where they obtained copies of their sisters' birth certificates. That afternoon Klyberg told them he was taking them to Holland.

Next morning in Rotterdam Klyberg again asked if they knew why they were there. When Fanny repeated that they were to be actresses, Klyberg told them that they were to be prostitutes. Fanny angrily said she was going back to England, but instead was persuaded to go with Jennie to a brothel in the Hague. They were interviewed by the proprietress, and next morning Jennie was examined by a doctor, after which she was driven to a police station where she was registered.

Fanny was told the brothel did not want her, and Klyberg, after making unsuccessful sexual advances to her, began a tour of brothels, trying increasingly desperately to sell Fanny. He started at

£12 and progressively dropped the price. In the end, in spite of all his expense, Klyberg had to pay her return fare to London. White slavery, if it existed at all, was clearly neither a flourishing nor a highly profitable business.

Triumphalist meetings of puritans followed the passing of the Criminal Law Amendment Bill. At one in Hyde Park soon after-wards the crowd was estimated at between 100,000 and a quarter of a million people. They hailed the decision to form a National Vigilance Association for the 'enforcement and improvement of the laws for the repression of criminal vice and public immorality'. The NVA was the most powerful and successful of the puritan organisations. It quickly showed its intolerance, in prosecuting brothels, dealers in indecent books and men for offences against women. Josephine Butler, who had become a member, was appalled and tried to stop the growing intolerance but even she with her record of fighting for women's rights was unable to halt the rush into repression. In the first twelve months the NVA was involved in 105 prosecutions. 'In the ten years before of the Criminal Law Amendment Bill legalised summary prosecutions of brothels, there was an annual average of 86 prosecutions of bawdy houses in England and Wales. Between 1885 and 1914 this average jumped to over 1,200'(Fisher, *Scandal*, 1995).

In cities throughout Britain lodging houses and brothels were closed. Manchester was said to have reduced the number of brothels in the city from four hundred to ten by the early 1890s. In London the casualties were greater: according to Roberts in *Whores in History*, seven hundred brothels closed in south London between 1894 and 1912, and five hundred went in central London in the same period. The great days of brothel-keeping were over, and prostitution, once so public, became furtive. When the whores expelled from the brothels took to the streets they were prosecuted.

Posses of purity vigilantes harassed the staff and clients of brothels. 'In 1887, brewery heir turned purity fanatic Frederick Charrington rampaged through the East End of London with his supporters, closing down brothels and assaulting sex-industry workers – in one incident, Charrington was sued for kicking a brothel attendant in the stomach' (Roberts, ibid.). One result of this harassment was to force the street prostitutes to be increasingly furtive. They would take their customers into dark and dangerous back alleys and back yards to escape the attention of the police. As we have seen the vigilance campaigns in the East End have been blamed for the ease with which Jack the Ripper could find and kill poor and degraded prostitutes. And the NVA enforced the old double standard: unrepentant prostitutes were harassed and prosecuted, their male customers went unscathed. This had been enshrined in a Royal Commission report of 1871 thus:

> We may at once dispose of any recommendation founded on the principle of putting both parties to the sin of fornication on the same footing by the obvious but not less conclusive reply that there is no comparison to be made between prostitutes and the men who consort with them. With the one sex the offence is committed as a matter of gain, with the other it is an irregular indulgence of a natural impulse.

There is no doubt that in areas where prostitution was a public nuisance there was support for the NVA. A chemist in Euston Square wrote to the local association of the

> great nuisance caused by the prostitutes infecting this district, and [I] shall feel obliged by your using your authority in removing the same. It is of very common occurrence, for my doorstep to be used by these women, for disgusting purposes, and the language used by them is simply disgraceful. (Bartley, *Prostitution*)

A resident of Endsleigh Gardens wrote to an association of the

> fearful prevalence ... of a gross state of street prostitution attended by features of a very disgusting character, particularly between the hours of 10 and 12 at which it is not fit for any

respectable female to walk about and young men cannot do so
without molestation. (Bartley, ibid.)

There were complaints from residents in Euston Road of women of
'loose character' frequenting the area night after night, and of a number
of brothels masquerading as hotels on Euston Road and King's Cross –
still a stronghold of prostitution today. In 1901 a petition with 8,500
signatures complained to the Home Secretary of the

> existing disgraceful condition on the streets of the parish and
> its vicinity resulting mainly in the opinion of your petitioners
> from the unsatisfactory state of the law as regards brothels and
> common prostitutes. The way in which the latter (dressed and
> conducting themselves in such a manner as to leave no doubt
> as to their vocation) infest the streets in the south part of the
> Parish is disgraceful. (Bartley, ibid.)

The effectiveness of the NVA depended on the willingness of the
police to act. The NVA put pressure on the London parish vestries,
and they in turn urged the police to keep watch on brothels and
collect evidence for prosecutions. 'At first, the London police were
willing to do this, observed alleged brothels and furnished reports
of them to the Vestries who in turn prosecuted or warned them'
(Bartley, ibid.). In 1887 the new Metropolitan Police
Commissioner, Sir Charles Warren, called off this surveillance,
saying it was not part of police duties. Warren believed that his
officers had more important crimes to deal with. He also
complained that the vestries warned rather than prosecuted brothel
owners. The vigilance societies were

> in the habit of routing out the brothels from the back slums and
> driving them into respectable places . . . and as long as there is
> a demand for prostitutes on the part of the public there is no
> doubt they will exist in spite of the Vestries and Vigilance
> Societies, and the more they are driven out of their . . . back
> slums, the worse it becomes for law and order and decency.
> (Bartley, ibid.)

Warren preferred a policy of containment, as the police had earlier in the century. The police were generally hampered by the difficulty of proving soliciting, since prostitution itself was not a crime. A series of mistakes and malicious prosecutions by officers led to a Royal Commission. In July 1887 a Miss Cass was arrested for soliciting. The magistrate discharged her but wrote down her occupation as prostitute and warned her about her future conduct. Miss Cass, who was a respectable dressmaker and a member of the 'eminently respectable' Girls' Friendly Society, vehemently protested her innocence. The press took up her case, there was a debate in the House of Commons 'leading up to an adjournment of the House', the home secretary resigned and there were enquiries into the conduct of the magistrate and the arresting constable, a PC Endacott. That officer had perjured himself by testifying that he had seen Miss Cass on the streets a number of times. He was charged with perjury but acquitted on the directions of the judge at his Old Bailey trial, and later reinstated as a constable. The chief commissioner issued instructions to his officers that women were not to be prosecuted without corroborating evidence. The number of prosecutions fell, from more than 6,000 in 1880 to fewer than 4,000 in 1890. The police feared that they did not have the backing of the courts, and were reluctant to arrest prostitutes. Some magistrates would not convict unless the person solicited was present in court. Police evidence to a Royal Commission in 1908 said:

> the main difficulty in enforcing the law is caused by the over-sensitiveness and impatience of the public whenever there seems ground, however slight, for alleging that there has been a mistake in arresting a woman on the charge of solicitation. The proceedings of the Metropolitan Police are widely reported in the newspapers, and if a magistrate refuses to convict . . . a wave of indignation passes throughout the community.

Sometimes, however, the harshness of the NVA was equalled by the police in their treatment of the poorer prostitutes. Police had long preyed on prostitutes and brothels, demanding protection money and sexual favours. 'They realised that where street walkers were concerned, respectable society was wholly indifferent to what they did'. (Fisher, *Prostitution and the Victorians*). In the autumn of 1895 the police went too far when they arrested two highly respected professional men in a manner that suggested people were no longer free to walk the streets.

The first man, Ray Lankester, a professor of anatomy at Oxford University, was arrested for obstruction in October. He had witnessed and protested about the brutal arrest of a prostitute. He went to talk to another prostitute nearby about the arrest and a policeman told him to move along. When he refused he was arrested and held in a cell for two hours. At his trial the magistrate was so partial to the police that Lankester's lawyer, Sir George Lewis, retired from the case, protesting: 'It seems to me, Sir, that you have absolutely made up your mind...instead of listening to any argument...you have interposed at every moment...' Lankester was found guilty of obstruction. He wrote in a letter to *The Times*:

> On my way from my club I stopped to ask some woman the explanation of an unusual scene of cruelty which I had witnessed. Before I had time to get an answer I was brusquely accosted by a policeman, and within three minutes...seized by both arms and taken to a police station...I ask whether it is tolerable that a man perfectly well known, talking to another person in the street...should be ordered to move on, and that on his remonstrating...he should be liable to be seized and treated as the vilest criminal?
>
> It is time that a departmental inquiry was held, in view of the allegations of violence and concerted perjury which have been repeatedly made against a portion of the police. These are not the only charges made, for it is a matter of common report that they level blackmail on the women of the street, and receive bribes from persons whom they have arrested.

Early in November George Alexander, proprietor of the St James's Theatre, was arrested for indecent behaviour. He had gone to a friend's house near his own, and on his way back was accosted by a half-starved prostitute. Seeing, as he said, that the woman was 'poor, miserable, starved and ill-clad', he gave her some money. A constable approached and accused him of 'having connection' with the prostitute. Among witnesses to his character at the court hearing was Arthur Wing Pinero, the playwright. Alexander was acquitted and two days later appeared on the stage of his theatre, where he was cheered by the audience.

The impact of the puritan moralists on prostitution was considerable. For a while whores were driven from the more fashionable streets, many brothels were closed and vice went largely underground. But in one sense the puritan campaign failed: prostitution was not eliminated entirely, as the puritans believed it could be. Indeed, the campaign seemed to prove that what the Victorians called The Great Social Evil could not be beaten by repression. Could it be beaten by openness? In her pamphlet *The Great Scourge and How to End It* of 1913 the suffragette leader Christabel Pankhurst (daughter of Emmeline Pankhurst) sought to break the taboo on discussing prostitution and venereal disease.

> Men writers for the most part refuse to tell what the Hidden Scourge is, and so it becomes the duty of women to do it. The Hidden Scourge is sexual disease, which takes two forms – syphilis and gonorrhoea. These diseases are due to prostitution – they are due, that is to say, to sexual immorality. But they are not confined to those who are immoral. Being contagious, they are communicated to the innocent, and especially to wives. The infection of innocent wives in marriage is justly declared by a man doctor to be 'the crowning infamy of our social life'.
>
> Generally speaking, wives who are thus infected are quite ignorant of what is the matter with them. The men who would think it indelicate to utter in their hearing the words syphilis and gonorrhoea, seem not to think it indelicate to infect them with the terrible diseases which bear these names...
>
> To discuss an evil, and then to run away from it without suggesting how it may be cured is not the way of the Suffragettes, and in the following pages will be found a proposed cure for the great evil in question. That cure, briefly stated, is Votes for Women and Chastity for Men...

The First World War, and with it official campaigns against VD that would bring the subject into the open, were not far off. But Pankhurst's pamphlet shows that as late as 1913 the taboo was still in force.

There was an echo of the Modern Babylon scandal in 1912, when W T Stead drowned on the *Titanic*. Moralists who had been pressing for a White Slave Act renewed their efforts as a tribute to his pioneer campaigns. The bill was eventually passed, but prostitution went on as before.

During the whole of the period we have been considering the connection between public houses and crime, particularly prostitution, was obvious. Thieves used taverns and public houses to plan their crimes and to divide the spoils. Prostitutes sought solace and customers. Drunkenness was rife, making it easier for the women to arouse an interest in their bodies. In 1833 nearly 30,000 people were charged with drunkenness in the London Metropolitan Police area. In 1948 there were only 32,871 prosecutions in the whole of England and Wales. The drunkenness of the Victorians has been described by Henriques as 'the finest hand maiden' of prostitution. 'The women I have placed in institutions tell me that their best time is when men are excited with drink; they come out of the houses at 11, 12 or one o'clock in the morning, and during those hours they have more command over the men than at other times...' (Henriques, *Prostitution and Society*, vol. 2).

One notorious public house was the Eagle tavern in the City Road, described in the *Report on Public Houses* as 'the most detrimental place...as far as women are concerned'. It had a large theatre and the entertainments attracted young women, some of whom were whores and others who were seduced into prostitution there while drinking. It had a garden 'with alcoves and boxes' which attracted young people in their cups: 'lads and young persons are taken in there, and plied with drink.'

No gentleman, well-dressed, can promenade there without being solicited by a female to go to houses of accommodation outside, whether he be aged, middle-aged or young. I had not sat down five minutes when I was solicited twice and told there were houses outside for me to go to...If you walk from the Angel in the City Road down to the corner of Tottenham Court Road, there is no place in London where there are so many disreputable women as will be found in that one walk...

During the nineteenth century some morals campaigners fought a determined but losing battle to close down the worst establishments. They were up against powerful vested interests, particularly the brewers, who were making a fortune from the most disreputable of the public houses.

The parish of Shadwell in Stepney was the scene of a lengthy struggle between the parish trustees and corrupt officials, particularly a crooked brothel-keeper and powerful local government magnate named Joseph Merceron. In 1819 the *First Report from the Committee on the State of the Police of The Metropolis* told how the area had become plagued by prostitutes who used 'the superabundance of public houses' in the area. The report stated:

some of them for a long time past have been the constant resort of the most abandoned and profligate women; and being in a situation affording a peculiar convenience for their evil practices, and purposely fitted for their accommodation, they have occasioned the increase of the worst kind of houses of ill-fame, the inhabitants whereof bid defiance to all decency and restraint. The prostitutes and procuresses filled the streets both night and day; and the parishioners have been thereby deprived of their trade; for those public-houses, being situated in the High Street, it was impossible for respectable persons to approach the shops without having their eyes and ears offended by scenes and language the most awful and disgusting...the parish appeared as if it were doomed to be the receptacle of all the profligates of the neighbourhood.

The exasperated residents complained to the parish trustees and the magistrates. They claimed their servants and sons were constantly exposed to seduction, 'and too often became a prey to the wretched beings with whom they were continually surrounded'.

Constables and the watch were bribed to look the other way. The
parish trustees set up their own patrols and found a deplorable state
of affairs. Dance halls attached to the public houses were being used
by prostitutes to pick up clients who were taken to nearby brothels,
in some cases also owned by the pub landlords.

The trustees applied to the licensing magistrates to have the
licences of the pubs suspended. Their petition was accepted with
great reluctance, but the licences were suspended pending an appeal
by the publicans. The Committee on the State of the Police reveals
the network of corruption which the parish trustees were up against:
'The most notorious of these houses was the Duke of York, kept by
— Hennekey, but supplied with porter by Messrs Meux and Co.
who had lent a large sum of money upon the house, and which was
producing an immense return, the draught of beer and spirits being
enormous'. In the interval before the hearing Meux and Co. did
everything they could to get the petition thrown out. In the forefront
of this campaign was Joseph Merceron, himself one of the licensing
magistrates. The result, says the report on the police, was that the
local publicans, particularly Hennekey of the Duke of York, 'not
only continued their indecent practices, but with the greatest
impudence...defied and threatened the parish officers, insulting
them in the public streets and daring them to do their worst'.

Despite the powerful advocacy of Merceron and his friends the
licences of the three public houses were withdrawn for the coming
year. Eventually the brewers produced another publican, a man of
apparent good character named Birks, who promised to clean up the
place, and he was granted a licence for the King's Arms. 'Within a
month the King's Arms was engaged in the lucrative trade of
prostitution and liquor on an even bigger scale than the Duke of
York, Meux and Co. having paid for extensive alterations to be
carried out to the house.'

So the struggle went on. At one time the parish consulted the
attorney-general to see whether they could bring a criminal action
against the magistrates. He ruled that there was nothing to suggest
that they had acted corruptly, although they might have acted
against the public interest. Yet there undoubtedly was corruption in
the granting of licences.

sausage rolls. Merrick's prison survey showed that 14,000 out of the 16,000 prostitutes he interviewed were attracted by the promise of 'nothing to do; plenty of money; your own mistress; perfect liberty; being a lady'. These young women leap out of their context into our own times in a quotation from a brothel-keeper to the 'Maiden Tribute' journalist W T Stead: 'at fourteen and fifteen they begin to want clothes and things which money can bring, and they do not understand the value of what they are parting with in order to get it.'

In the chapter 'Mean Streets' we have seen what life was like for the eighteenth-century streetwalker. What was life like on the streets in the second half of the nineteenth century? Obviously it differed according to the area, the kind of client, the economic climate, the time of year, the attitude of the police, the age and attractiveness of the prostitute. When times were good and the girl could take her clients to a room in an accommodation house it was probably as good a life as a working-class girl could expect. But there were dangers and, particularly, hardships. The 'roving correspondent' James Greenwood was allowed to examine the street clothing worn by prostitutes interned in the Westminster House of Correction. 'Nothing is more common than for these poor creatures to be found wearing a gaudy hat and feather and a fashionably made skirt and jacket of some cheap and flashy material and nothing besides in the way of under-garments but a few tattered rags that a professional beggar would despise.'

Greenwood wrote in *In Strange Company: The Notebook of a Roving Correspondent* that on bitter winter nights the women had to walk the streets 'with their wretchedly thin shoes soaking in the mud and their ill-clad limbs aching with cold'. Although there was clearly some element of competition for customers, and new girls would be warned off the 'beats' of regulars, with or without violence, prostitutes tended to give each other friendship and sympathetic companionship, and this may have been another of the attractions of the life. Prostitutes would lend each other money or items of clothes, raise collections for funerals or to help pay doctors' fees. Mary Higgs, one of the many intrepid souls who ventured into the lower depths in an attempt to reform the young women she found there, described the scene in a prostitutes' lodging house where the girls had gathered in the kitchen. They are clearly enjoying each other's company:

> Round the fire was a group of girls far gone in dissipation, good-looking girls most of them, but shameless; smoking cigarettes, boasting of drinks or drinkers, using foul language, singing music-hall songs or talking vileness. The room grew full . . . a girl called 'Dot' danced the 'cake-walk' in the middle of the room.

Researchers were able to dispel one of the many myths about prostitutes – that they lived short and squalid lives and died of disease or violence. According to Acton in *Prostitution Considered*, the road to ruin was in fact healthier than the life their decent working-class sisters were living. Acton was able to compare the health of prostitutes and respectable women. In a telling passage he comments:

> If we compare the prostitute at thirty-five with her sister, who perhaps is the married mother of a family, or has been the toiling slave for years in the over-heated laboratories of fashion, we shall seldom find that the constitutional ravages often thought to be a necessary consequence of prostitution exceed those attributable to the cares of a family and the heart-wearing struggles of virtuous labour.

Acton adds that he had every reason to believe 'that by far the larger number of women who have resorted to prostitution for a livelihood return sooner or later to a more or less regular course of life'. Most were on the look-out for a suitable husband and a surprising number succeeded in finding one. Occasionally, as we have seen, they were men of high social standing.

Vice and War

During the early years of the twentieth century some redrawing of the map of prostitution took place. While Piccadilly and the Haymarket remained the focus of the trade, the Strand and Fleet Street, for centuries among the most important thoroughfares for whores, lost their popularity as the centre of the entertainment industry moved west. Charing Cross station remained important: stations, with their hotels and boarding houses and well-off commuters, drew whores to what had otherwise become respectable areas. Victoria station was one of the few important pockets of prostitution remaining south of the river.

The First World War saw a huge increase in the demand for prostitutes. Men on leave from the trenches or mobilising in London did not find sexual continence appealing. At the same time, commentators noticed that prostitutes had become more flagrant. Sir Max Pemberton, a writer of adventure stories, pointed out the dangers in 'The Grave Sex Plague', a series of articles in the *Weekly Despatch*:

> A young officer who came from Scotland to a hotel near Regent Street . . . From its door to the Piccadilly Tube, a walk of a few hundred yards, he was accosted sixteen times – sometimes by those who appeared to be mere children. To a relative who met him later he said: 'No healthy lad could withstand this kind of temptation.' It is a true saying. They cannot, and we should not expect it of them. It is our part to remove that temptation from their path . . . There is no city so

absolutely vicious as London has been since the outbreak of
the war... We do not wait for dark in the West End to open this
dance of death. From the early hours of the afternoon the
soldiers' steps are dogged by women. In the tea-shops, in the
hotels, in kinemas, in music-halls they wait for them. He must
jostle them upon the pavement and have them at his elbow
whenever he stands to greet a friend. And 70 per cent of them
are diseased, as one great authority computes...

The war also saw the introduction of an officially sanctioned
'morals police' composed of women, some of them former
Suffragettes. Two different organisations, the Women Police
Volunteers and the Women's Patrols, roamed parks and cinemas,
warning copulating or groping couples and witnessing police arrests
of homosexuals caught in the act. The women doubtless enjoyed
this unique and brief freedom to be voyeurs, but some officials were
horrified. After hearing a case where a prostitute told a policeman to
'fuck off', a Marlborough Street magistrate told five of the
patrolwomen that it was disgraceful that they had listened to such
filth. Patrolwomen who saw two men indulging in fellatio in Hyde
Park were said to be 'not only willing but anxious' to give evidence
before the trial; on the other hand, two patrolwomen who saw a
corporal copulating with a woman clerk from Harrods in the same
park refused to appear in court.

The patrols also enforced curfews for girls, and had powers to search
women's houses for enlisted men and put a stop to private drinks
parties. They were active in the vicinity of army camps where they
sought to restrain young girls suffering from 'khaki fever', much as
dollymops had suffered from 'scarlet fever'. They tried 'to safeguard
our girls from the result of unnatural excitement produced by the
abnormal conditions now prevailing'. Max Pemberton, who had earlier
warned of the dangers to soldiers from diseased prostitutes, decided in
1917 that the snooping was making it impossible for soldiers on leave
to have any fun – 'the prude on the prowl has ruined London.' Dance
halls had been closed and even to kiss a girl in Hyde Park had become
a crime, he said. But more sinister pleasures were still available, he
suggested, quoting an officer:

At night we used to dine at the Savoy and afterwards have a jolly little dance in the rooms off the Palm Court. You can't do that now – it's become wicked. But I tell you what you can do. You can settle up about midnight and go to a house in a by-street not three hundred yards from the Criterion Theatre – and if you've got the entree, you can open the door up on the first floor, find yourself among a dozen couples who haven't troubled the tailor or the costumier; you can dance and drink with them until the cows come home, and see an orgy which would make Cleopatra blush. And that's the only kind of amusement you seem able to provide for us.

Instead of giving soldiers going to France in 1914 condoms the army gave them a leaflet signed by the Secretary of War Lord Kitchener, a bachelor:

Your duty cannot be done unless your health is sound. So keep constantly on your guard against any excesses. In this new experience you may find temptations both in wine and women. You must entirely resist both temptations, and while treating all women with perfect courtesy, you should avoid any intimacy. Do your duty bravely. Fear God, honour the King.

There was a fear that by giving the men condoms or the effective treatment of calomel ointment and permanganate of potash the army would be seen to be condoning vice. General Childs of the War Office said there would be questions in the House of Commons 'which it would be impossible to answer'. After a royal commission on VD reported in 1916 the army finally approved some form of treatment, but it was not clear what. To make the matter more confusing, the Army Council said it rejected any kind of preventive that might 'afford opportunities for unrestrained vice'.

The result of the confusion was that men went on getting VD, sometimes more than once. Some may even have courted it, as a dose of VD meant a month out of the front line. There were more than 100,000 cases among troops in the UK during the first three years of the war, and a quarter of a million among British forces in France.

Colonial troops had higher rates of infection than the British army, even though they were given condoms. According to Paul Ferris in *Sex and the British*, the attitude of the British authorities toward brothels and street prostitutes infuriated colonial governments. The Prime Minister of New Zealand, W F Massey, saw hordes of prostitutes working in the Strand. He recalled that the parents of soldiers had written to him asking that their sons be forbidden to visit Paris, not realising that London was worse.

The war ended on Monday 11 November 1918, and that night people – many of them total strangers – reeled through the streets shouting, singing, kissing and copulating in doorways, alleys, parks, taxis. Sexual relations had been changed in profound ways. Mass education of the troops, however tentative, on the dangers of venereal disease did much to break the old taboo on the subject. And the employment of women in factories and on other forms of war work led to the sexual liberation whose results are still with us. Once men could have sex outside marriage with women of their own class there was less need for prostitutes, at least by young men who were attractive to women.

The sexual revolution that followed the war, largely a metropolitan phenomenon, brought predictable howls of outrage and protest. Short skirts, the new dance crazes, flappers, night clubs, cocktails, divorce, jazz; all were signs of a moral universe in turmoil. Those who liked to be scandalised read the *News of the World* on Sundays. There they could read about the night-club owner Kate Meyrick, 'Queen of the Night Clubs' in twenties London. Kate, famous as the first woman in Ireland to ride a bicycle, was abandoned by her doctor husband, leaving her at the end of the First World War with eight children to support, including two sons at Harrow and four daughters at Roedean. Some married into the aristocracy. While in Ireland Kate, who was well-born, had mixed in upper-class society. She tells in her autobiography *Secrets of the 43* how she met the Duke and Duchess of York, later to be sovereigns of Britain.

Her first venture into clubs was as co-manager of Dalton's in Leicester Square, a frequent target for the police because of its reputation as a pick-up point for prostitutes. At the time she had never even been in a night club, and didn't realise that some of the well-dressed customers were gangsters, usually from the Darby Sabini gang which dominated the underworld until the Second World War. They drank freely and refused to pay. One night after a quarrel with a customer who called the gangsters 'Cads', one of them pulled a revolver and shot the place up. Finally Kate refused to let them in, and one of them knocked her out. The following day another gangster came to apologise, explaining that the culprit was an outsider who had been given a beating he would never forget. The Sabinis were experts in unsubtle violence, and the beating would certainly have been memorable.

Although already in her forties, Kate went on to open dozens of clubs, frequented by bohemians such as the artists Augustus John and Jacob Epstein and the writers Joseph Conrad and J B Priestley, as well as gangsters, aristocrats and whores. Eventually fines gave way to spells of imprisonment, and Kate, her health broken, decided to retire. Just before she died at the age of 56 she wrote her memoirs, which end with the words: 'What does the future hold in store? It may hold disappointment, perhaps. But one thing I know it can never, never take away from me, and that is the love of Life, real Life, brilliant and pulsating.' When she died a year later dance bands in the West End fell silent for two minutes as a tribute.

Another story that intrigued readers of popular papers was that of the brothel-keeper Queenie Gerald. Her modest establishment in the Haymarket was raided by police in June 1913. Queenie was in the bathroom with two girls, aged seventeen and eighteen, who were said to be 'almost nude'. Queenie, an attractive 26-year-old, said to the officer in charge: 'This is a surprise.' She claimed she was giving the girls a bath. Police found some letters from men, a revolver, a whip, a cane, some photographs and rather a lot of money – more than two hundred pounds. Queenie pleaded guilty to living on immoral earnings and was sent to prison for three months. That should have been the end of it, but there were rumours that things were not quite right, that virgins were being procured for wealthy men. Keir Hardie, the Labour MP, harassed the home secretary, the Pankhursts weighed in, and eventually the affair was aired in the Commons. There was no real evidence of virgins or white slavery, but it all made good copy for the newspapers. Queenie was still in business in the 1920s.

In the 1930s women could make a good living working on the streets. Inspector Fred 'Nutty' Sharpe, who in the mid-thirties was head of the Flying Squad, estimated that in a four-hour day or night they could earn between £15 and £20: at the time, a girl working in a shop would earn about £2 a week. A woman police officer remarked on the friendliness of the prostitutes to their rivals on the streets. 'They are a friendly lot, ready to help one another, exchanging clothes with each other and even loaning small sums to a rival down on her luck and out of business for the time being.'

French prostitute Marthe Watts, who became part of the Messina vice empire, came to England in 1937 and at first found the climate and the long hours spent streetwalking difficult. But after she got a regular 'beat' on Bond Street she made a good living. Some of the Englishman's sexual preferences surprised her: she wrote that she was 'astonished' at the number of men who wanted her to tie them up and beat them.

The structure of prostitution had not changed greatly since Victorian times. Edward Smithies in *Crime in Wartime* says that the women were divided into three main groups:

> Those who did not solicit on the streets, but relied upon introductions and arrangements by telephone to obtain clients; those who did solicit outside but took their clients either to their own flats or to houses of assignation; and those who solicited and had sexual intercourse outside. As they grew older, prostitutes tended to move from the first group to the second, though the situation was always changing.

At the upper levels of the profession the girls lived in style, with flats in Mayfair or another fashionable district, maids and motor cars. The flats would be luxuriously furnished and the clients would expect and be prepared to pay a high price for their pleasure.

There were also expensive private hotels which were really brothels. London had a number of these in the late 1930s. One in the Marylebone Road had rooms at the front which were 'luxuriously furnished' while those at the back were cheaper. Apart from catering for prostitutes and their clients the hotel had another peculiarity: genuine travellers who turned up with luggage were turned away.

Further down the scale there were blocks of flatlets let wholly to prostitutes. Several streets in the fashionable West End contained a number of these dwellings, one of them Upper Berkeley Street. Some prostitutes preferred self-contained flats which they could share with a friend, partly to save on the rent and partly as a form of protection against dangerous clients. This unfortunately left them open to the accusation that they were keeping a brothel. A magistrate warned one prostitute who shared a flat in Baker Street in order to halve the 'very substantial' rent of £3. 15s. a week that she ran this risk. It was an example of the friendly decency with which London magistrates treated the girls who were brought before them. Foreigners were surprised: when the American broadcaster Alexander Woollcott was asked after a visit to Bow Street what had impressed him most he replied: 'The old-world courtesy with which your magistrates treat your whores' (Smithies, ibid.).

Other accommodation was provided for prostitutes by shop-keepers, caretakers and private householders. A dress designer who rented an expensive apartment near Grosvenor Square allowed it to be used for prostitution. Men would phone her and ask her to find them a girl. She would call one of the 52 women whose numbers she kept in a book, and the man and the woman would meet at the flat. In some ways this system resembles present-day escort agencies, particularly in its reliance on the telephone, although the woman could probably have been prosecuted for running a brothel.

Some prostitutes preferred to solicit and have sex in the open air. It saved renting an expensive flat, and it meant they could refuse some of the clients' demands – such as insisting that they took their clothes off. Hyde Park was, naturally, a particular favourite for the women who worked around Marble Arch and the Bayswater Road.

Prostitutes could also find clients in night clubs. Henriques says that just before the Second World War there were in the streets 'near the Odhams Press building [off Covent Garden] several clubs, such as the Caravan, which combined indecency with prostitution'.

The Second World War brought what prostitutes later recalled as the 'years of plenty'. The rise in wages meant that more men could afford their services, and as demand began to outstrip supply prices rose. Prostitutes would also allow their clients less time – the beginning of the notorious 'short time'. This was usually ten or fifteen minutes, after which the whore's maid would knock on the door as a signal that it was time to go.

War changed the economics of the industry in other ways. Before the Blitz, the exodus from the city and particularly from the West End meant that prostitutes could rent apartments in 'respectable' blocks that were previously closed to them. After 1941 rents rose, and the prices the women charged rose with them. The arrival of the American Army in southern England affected rates: US army sergeants were paid four times as much as their British equivalents, and by 1945 US soldiers were being charged £5 for 'short time', which was more than British servicemen could afford.

These rates drew more and more women on to the streets, although it is impossible now to know just how many. It has been very conservatively estimated that there were 3,000 prostitutes in London in 1931, and 6,700 by 1946. Both these figures seem much too low. With war and the blackout arrived vast numbers of British and foreign troops, and women flooded into the West End to service them. Some were married women whose husbands were away from home in the forces, some young women who saw a chance to make easy money but had no intention of making a career of prostitution. Among these were a number of fourteen- and fifteen-year-olds. Doorways, parks and any dark open space were used. 'In the blackout, the whole of London served as Hyde Park, with couples copulating undisturbed in the darkness.'

By the end of the war there were so many harlots jostling each other for the best 'beats' that they were running out of space. This led to friction between established prostitutes, who believed they had rights to patrol certain streets or even just part of a street, and newcomers. The newcomers had either to colonise new areas, which might not be so lucrative, or buy out a prostitute who wanted to retire. 'In the mid 1940s the buyer paid the seller a percentage of her earnings for an agreed number of months, while the seller undertook to ensure that there was no trouble from girls with neighbouring or overlapping beats' (Smithies, *Crime in Wartime*).

Two men working for the Public Morality Council reported that in Soho at midnight they were approached by 35 women in just over a hundred yards. Four hours later seven of the women were still working. In another survey they found prostitutes who were French, Italian and German, as well as 'a large number of English and a goodly number of Welsh and North Country women'. Observers noted the fearless behaviour of the women. While others rushed to air-raid shelters when an alarm sounded, the prostitutes continued to patrol their beats apparently unconcerned.

The behaviour of the amateur harlots who flocked to London to exploit the young American servicemen in particular caused offence. Vivienne Hall, a secretary, wrote that the only girls who showed friendliness to the Americans were 'our most crude specimens of womanhood . . . doing anything they want them to do and fleecing them in payment – it's disgusting to see our young girls cheapening themselves and screaming about the West End; it's they and not the Americans who are bad' (Philip Ziegler, *London At War*.) A woman named Hilda Neal commented on the youth of the girls: 'Awful little flappers seize on them like limpets; many look about fifteen or younger . . . Judging from the couples I saw on the train on Saturday, the men looked quite a decent class, but the girls were of the factory type and loud at that' (Ziegler, ibid.).

When the *Evening Standard* began a campaign to clean up the streets the attitude of officialdom was that immorality was not a crime. In any case it would have been well-nigh impossible to police the vast shifting population of men and girls.

Just as the moral panic of the First World War had led to the setting up of a 'morals police', the Second World War produced Regulation 33B of the Defence of the Realm Act. This gave medical officers powers to request the examination of any woman suspected of being a source of venereal infection, although there were few instances of this now forgotten regulation being applied. The first case was brought before magistrates at York on 5 March 1943. It involved a young married woman in the East Riding of Yorkshire who was suspected of having infected two people. Requested to attend for examination, she twice promised she would and failed to do so. She was subsequently arrested on a warrant, pleaded guilty and was sentenced to two months' imprisonment. Under the regulation, as under the old Contagious Diseases Acts of the nineteenth century, quite innocent women might be arrested by mistake and suffer enormous indignity and public shame.

Conscription was a problem for prostitutes. In 1941 conscription was introduced for unmarried women aged twenty to thirty. There were exceptions, but most prostitutes fell into the categories likely to be called up. They avoided it by writing 'prostitute' in the occupation section of the call-up paper: 'The authorities did not want them mixing (and recruiting?) in the ranks' (Smithies, *Crime in Wartime*).

The condom had come of age. The London Rubber Company, which was making nearly four million a year in 1939, was then given a virtual government monopoly for the duration of the war and production rose to 120 million. The trade name Durex became the generic term for condoms.

British troops were provided with them, but VD was still common. Films were made and advertisements warning of the dangers placed in newspapers. The impact of the latter was spoilt, however, when press magnates persuaded the Ministry of Health that they were too hard-hitting. The words 'on or near the sex organs' were subsequently excised from a paragraph explaining where a syphilitic ulcer would first appear. The arrival of the American servicemen brought a wave of VD cases, and an intensification of the health campaign.

By 1944 there were fears that the fortunes being made by brothel-keepers would lead to corruption of the police, and magistrates began to crack down. Then attention turned to women soliciting on the streets, and arrests rose from 1,983 in 1945 to 4,289 in 1946 and 5,363 in 1948. This was partly due to the ending of the blackout: with the lights back on, it was obvious that there were far more women on the streets. But the war had caused a rise in demand for prostitutes' services, and with the departure of the Americans, prices fell and more men could afford to pay for sex. The eventual solution was the 1959 Street Offences Act, which forced the women to find less public ways of selling sex.

Vice Empires

Around the time of the First World War we see the first signs of violent organised criminals attempting to control prostitution. Victorian London had chains of brothels, but the sex industry consisted mostly of small-scale enterprises, pimps controlling a few women. Arthur Harding, a notable East End criminal who left an invaluable account of organised crime in the early years of the twentieth century (Raphael Samuel, *East End Underworld*, 1981) gives intriguing glimpses of criminals attempting to control sections of the East End vice trade, for instance the Jewish prostitutes. One of these criminals was a Jew named Isaac Bogard, known as Darky the Coon because of his dark complexion. He was involved in a feud with Harding, which led to beatings, shootings, and eventually to an ambush on an East End courthouse in which Harding's men set out to assassinate Bogard and another man while they were in police custody. Recalling the prostitution of those days, Harding explained:

> The brides [prostitutes] were mostly down the other end of Brick Lane where the lodging houses were in Flowery Dean Street [the notorious Flower and Dean Street]. The Seven Stars next to Christ Church School was mostly used by the ladies of the town, and the Frying Pan on the corner of Thrawl Street and Brick Lane was famous for being the center of the red light district.

There were many Jewish prostitutes in the East End, and a fifth of convictions for keeping brothels involved Jews. But it was not

329

really until the 1920s that the business threw up some major criminals.

Crime in London at that time and until the Second World War was dominated by a combination of Italians and Jews led by Darby Sabini, an Anglo-Italian who grew up in the Little Italy area around Saffron Hill. He despised but tolerated organised vice, and enforced among his own men a traditional Italian code of respect for women. On one occasion he was asked for help by the Italian father of a young woman, Anna Monti, who had been lured into prostitution by a vice king named Juan Antonio Castanar. Anna lived in Little Italy and her parents, like many other Italians in the area, regarded Sabini as someone who could redress wrongs that were beyond the law. Castanar, a Spaniard who drove a Rolls-Royce, was a famous tango dancer and had a dancing school in Archer Street, Soho. He used this to lure pretty young women into so-called white slavery abroad. He and a rival, a Frenchman of Italian descent named Casimir Micheletti, dominated the vice scene in the West End.

Sabini paid Castanar a visit and Anna, who had been sent to the Middle East, was restored to her family. But Sabini was not finished with Castanar. Within weeks his dance studio had been destroyed by fire, and shortly afterwards his headquarters were firebombed. The Sabinis were not suspected: instead rumours deliberately spread on the underworld grapevine put the Castanar and Micheletti gangs at each other's throats. There were stabbings and shootings, and questions in the House of Commons. Finally the two gang leaders were arrested and deported. Castanar tracked Micheletti to Montmartre and shot him dead. He was sent to Devil's Island.

The next overlord of vice in London was another foreigner, a Latvian known as Max Kessel or Red Max but whose real name may have been Emil Allard. In 1936 he was shot dead by a French-man, Marcel Vernon, and his body dumped in a ditch at St Albans. Vernon had escaped from Devil's Island, and after being found guilty and deported to France he was returned there.

His trial led to new speculation about the white slave trade. Vernon ran an extensive prostitution racket abroad with bases in South America, the US and Canada, in addition to his Soho establishments. His trial was told of young women being lured abroad with promises of jobs only to be tricked or forced into prostitution. The worst fears of the Victorian purity campaigners seemed to be confirmed. But a bestseller published in 1934, Henri Champly's *The Road to Shanghai*, gave an altogether different impression. Champly believed that most of the women went willingly and knew exactly what awaited them. They went in search of adventure and fortune, leaving a depressed labour market at home for at least the chance of steady earnings and perhaps marriage to a wealthy client. Once again the white slave trade seemed to be a chimera.

Without the toleration of the gangster Darby Sabini – and most of his rivals – the Messina brothers could not have dominated West End vice as they did from the 1930s on. The brothers were vicious and efficient, ruling by terror and amassing considerable wealth. Under their guidance prostitution became big business for the first time since the eighteenth century, but without the sense of style and fun.

There were five Messina brothers – Carmelo, Alfredo, Salvatore, Attilio and Eugenio. Their father Giuseppe, a Sicilian, had first been involved in keeping brothels in Malta, where Salvatore and Alfredo were born. After the family moved to Egypt, Giuseppe ran a chain of brothels in several cities until his success alerted the authorities and the family were expelled in 1932. They looked around for other markets for their talents and in 1934 Eugenio arrived in London, followed later by his brothers. The campaigning journalist Duncan Webb, who launched a crusade against the Messinas in the pages of the *People* newspaper, wrote:

> By bribery and corruption they organized marriages of convenience both in Britain and abroad to enable their harlots to assume British nationality. They ruled their women by persuasion, threat or blackmail and the use of the knife and the razor. They ruled the streets of the West End by similar methods. Indeed, so terror-stricken did the underworld become at the mention of the word 'Messina' that in the end they found little difficulty in building up their vast empire of vice.

It was said to be the Messinas who introduced short-time (see p. 326), or the 'ten-minute rule'. The Messinas' girls were regimented: they had to start work at four o'clock in the afternoon and carry on until six the following morning. By 1945 the girls were bringing in thousands of pounds a week for the Messina family.

Such wealth attracted the attention of rival pimps and also of the journalist Duncan Webb. He was already on the trail of the Messinas when a gang led by the Maltese Carmelo Vassallo started demanding protection money from the girls. Their demands were modest enough: £1 per girl per day. The girls were earning £100 a night each for the Messinas, who paid them £50 a week.

In a reprisal attack Eugenio Messina cut off two of Vassallo's fingertips. Eugenio was jailed for three years for this assault. His girls told the police about the Vassallos' protection racket. Policemen watched as the Vassallos drove up to some of the girls near Piccadilly, one of them shouting: 'It's better for you to give us the money, otherwise I will cut your face.' In the car the police found a hammer wrapped in newspaper, a knife and a cosh. Four of the Vassallo gang were prosecuted and given up to four years' penal servitude.

Questions were asked in Parliament, and the Home Secretary, Chuter Ede, was told that the Messinas were said to be making half a million pounds a year from prostitution and to have twenty girls working for them. Ede, nevertheless refused to order a special inquiry into vice in London, saying: 'Any inquiry would not help the police because their difficulties arise from the fact that, although they may have good reason to suspect such activities, they are sometimes unable to obtain evidence upon which criminal proceedings could be based.'

It was Webb who brought the Messinas down. Frequently threatened and occasionally attacked, he was an outstanding investigative reporter. 'The reason the underworld chaps talk to me is because they trust me,' he wrote. 'They know I cannot be bought or sold, nor is there a lot of which I am afraid.' When he heard a thug was threatening to cut his throat, he confronted him with the words: 'I am Duncan Webb. The last I heard of you was that you were going to cut my throat. Here is my throat. Cut it.' After he exposed the Messinas, Webb, a devout Roman Catholic, paid for an advertisement in *The Times* thanking St Jude.

The Syndicate

The long reign of the Messinas was over, but there was no respite for the girls who worked for them. Waiting in the wings to take over in the West End was the East End partnership of the Jew Bernie Silver and the Maltese 'Big Frank' Mifsud, soon to be known as the Syndicate. They had been running brothels and gaming clubs in the East End and moved into the vacuum left by the fall of the Messinas.

Silver, from Stoke Newington in north London, had been in the Parachute Regiment during the war. Discharged on medical grounds in 1943, he went into vice in the East End and kept a brothel in Brick Lane, becoming one of the Messinas' satellites. From these obscure beginnings he rose to found a vice empire and to be known as the Godfather of Soho. Duncan Webb called him 'one of the two most evil men in London'.

As he grew wealthier he acquired expensive tastes – he was buying a £27,000 yacht when he was arrested on vice charges in 1973. By then the partnership was making £100,000 a week, according to the police. Silver, sleek and well-dressed, looking like a Hollywood gangster, became an important figure in the Soho pornography industry. Mifsud, a former traffic policeman from Malta, described as aggressive, generous, forever buying drinks, was always loaded with money but dressed 'like a bum'.

They had watched the breakdown of the Messina empire and the internecine warfare of the Maltese factions which tried to replace the brothers. From a single club in Brewer Street, Silver and Mifsud expanded until they owned most of Soho's strip clubs. With Silver providing the brains and Mifsud the muscle, the Syndicate imposed a kind of peace in the area for two decades.

One of the threats to that peace was Tommy Smithson, a thug involved in protection rackets. In June 1956 Smithson was found dying from gunshot wounds outside a house in Carlton Vale in west London owned by the Maltese gangster George Caruana.

At the time, there were two theories about the reason for Smithson's death. One was that Maltese club owners had grown tired of his demands for protection money. The other, which eventually proved to be true, was that he had fallen foul of Silver and Mifsud. The senior Scotland Yard detective Bert Wickstead called the killing 'a landmark inasmuch as it let every other contender for the vice position in the West End know that the Syndicate were in pole position and would brook no interference to thwart their powers'.

Bert Wickstead had been investigating the Syndicate and its methods. He found that Silver had added an ingenious twist to the selling of sex by letting flats to prostitutes at exorbitant rents – flat farming, as it was called. The girls had rent books showing they paid between £3 and £5. In fact they were paying far more – £25 to £30. They were also contributing large sums from their earnings. To maximise the use of the flats the girls worked in shifts, one shift beginning in the early afternoon and working through until the evening, the other then taking over and working until the early hours of the morning.

Silver was tried but acquitted. When Wickstead tried to move against the Syndicate, in October 1973, the pair fled abroad after being tipped off by a detective in his squad that they were about to be raided. Wickstead later wrote that he had 'enlisted the aid of the press' by persuading them to print stories with headlines like 'The Raid That Never Was'. The idea was to make the Syndicate think that he had given up the hunt. Silver appears to have fallen for this line, and the following month he was back in London when Wickstead struck again.

Silver was arrested at the Park Tower Hotel in London, where he was having dinner with a girlfriend. He was taken to Limehouse police station in the East End; Wickstead felt he could trust the offices there better than he could those at West End Central. Then

Wickstead raided the Scheherazade Club in Soho, where some of Silver's henchmen were drinking and dancing. Wickstead stepped up on to the stage to announce that everyone was under arrest. Buses took the guests, staff and even the band to the station at Limehouse, where the party continued. Wickstead recalled: 'I put them all in the charge room and they were thoroughly enjoying themselves, the band was playing and everybody was singing.'

Silver went on trial at the Old Bailey in September 1974. The Syndicate was accused of running what prosecutor Michael Corkery called 'a vicious empire . . . an unsavoury world of prostitutes, ponces and pimps'. After a trial that lasted 63 days, Silver was found guilty of living on immoral earnings. He was given six years in jail and fined £30,000. Six Maltese men were also jailed, the judge, Lord Justice Geoffrey Lane, telling them: 'The profits you reaped were enormous.' There had been reports that the Syndicate had salted away £50 million in Swiss bank accounts. Mifsud, who had been in hiding in Austria, was extradited and sentenced to five years' imprisonment, then freed on appeal. He died in Malta in 1999.

Just how violent the Syndicate was prepared to be was suggested by a witness at a trial, Joseph Spiteri, who screamed at Silver: 'He has blood on his hands. He killed the girl I was living with and six other girls. He was the head man. He is a bloodhound. He killed the girl and framed me.' When defence counsel asked why the police failed to act Spiteri replied: 'They used to run the police.'

The Syndicate was now a spent force, and others moved in. However, the great days were over for both the gangsters and the old-style vice business.

In 1969 Joseph Wilkins, a former used-car salesman who had interests in one-armed bandits and night clubs, took over Winston's, fashionable with middle-aged businessmen looking for 'hostesses'. He also had interests in the 800 Club in Leicester Square, once a haunt of Princess Margaret, the Islet Town Club in Curzon Street and the Crazy Horse Saloon in Marylebone, once run by former Rolls Razor washing-machine tycoon John Bloom.

When Wilkins applied for a licence for Winston's its former owner, Bruce Brace, claimed Wilkins had used strong-arm tactics to take over the club. Wilkins admitted that he had paid no money for the 27,000-member club, but claimed he had settled debts of £6,000. He got the licence, but the club soon closed.

Before long, Wilkins and some of his staff found themselves in trouble with the law. There were allegations that drunken punters were being robbed after visiting his clubs, and he was charged with conspiracy to pervert justice over licences. He was acquitted, but while awaiting trial on another conspiracy charge he and an accomplice were shot and wounded in Beak Street. His wife claimed the Kray twins, who were serving life sentences, were behind the shootings.

A penniless Polish refugee who came to Britain at the end of the Second World War gave his name to a vicious new kind of racketeering. Perac or Peter Rachman built up a property empire in the Notting Hill, Shepherd's Bush, Paddington and Earl's Court areas during the late 1950s and early 1960s. While working as a clerk in an estate agent's he realised the opportunities the 1957 Rent Act gave to unscrupulous landlords. They could now charge new tenants much higher rents than existing tenants, whose low rents were legally protected. All the landlord had to do was persuade or force the existing tenants to leave. The process of getting them out, by fair means or foul, was known as 'Rachmanism'.

Rachman began buying up the leases of large Victorian terraced houses let as flats. Savage dogs were used to assault tenants, intolerable neighbours were installed and held all-night noisy parties, essential services were cut off. Housing was in short supply and Rachman could let squalid flats at exorbitant rents. Many of the tenants were prostitutes. Some of the properties became brothels.

Soon Rachman was a millionaire and began to attract the attention both of the police and of other underworld figures. The police found it impossible to prove he knew his properties were being used as brothels, but the Kray twins, East End gangsters with a growing reputation for violence, found Rachman an easy target. When he refused to pay protection money the Kray mobsters attacked his rent collectors. As Reggie Kray put it: 'He had to pay up – it was either that or his rent collectors were set upon. They were big, but our boys were bigger.' Rachman finally deflected the twins' attention by suggesting that they could easily 'persuade' the owner of a successful night club, Esmeralda's Barn in Wilton Place off Knightsbridge, to sign it over to them. He was right, and for some time the twins were too busy with their new club and their other rackets to bother him. Rachman was free to enjoy his Rolls-Royce, his large detached house in Winnington Road, Hampstead, with its two uniformed maids and gardener, and nights out with the retired London crime overlord Billy Hill, his mistress Mandy Rice-Davies and Christine Keeler, two of the girls in the Profumo scandal. He died in 1962 at the age of 42.

Street prostitution continued to be an embarrassment after the Second World War, particularly during 1953 when the coronation drew many visitors to London. Dr Alfred Kinsey, the American sexologist and author of the famous Kinsey Report, claimed he saw a thousand prostitutes at work in the West End one Saturday night in 1955. 'I have never seen so much nor such aggressive behaviour anywhere else,' he said.

*Before the act: streetwalkers ply their trade in Soho before the 1959
Street Offences Act made it too expensive by raising fines.*

Statistics suggested that there had been a big increase in the amount of prostitution. In 1958 there were 16,700 convictions, greatly above wartime figures and more than 50 per cent above the average for the years 1952–55.

> The curious investigator in the 'fifties could see evidence on the pavements, in Hyde Park, in doorways and alleys and under railway arches. From the edge of Notting Hill in the west, down Bayswater Road, through the Park to Piccadilly, and eastwards to Stepney, he could expect to be accosted at every few yards except across the City 'gap' from east of Charing Cross Road to Aldgate Pump. Similarly a walk north–south from Maida Vale, through Paddington to Victoria, or at a slightly different tangent from the mainline railway stations of Euston, St Pancras and Kings Cross, brought the same sights. The one-mile 'Prostitutes' Row' from Piccadilly to Waterloo Bridge had stretched over seven miles with only a one-mile break. (John Gosling and Douglas Warner, *The Shame of a City*).

There was certainly plenty of anecdotal evidence: citizens complained of having to clear contraceptives from their front gardens, and others that couples were copulating in Hyde Park in broad daylight. One of those scandalised was Billy Graham, the American evangelist. He commented on the antics he saw: 'It looked as though your parks had been turned into bedrooms, with people lying all over the place.'

The street girls operating on the eve of the Street Offences Act of 1959 can be categorised by price. Those who charged the highest prices were the girls in Mayfair, who were naturally the most attractive. Next came the streetwalkers of Soho and Piccadilly. A further rung down the ladder were the girls in Hyde Park, Bayswater, Victoria and Maida Vale, and below them were the Euston–King's Cross women. As ever, the tarts of the East End were at the bottom of the earnings league table.

It is interesting that prostitution had returned to Stepney, a fact Gosling and Warner attribute to the arrival of many single black men. In 1952 the black journalist Roi Otley wrote of the area around Cable

Street: 'Today, down by London dock in about a square mile of back streets there exists a dismal Negro slum. The neighbourhood, situated in the borough of Stepney, abounds with brothels and dope pads in tumbledown old buildings' (Roi Otley, *No Green Pastures*, 1952).

The Conservative home secretary, Sir David Maxwell-Fyfe, decided in 1954 to order an inquiry into prostitution and homosexuality. John Wolfenden, an academic, who described his committee as 'we poor innocents', was given the task of examining the state of the law. Their 1957 report proposed heavier fines and even imprisonment to stop prostitutes making a nuisance of themselves. The committee also recommended that what homosexuals did in private was their own concern, as long as they were over 21 years of age. Two years afterwards the proposals on prostitution became law. Eight years later the law on homosexuality was changed as the Wolfenden committee had suggested.

The Street Offences Act drove most of the prostitutes into the shadows. The estimated 5,000 women needed somewhere else to ply their trade. A few may have joined the ranks of the 'call girls', the elite of prostitutes, but most of them did not have the requisite looks or polish. Others put their cards in the windows of small shops. These women first of all described themselves as French, and later, as the imagined attractions of different nationalities changed, perhaps under the influence of the cinema, as Scandinavian.

Another outlet was the escort agency, and Joseph Wilkins had the foresight to get in early. He was behind the Eve International, Playboy Escort, Glamour International and La Femme agencies. Eve International was said to have 200 girls on its books, charging from £14 a night upwards and bringing in £100,000 for the agency. When Wilkins was charged, with his wife and henchmen, with living off immoral earnings, his girls were said to be charging £40 for a 'quickie' and £100 for 'longer', and making £400 a week each for themselves. Wilkins was jailed for three and a half years, reduced to two years by the Court of Appeal. Although he was later involved with a long-firm fraud – a kind of credit swindle – and drugs, his brief spell as a vice king was over.

Some girls used near-beer joints, which did not have a licence to sell alcohol, as places to pick up clients. They also began to advertise in phone booths all over London, which were soon wallpapered with explicit cards complete with photos. Vigilante groups would go round the booths ripping these up, and men employed by the girls would follow, pasting up replacements.

The film industry contributed innumerable 'starlets', who seldom or never acted in films but nevertheless made a good living as the companions or accessories of the rich and famous. In 1960 it was estimated that while her looks lasted such a girl could make between £300 and £500 in a weekend at some foreign resort or in London during 'the season'. Although in effect they were selling sex to a succession of men, these women would not have considered themselves prostitutes.

The Soho vice industry had burgeoned after the war as racketeers bought up the leases of premises housing small businesses as they expired and let and sublet them to prostitutes. Parts of the premises were turned into sex shops. In the 1980s new legislation enabled Westminster City Council to refuse licences to sex shops, and the police clamped down on what was left of the peep-show and porn clubs. Today even the miserable sex and porn shops seem to be on the retreat. However, the escort agencies are flourishing, as are the prostitutes, and there are still some strip clubs where customers are charged up to £10 for a bottle of alcohol-free lager. In others, customers who paid a £10 entrance fee were expected to buy the 'hostesses' fake champagne at £50 a bottle.

In the 1980s and 1990s Old Compton Street gained a sprinkling of gay pubs and clubs. According to the *Independent* in February 1991, presiding over the strip clubs was Jean Agius, another Maltese – 'short and thin with sparse hair, pale and very unhealthy-looking. Over a track-suit he wore a showy but moth-eaten fur coat. It was all slightly sad.' Nevertheless, the newspaper pointed out that he owned a Rolls-Royce Corniche and a Bentley.

In some parts of the city, however, prostitution went on in the same old way. A prostitute named Anita went to work in a block of flats in Soho in the early 1980s after being told that she could earn £400 a day there. Conditions in the run-down block could have been organised by Marthe Watts, the Messinas' whore and madam forty years earlier. Anita recalled:

It was ten pounds a time, straight sex, eight minutes. Then the maid would knock on the door and if he wanted to stay longer it was extra money: plus if he wanted you to take your top off it was an extra five pounds, everything was always extra... you always had six or seven waiting to come in, the door never stopped, and it was a twelve-hours shift. The insides of my thighs used to kill. (Roberts, *Whores in History*).

Bawdy, Lewd Books

As long ago as the 1660s there was a trade in frankly pornographic books. Pepys bought *L'Eschoole des Filles* in 1688 and found it 'the most bawdy, lewd book that ever I saw, rather worse than *La puttane errante* [by Pietro Aretino] so that I was ashamed of reading it'. Interestingly his copy came in plain binding. He resolved 'as soon as I have read it, to burn it, that it may not stand in my list of books, nor among them, to disgrace them if it should be found'. He did burn it, having read it first, and recorded that it was a 'rightly lewd work, but not yet amiss for a sober man to read over to inform himself in the villainy of the world.'

In the middle of the seventeenth century the establishment had been shocked by the book *The School of Venus*, perhaps not because it included all the four-letter words, which were then in common use, but because of its democratic attitude to sex. A worldly young lady, Fanny, is asked by the innocent Katy 'whether this pleasure could be partaken of by others than maids and young men?' Fanny replies: 'All people of all ranks and degree participate therein even from the king to the cobbler, from the queen to the kitchen-wench. In short, one half the world fucks the other.'

At the beginning of the eighteenth century London's main pornographer was Edmund Curl, who seems to have become the first Englishman to be convicted for publishing erotica when he was arraigned over *Venus in the Cloister, or The Nun in her Smock* in 1727. Defoe called his books, which included *The Treatise on the Use of Flogging in Venereal Affairs*, 'lewd, abominable pieces of bawdry'. Curl replied with a pamphlet in which he justified porno-graphy on the basis that if vice exists it is better to admit it than to cover it up.

In the nineteenth century the authorities began a more systematic prosecution of the publishers of what were seen as obscene books and newspapers. In 1830 there was a successful prosecution over the Marquis de Sade's *Juliette*, and publishers were repeatedly indicted over John Cleland's *Fanny Hill or Memoirs of a Woman of Pleasure*. The book had been banned on its publication in 1749 and was prosecuted again on its revival in 1963 under the Obscene Publications Act. Clearly copies were readily available: Arthur Wellesley, the future Duke of Wellington, took several copies with him when he went to India.

Some of these prosecutions were private actions brought by the Society for the Suppression of Vice, which was founded in 1802. The wit Sydney Smith called it 'a society for suppressing the vices of those whose incomes do not succeed £500 per annum'. Over the next fifty years the society brought 159 prosecutions, almost all of them successful.

It was just one of the social purist groups which sought to make men moral. Some of the more radical souls in the Church of England were 'against the popular press, cheap novelettes, sensational periodicals and "penny dreadfuls"' (Bartley, *Prostitution*). Even birth control literature and advertisements for medicines which induced abortions were condemned because they appeared to condone sex outside marriage. 'Similarly, men were prosecuted for giving lectures on health, biology and science, because they were considered to be "full of obscene language, unfit to be given in public".' (Bartley. ibid.). The London Council was urged to obliterate obscene graffiti in its lavatories, and the London Council for the Promotion of Public Morality and the NVA campaigned successfully against 'living statuary'. These were teenage girls in flesh-coloured tights who would sing behind a curtain and then be revealed standing about in elegant poses. Morals patrols saw that courting couples in parks behaved decently. But it was mainstream pornography that evoked the full rigour of all these agencies.

Novels exhaling its stygian stench burden news-stand and book agents' baskets. Papers teeming with salaciousness obtain readers by the hundreds of thousands, and drive out of the market self-respecting and decent publications...Theatrical posters...are to our young people unmistakable object lessons in lasciviousness; and the stage...not unfrequently becomes the panderer to lowest passions. (*The Pioneer*, January 1894)

Police in London raided a house in the West End and 'made an extensive seizure of indecent pictures and books, which, judging from the price at which they were sold, could only have been bought by the wealthy people in Society' (Bartley, *Prostitution*). Street hawkers were prosecuted for selling indecent photographs. The publisher Vizetelly was jailed for three years for publishing 'indecent literature', which in this case included Zola's *La Terre*, 'the obscenity of which is so revolting and brutal' that it was banned and destroyed. There were 'obscene' Christmas cards, theatrical and music-hall posters and advertisements. A peddler was convicted of publishing an 'obscene' tooth-pick case: it had on its inside lid a picture of a copulating couple.

One of the centres of the trade in pornography was the tangle of streets later swept away by the building of Kingsway and Aldwych. The most important concentration was in Holywell Street. It was in this area that William Dugdale, Edward Dyer and other pornographers plied a lively trade, spied on by the agents of the Society for the Suppression of Vice. The record of one prosecution gives a flavour of the agents' methods.

I went to the shop two or three times before the day when the sale took place, and bought several innocent publications. On the day in question the prisoner showed me a French print in the window, which I had asked to see. I asked him if he had anything more curious, and he at length invited me to go into the back shop. He then showed me several indecent prints. I asked him the price, and selected two which I produce. These form the subject of the present indictment.

William Dugdale was an important pornographer and his premises in Holywell Street were raided several times. In September 1851 a force of constables led by an inspector of the Thames Police accompanied by men from the Society for the Suppression of Vice descended on Holywell Street. They were spotted by Dugdale's look-out, who warned his employer. Those inside the shop locked and bolted the doors, and people in houses and shops nearby emerged and menaced the police and the vice society men, who were trying to break in. The reinforced doors withstood this attack, but after ten minutes Dugdale opened up and invited the police in. Many of the incriminating prints had been burnt while the siege went on but the police took away a large quantity of books, prints, catalogues and plates. Dugdale was jailed for two years.

In May 1857 the country got its first Obscene Publications Act. The Lord Chief Justice, Lord Campbell, had described obscene publications as 'more deadly than prussic acid, strychnine or arsenic'. The test of obscenity was later defined as whether the material was likely to 'deprave and corrupt'. Within two months the Society for the Suppression of Vice announced that it had seized thousands of obscene prints, hundreds of books and engravings. Eleven years later the society declared that a new front had been opened in the war between it and the pornographers – the stereoscopic viewer and the improved postal service had introduced 'a new phase . . . in the history of vice'.

Henry Mayhew had conventional Victorian views on pornography and censorship. He wrote: 'Until very lately the police had not the power of arresting those trades who earned an infamous livelihood by selling immoral books and obscene prints. It is to the late Lord Chancellor Campbell that we owe this salutary reform, under whose meritorious exertions the disgraceful trade of Holywell Street has received a blow from which it will never again rally.' Yet, eleven years after the Obscene Publications Bill was passed, the *Saturday Review* wrote of Holywell Street: 'the dunghill is in full heat, seething and steaming with its old pestilence'. The Society for the Suppression of Vice had to admit that for all its zeal in prosecuting pornographers, they showed 'a tendency to revive'.

Towards the end of the Victorian era the volume of pornography was still growing, with titles such as *Lady Bumtickler's Revels* and

Raped on the Railway: A True Story of a Lady Who Was First Ravished and then Flagellated on the Scotch Express becoming popular. Some respected writers were secretly involved, including the journalist and author George Augustus Sala. He was known among the respectable classes for *Twice Round the Clock* his account of London life of 1858, and as war correspondent for the *Daily Telegraph*. In more louche circles he was known for books such as *Miss Bellasis Birched for Thieving*, a tale of middle-class depravity set in a Brighton girls' finishing school. Readers with a taste for flagellation are treated to accounts of the girls being chastised while their spiritual adviser, the Reverend Arthur Calvedon, watches through a spy-hole. Afterwards the school's proprietor, Miss Sinclair, assuages his lust. Sala also wrote *Prince Cherrytop* and *Good Fairy Fuck*.

Perhaps the most important writer of pornography was the poet Charles Algernon Swinburne. His splendidly subversive *La Sœur de la Reine* is the tale of Queen Victoria's twin sister, a Haymarket prostitute. The queen herself is subject to fits of ungovernable passion, and is seduced by William Wordsworth after a particularly suggestive reading of his poem 'The Excursion'. Afterwards her rampant sexual needs can only be satisfied by two very unlikely historical figures, Lord John Russell and 'Sir Peel'. This stuff was too hot even for John Camden Hotten, publisher of expensive pornography for well-heeled Victorians, including *Lady Bumtickler's Revels* and *Madam Birchini's Dance*. Swinburne's pornography circulated in manuscript form only.

Soho had been a centre of vice for centuries, and when Holywell Street and the surrounding area were demolished the pornographers found a new home there and in nearby Charing Cross Road. By the 1940s it was London's main centre for what was quaintly called 'erotica', although the insipid wares on offer, on the same lines as the fifties magazine *Health and Efficiency*, were unlikely to inflame. Somehow the area, with its tarts and foreign restaurants and intriguingly bohemian atmosphere seemed perfect for this furtive trade. The first shops were discreet almost to the point of invisibility. There would be a front section which gave little away, and a curtained-off rear where the 'more interesting' wares could be inspected. There was no browsing: customers would dive in and depart within minutes, having parted with a surprising amount of money for something in a plain brown parcel.

In the fifties the police had a home office list of more than a thousand banned books. It included the works of Hank Janson and a novel by Maupassant, Defoe's *Moll Flanders* and James Hanley's *Boy*. Hundreds of magazines were also banned.

Much of the material sold in the 'dirty book' shops came from America. The magazines had titles like *Razzle* and *Silk Stocking Stories*. Also on the banned list were *Jiggle*, *Titter*, *Oomph*, *The Romance of Naturism* and *Fads and Fantasies*. The more expensive items came from Paris. While the trade was in this state of innocence it was dominated by a few colourful characters, among them Ron 'The Dustman' Davey, who had indeed been a dustman with Hammersmith Council. He got into the pornography trade by selling photographs of women members of a nudist club he belonged to. Pictures of women wrestling were particularly popular, as he later recalled.

Davey produced his own wares on primitive printing machines, yet despite the poor quality could not keep up with demand. 'So popular did Davey's books become that they became known throughout the trade as "MDs" – short for the Millionaire Dustman' (Tomkinson, *The Pornbrokers*).

Another figure to emerge in the fifties was Ronald Eric Mason, known as John Mason, who made one of the biggest porn fortunes. He would later claim that he started bribing police officers in 1953, and that in all he had paid off a total of 148 officers. These included Detective Chief Superintendent Bill Moody, to whom he once gave £14,000 to get a friend off a criminal charge.

At first the police extortion was relatively modest, but any inhibitions that officers may have had were washed away by the tidal wave of money, gifts, holidays and free sex that came their way during the Soho pornography boom of the 1960s and 1970s. Some members of the Yard's Obscene Publications Squad – known as the Porn Squad and the Dirty Squad– including officers up to the rank of commander, saw to it that free-market economics applied to the flood of blue films and girlie magazines. In return, pornographers including Jimmy Humphreys and Mason paid the officers anything from £2,000 to £14,000 to open new shops and a weekly £500 to be allowed to operate them, while the wholesalers who imported the pornographic films and books paid £200 a week. They could afford it: one of them, Big Jeff Phillips, drove a Rolls-Royce and lived in a manor house in Berkshire.

The greed and indiscretion of the police knew no bounds. John Mason was given a CID tie to wear on his visits to the storeroom in Holborn police station where confiscated pornography was stored. Some of it had been taken from his own shops – from time to time the Porn Squad had to raid the premises of their clients. Mason was allowed to buy back his own material from the police station.

Bernie Silver, the vice racketeer who had taken over the Messina vice empire, was the most important figure in the early years of the porn revolution, but the most colourful was Jimmy Humphreys, who with his wife Rusty would eventually bring about the downfall of the Porn Squad. Born in Southwark in 1930, Humphreys numbered such well-known local criminals as Mad Frankie Fraser, Jimmy Brindle and the Great Train Robbers Bruce Reynolds and Buster Edwards among his friends. After a routine career of minor crime, in 1962 he opened a club in Old Compton Street in Soho. There he met and married June Packard, a dancer who reinvented herself as Rusty Gaynor, queen of the Soho strippers.

Rusty, whose father was a respectable master-builder, had started out as a chorus girl, but soon grew more ambitious. She hired choreographers and arrangers and went to Paris to see what she could learn from the Folies Bergère. The Humphreys acquired several clubs, in which strippers danced to taped music.

As their empire grew, they naturally came into contact with members of the Porn Squad. Many of these officers, already corrupt, were attracted by the obvious signs of prosperity around the couple: by now the Humphreys owned, along with their clubs, a large manor house in Kent and a flat in Soho. Soon the pornographer was entertaining senior officers and their wives, who would invite Humphreys and his wife to join them at a good restaurant. At the end of the night Humphreys would be expected to pay the bill.

Every bribe and gift and dirty weekend with Porn Squad members and girls from his clubs at his holiday home in Ibiza was secretly recorded by Humphreys in a series of diaries which he kept in safety-deposit boxes. Among the senior officers mentioned in the diaries were Commander Wally Virgo of the CID, Bill Moody, head of the Obscene Publications Squad – the greediest of all – and Commander Ken Drury, head of the Flying Squad.

Drury, a picaresque character, was arguably the most corrupt officer in London. By a delicious irony he had been one of the chief investigators in a case of police corruption exposed by *The Times*. His appetite for the hospitality of porn dealers was so gross colleagues worried that he was putting on too much weight, so Humphreys gave him an exercise bicycle and a rowing machine.

It is hard to comprehend how men like Drury got away with it for so long, unless one understands the climate inside the police force at the time. According to Frank Williamson, an inspector of constabulary, there were three types of officers at the Yard: those who were corrupt, those who were honest but turned a blind eye to the corruption, and those who were too stupid to realise some of their colleagues were corrupt.

In the late 1960s Humphreys, trying to sell obscene books from his Soho premises, was meeting resistance from the Porn Squad, who wanted to keep tight control on the racket. At a dinner in the Criterion restaurant in 1969, when he and Rusty were guests of senior detectives including Wally Virgo, Humphreys complained that Bill Moody would not give him the all-clear to start trading. Bernie Silver, who was also present, offered to introduce him to Moody, and eventually a deal was done. As Humphreys recorded in his diary, the price was an initial £14,000 and then £2,000 a month to keep the police off his back. And Silver was to become his partner, at Moody's insistence.

The uneasy partnership was soon in trouble. While Silver was out of town Humphreys had an affair with his mistress, Dominique Ferguson. Silver threatened reprisals, and Drury charged £1,050 to straighten matters out. Then Rusty was jailed for three months for possessing a gun.

Meanwhile investigators for the *Sunday People* had been looking at the new porn empires, and in 1971 the paper named Silver and Humphreys, among others, as pornographers. It also claimed there was police corruption, but a police investigation came to nothing.

In February 1972 the paper returned to the attack. Under the headline 'Corruption, the charges against the police' it stated:

Police officers in London, particularly some of those attached to Scotland Yard's Obscene Publications Department, are being systematically bribed by dealers in pornography. It is this that largely explains why their businesses flourish; why immense stocks of 'dirty' books, magazines and films are not confiscated. That is the unanimous opinion of the *Sunday People* reporters who have been investigating pornography in Britain.

One porn dealer told the paper that he paid certain officers in the Obscene Publications Squad an average of £1,500 a year. The money would be handed over in a pub or a restaurant. A blue-film maker said he had paid a detective sergeant £30 to get a prosecution dropped, and was told that a licence to operate would cost him £200 a month plus a percentage of the profits. The manager of a film club said he had paid off thirteen officers over the years, while others had borrowed blue films from him.

What sealed the fate of the corrupt police was a photograph on page one of Drury on holiday in Cyprus with Humphreys and his wife. Drury and his wife had been their guests during the two-week stay in Famagusta, and Humphreys had paid most of the costs, which came to more than £500.

Drury, who had signed the hotel register with his police rank, tried to brazen it out, claiming that far from being on holiday, he had been on the trail of escaped Great Train Robber Ronnie Biggs. Humphreys backed him up, but anti-corruption officers who were now investigating the links between police and pornographers did not believe either of them. In March Drury was suspended from duty and on 1 May he resigned. He sold his story to the *News of the World* for £10,000, claiming in the paper that Humphreys was a police informer, a 'grass.'

Humphreys had other problems. Peter Garforth, a thief who had an affair with Rusty before she knew Humphreys, was attacked and badly cut up. He named Humphreys as one of his attackers. The pornographer fled to Amsterdam, but was arrested and sent back to Britain, where he was jailed for eight years.

A detective named Gilbert Kelland, later an assistant commissioner, was appointed to head the investigation into police corruption. He visited Humphreys in Wandsworth prison and for three months listened in astonishment as the pornographer told in great detail the story of the corruption of the Obscene Publications Squad. To back up his claims Humphreys had his diaries.

In February 1976 Drury, Virgo and Moody were arrested in a series of dawn raids. At the same time dozens of other officers were taken in. It was the biggest police scandal since 1877, when several of the senior detectives at Scotland Yard were convicted of accepting bribes. The judge, Justice Mars-Jones, estimated that Moody and Virgo had between them taken £100,000 from the pornographers, 'on a scale which beggars description'. It emerged that Moody had organised the taking of bribes 'as it had never been organised before', to use his own words. His superior officer, Virgo, oversaw a cover-up, seeing to it that six previous allegations of corruption in the Obscene Publications Squad were quietly dropped. Both Virgo and Moody were sentenced to twelve years in prison, although Virgo was freed after ten months.

Drury got eight years: of the 74 officers investigated, twelve resigned, 28 retired, eight were dismissed and thirteen were jailed. It was clear that the Yard had been the biggest criminal organisation in London. Kelland wrote in *Crime in London*: 'We strongly believed that, for the eventual benefit of the force, the crow of corruption had to be nailed to the barn door to convince and remind everyone of the need for positive action and eternal vigilance.'

Humphreys was given a royal pardon in 1978 for his part in this coup, and released. He and Rusty left the country and he became a bookmaker in Mexico and Florida. But by the nineties they were back in England, renting flats to prostitutes. It is said that Rusty occasionally acted as a 'maid' for the women. In summer 1994 they were both jailed for eight months.

After the trials the Obscene Publications Squad was disbanded and their role was taken by a squad of uniformed officers. There was much for them to do: a new generation of young pornographers had moved in and business was booming as never before. Videos and

older clients explained why he was charged less: "I only pay £15 because I don't go with a girl because I'm impotent.'"

When those who were still capable of enjoying the girls had sex they gave them the vouchers. At the end of the party each girl would give Cynthia the vouchers she had collected, and would be paid pro rata.

The middle-aged and elderly customers – politicians, barristers, clergymen, businessmen and other professionals – were ferried to Streatham police station for questioning. Sixteen months later, by which time she was a national celebrity referred to in the tabloid newspapers as 'Madam Sin', Cynthia Payne went on trial at Inner London Crown Court. There was only one defendant: the other women involved were not charged, nor of course were any of the customers. Because of widespread and sympathetic coverage by most newspapers, the public faced consciously, perhaps for the first time, the hypocrisy of the law, the double standard that punished women for meeting a demand created by men. There was genuine shock when Judge West-Russell sentenced Cynthia to eighteen months' imprisonment for keeping a disorderly house. This was reduced on appeal to six months. She was also heavily fined.

Four days later the *Spectator* published an editorial which pointed out that not only had the customers gone free, they had also gone unnamed.

It is difficult to discern any justice in this very typical case. The punishment itself is altogether excessive: nothing is gained in imprisoning Cynthia Payne and her kind unless they have corrupted the young and innocent. The transactions between Mrs Payne, her male clients and the women in her house were transactions between freely consenting adults. According to the law, the men committed no offence, and if the women did, they were not charged with any. Only Cynthia Payne is regarded as legally culpable, even though she, the men and the women were all engaged in the joint exercise of an improper Christmas party.

The law has been enforced, but justice has manifestly not been done. The quite unnecessarily severe sentence apart, there remains an outrageous indecency in the law as it stands and is enforced. If prostitution be an offence punishable at law, then a law should be written and enacted to this effect; and, if offence it be, then the man and woman, clearly sharing the offence, should be held to be both of them culpable. Commonsense would go further, and say that, of the two, the man – who, after all, is creating the demand and supplying the cash – is the more responsible for the illegal enterprise, the more culpable and the more appropriate to be punished.

But our legislators have not wished prostitution as such to be an offence, precisely in order to avoid the punishment – and the publication of the names – of the men whose demands create the supply...

In prison, Cynthia thought that one day she would like to run a home for the elderly with special wards for the disabled. Those who couldn't afford to pay for sex would get it free on the National Health Service. Instead she went on the after-dinner speaking circuit, sometimes for charity. In 2000, at the age of 67, she reflected on fame without fortune. Two films which had been made about her life had brought her only £10,000, she said in a *Daily Express* interview, and she never made much money from her sex parties, either. 'I charged only £15 initially and I was being fiddled by some of the girls. I also offered money-back guarantees, £5 discounts for old-age pensioners and free access to the parties for disabled people. I was just too soft – I was not hard and ruthless enough.'

In 1963, when London was swinging, the porn boom was getting under way, the Krays were building a gangland empire based on terror and the older generations feared that standards were slipping, the establishment showed that when its vital interests were threatened it could still be ruthless, even vicious. The Profumo affair ruined the career of a senior Conservative politician and the backlash cost a man his life. Christine Keeler, a weak young woman hopelessly adrift in louche circles, never found her feet again.

It began with a chance encounter. John Profumo, the Minister for War, was a guest of Lord Astor at his estate at Cliveden. After dinner one evening he met Christine Keeler by the swimming pool. When he returned to London he rang her and they began a brief affair.

Keeler had come to London at the age of sixteen after an unhappy childhood at Wraysbury in the Thames Valley. She got work at Murray's Cabaret Club, where she met Mandy Rice-Davies. She also met the society osteopath and artist Stephen Ward, who numbered many rich, aristocratic and famous people among his patients. Ward was fifty at the time of these events. He had many lovers, some of them prostitutes, and his other weaknesses included name-dropping and hob-nobbing with peers. He was good-looking in a drawn, world-weary kind of way and was said to have great charm. He and Keeler became lovers, although she too had many other affairs, including, she claimed, one with Captain Ivanov, the Russian naval attaché. At the time she met Profumo she had been staying at a cottage in the Cliveden grounds let by Lord Astor to Ward, who was also a friend of Ivanov.

The links between Ward, Ivanov and Profumo became known to the security services, and eventually Sir Norman Brook, Secretary to the Cabinet, mentioned this to Profumo. The minister quickly

Doomed friendship: Stephen Ward with Christine Keeler. He was found guilty of living off prostitutes, but died of a fatal drugs overdose.

broke off his affair with Keeler, and there the matter might have ended, had it not been for Christine Keeler's complicated love life.

In October 1962 there was a fight between two of her lovers, both West Indians, and one, John Edgecombe, slashed the face of the other, Lucky Gordon. The following month Christine paid a visit to her friend Mandy Rice-Davies, mistress of the rack-renter Peter Rachmann, who was living at Ward's flat in Wimpole Mews. Edgecombe turned up and when the girls refused to let him in he opened fire on the door with a pistol. He was arrested and the press began to take an interest in Keeler and Ward. When Keeler told them she had been sleeping with both Profumo and Ivanov a first-rate scandal broke.

In the Commons Profumo felt he had to deny the rumours that were now circulating. He claimed there had never been any impropriety between him and Christine Keeler, and threatened to sue anyone who repeated the allegations. Then the home secretary asked the commissioner of police to investigate the affair. Police put pressure on Ward, who wrote letters to senior politicians and the press saying that 'my efforts to conceal the fact that Mr Profumo had not told the truth in Parliament made it look as if I myself had something to hide.' On 29 May 1963 the lord chancellor began a further investigation and three days later Profumo confessed to his wife, the actress Valerie Hobson. Profumo issued a statement saying that he had lied to the House of Commons, and then resigned.

The hounding of Stephen Ward began, although it never became clear at whose insistence this was. Dozens of potential witnesses were interviewed by the police, some of them several times. On 22 July 1963, Ward appeared at the Old Bailey. There were five charges, mainly of living on the earnings of prostitutes. During the trial Keeler and Rice-Davies, among others, admitted selling sex in Ward's flat and giving him money although they explained that when he could afford it he gave them more money than they ever gave him. Nevertheless Ward was found guilty. By then he was beyond the reach of his persecutors, having taken a fatal drugs overdose. Keeler was sent to prison for other offences. Writers about the affair have doubted whether she and Ward were guilty.

Good-time girls: Christine Keeler (right) and her friend Mandy Rice-Davies. Mandy easily floated to the top of the louche world of sixties London. Christine sank.

Sex and the City in the 21ˢᵗ Century

The sex industry has an exemplary record of adapting to change, and it is still changing today. There is relatively little street prostitution, particularly in central London:[11] massage parlours are thriving, escort agencies cater for the wealthy client and there are suburban brothels in surprising places. One at Crayford in Greater London was over a bookshop I visited frequently. It had a separate entrance and was in no way connected to the bookshop or its owner. It was all very prosaic. We could hear customers going up the stairs to the reception area, and business was never brisk, although we were not there in the evenings. In the early afternoon the women would leave to pick up their children from school, and would later return, frequently driven by their partners. The police were said to treat it with benign indifference as long as there was no trouble.

Recent surveys have shown that changes in the patterns of street prostitution affect all the 'hot spots' in the city. These include Paddington, Tottenham, Whitechapel, Mayfair, Soho, Stoke Newington, Streatham, King's Cross and Brixton, although this list may be out of date because local action by the police can drive the women out of one area to colonise another, temporarily or permanently. A report by a team under Professor Roger Matthews of Middlesex University (*Prostitution in London: An Audit*) found that street prostitution overall was declining, with only 1,100 'known' women involved in any one year and as few as 115 being on the streets on any one night. Whatever figures we accept for Georgian and Victorian prostitution there has obviously been a very great decline, even in fairly recent times. The Wolfenden Report which led to the Street Offences Act of 1959 pointed out that in 1953 there were 6,829 prosecutions of women working in the West End alone. Now there may be fewer than 200 women working in that area. Matthews concludes that the decline is 'partly due to pressure from the local community, police intervention and a growing awareness of the dangers of working on the streets'.

At the same time there has been an increase in 'off street' prostitution, in saunas and massage parlours, clubs, hostess bars and private flats. At the top end of the trade escort agencies are flourishing. Matthews does not believe there is a link between the decline of street prostitution and the rise in its off-street conterpart – few street prostitutes make the transition to off-street work.

The Matthews study is the first major survey of prostitution in London since the Second World War, and its findings and conclusions are worth examining in some detail. Although for various reasons the King's Cross area is the one most people will think of as a typical hot spot for vice, Matthews shows that Paddington has about eight times as many women on the streets – 400 compared to 50. 'This is probably not surprising since Paddington in fact involves three distinct areas centred around Sussex Gardens, Cleveland Square and Porchester Gardens. Sussex Gardens is the most active of these areas and it is the case that of the 16 women reported to be on the street on an average night the majority will be located in Sussex Gardens.'

The age range of the women involved is what would be expected from a reading of Victorian surveys. There were a few girls under the age of sixteen – one was thirteen – and 5 per cent of them were over 40. The majority of them were in their twenties and thirties – 28 per cent between 21 and 25, 22 per cent between 26 and 30, 16 per cent between 31 and 35, 12 per cent between 36 and 40. Using police categories of ethnicity we get the following figures: 78 per cent were white, 16 per cent Afro-Caribbean, 3 per cent Asian and 2 per cent Mediterranean.

The survey found that a 'significant percentage' of street workers are 'away day' women, that is sex workers who come to London from other parts of the country for short periods. Monica Coghlan, the prostitute the author and politician Jeffrey Archer famously denied having sex with, used to commute from a northern city. Police records show that most of the women come from Birmingham, Nottingham, Wolverhampton and Bradford. 'They may be drawn to the capital because of the promise of higher earnings or because they find it difficult to work in their own area ... Interviews with police officers suggest that many of these women are finding the streets of London a relatively hostile environment in which to work, and are consequently either staying in the capital for shorter periods of time or are not returning once having left.'

The survey gives important new information on earnings, which show the same variation in rates for different areas that has persisted over the centuries. 'Whereas women working in Whitechapel are currently charging between £10 and £40, depending on the service provided, prostitutes in Mayfair are earning in the region of £100 per client.' Overall, the average charges for different services were: £20 for hand relief, £30 for oral sex and £50 for 'full sex'. 'The cost of additional "special services" would be extra.'

Perhaps the most valuable part of the survey concerns women working from private premises, and those working for escort agencies. It confirms that the latter are the elite of whoredom. It also gives statistics for saunas, massage parlours, hostess bars and clubs.

To arrive at a total for women working from private premises, the survey team checked the phone numbers on cards in telephone boxes, interviewed a 'cardman', one of those who paste up the cards for the prostitutes, and searched all the local papers in the London area for advertisements as well as free papers and other relevant journals. British Telecom was asked to help with numbers, as some premises had more than one phone.

It is apparent when investigating this aspect of the trade that the number of women operating in this form has increased substantially in recent years. According to British Telecom it was only about ten years ago that women started to advertise by placing cards in telephone boxes, and that over the past decade these telephone boxes have become increasingly covered in cards advertising sexual services. These cards are not only becoming more prevalent, they have also become more explicit. A few years ago the cards were relatively plain, and the wording was suggestive rather than overt. What is also noticeable about the cards which are currently to be seen is that a significant percentage cater for specialist tastes, while a number are written in foreign languages and are clearly advertising the services of women from abroad, and are presumably aimed at men of different nationalities.

For some time these cards appeared only in boxes in central London, but now cards are appearing in areas such as Camden and Kensington. Between 1994 and 1997 the number of boxes affected rose from 600 to 1,000. Attempts by British Telecom and Westminster Council to clear up the boxes are frustrated by the cardmen, who paste up replacements as fast as the cards are removed. In one eight-week period more than a million cards were removed. These would have cost the whores involved £150,000 to have printed.

The survey team interviewed some of these women about their charges and the number of clients they accepted. 'Full sex' cost anything from £40 to £100, the average being £60. Average for hand relief was £30, for oral sex £40 and 'special services' £100 or more.

One woman had only four or five clients per week but charged them each £100 or more. A woman who worked a five-day week had about fifty clients in that time. The survey team estimated that there were approximately 16,000 clients per week for women working from private premises. The women were earning on average at least £1,250. Out of this they have to pay rent, the costs of their cards and other advertising and the wage of a maid.

Professor Matthews found that police and local authorities tolerated massage parlours, which are arguably brothels, although it might be hard to prove it. Generally they act against them only when the public complain or 'if they come to police attention as part of a particular operation'. Where police did prosecute and the massage parlour had to close, it probably soon opened again elsewhere under another name. 'Despite occasional closures the massage parlour and sauna business in London appears to be thriving.'

The survey concludes that at the time it was carried out there were approximately 185 such illicit establishments in the city. They charge clients an entrance fee of £10 or £15. The client then chooses a girl and goes with her to a private room to negotiate the cost of sex. Because the manager is not party to this negotiation and in theory does not get any of the money it might be impossible to prove brothel-keeping.

Charges in these parlours are roughly in line with those charged by the phone-box whores: £30 for hand relief, £40 for oral sex and £60 or more for full sex.

Professor Matthews says that at the time of the survey there were about seventy escort agencies in the city. The client gets the agency's phone number from an advertisement and the agency puts him or her in touch with the 'escorts' it has on its books. 'Clients are normally given a verbal description of the women available over the telephone, while in some cases the agencies may circulate photo-graphs of the women, or the transaction might be arranged as a "blind date". Either way, the agency itself charges a fee for introducing the client to the woman (or man) which ranged from £30 to £55 with the average fee being around £40.' One agency which charged £55 also charged £250 an hour for the escort. This agency had twenty women and thirty men on its books.

An important new factor in prostitution is drugs. Professor Matthews' study says that heavy use of drugs, particularly crack cocaine, by prostitutes may be reflected in the price of sexual services. Other recent surveys suggested that drugs increase the danger that the women will have unprotected sex. 'It is also suggested that they are likely to feel pressured, because of the need to earn quick money, to either provide sexual services at lower prices or engage in activities which may be unsafe.'

Studies in the King's Cross area of north London show that many of the women are drawn to it because it is known to be 'a thriving sex market where drugs are readily available' (May, Harocopos and Turnbull, *Selling Sex in the City*, 2001). A team from the South Bank University interviewed 55 women aged between seventeen and 47. Apart from the very important drugs element and the absence of absolute destitution the findings resembled those of surveys a hundred years or more earlier. Most told of unhappy childhoods, with sexual or other abuse. More than half had spent some time in local authority care. About the same proportion left school without qualifications.

The earliest age at which any of the women began selling sex was thirteen, and the average age for this event was twenty. They worked an average of six days a week, had an average of 26 clients and earned an average of £700 a week. This suggests they were charging the clients between £25 and £30 a time.

All but two of the women interviewed took drugs: 23 used crack cocaine, and 24 used heroin. They spent from £10 to £2,000 a week on drugs.

Some enjoyed sex work. 'I like meeting people, the money, and hours are flexible.' 'I like robbing men. I can use my brains and their stupidity, and earn loads of money.' The majority, however, disliked the work. The clipped quotes given in the survey cannot hide the raw pain and shame of some women: 'I dislike everything. It feels like you are being raped half the time; mauled. I despise the men, I despise the job.' 'I dislike having to have sex. Not knowing who you are dealing with. Feeling horrible and dirty.'

Why do they do it? Twenty said money was the deciding factor. 'For six, it was a matter of economical survival: "I had no money and I was on the street. I didn't know what else to do, so I just walked around Sussex Gardens watching others and picked up how to work."' Some said they had been pushed into it by men. 'My ex-husband started me off. He forced me into it. He was 22 years older than me and I was very naive and young.'

Pimps use drugs to ensnare the women and then to keep them on the streets. In 1999 the Home Office report *Street Business: The Links Between Sex and Drugs Markets* described crack cocaine as a drug which 'facilitates' prostitution. Customers for both sex and drugs are attracted, and the pimps make money from both.

A survey of sixteen pimps, carried out in 2000 for the Home Office (May, Harocopos, Hough, *For Love or Money: Pimps and the Management of Sex Work*) gives valuable insights into a neglected aspect of the sex industry. These men managed between one and nine women each, earnings ranged from £500 to £7,000 per week, 'and only three claimed to split earnings equally with their workers'. The pimps were heavily involved in drug dealing and use, and in other serious crimes.

The pimps and their women differed sharply on the question of the benefits of pimping. Twelve of the former said the protection they offered was a benefit. One of the women said: 'They like to make you think there are benefits but there are none, unless you like being scared to death and beaten up.'

Violence was a common factor in the relationship between pimps and their women. 'One day he wanted more money, he owed someone. I was ill and didn't want to go out. I got a fractured skull for that one.' 'I call it domestic violence. He beat me up and hospitalised me, but I dropped the case. I had a broken foot, a black eye, a punctured ear drum, a cut throat and I lost my baby – I was five months pregnant at the time.'

Complaints to the police about violent pimps are rare. The women blamed lack of effective protection. In November 2001 *Time Out* quoted Hilary Kinnell of the Safety Violence and Policing Group, a national umbrella of organisations working with prostitutes: 'Violence against sex workers is not regarded as a police priority. The police have limited resources and the women are often not prepared to report incidents because of the hostility they feel the police have towards them.'

For illegal immigrants the fear of being deported is another reason for not complaining. Gangs bring at least 1,400 women into the UK each year to work as prostitutes. The women incur large debts to pay the smugglers – anything from £5,000 to £20,000. Once here they are sold to a pimp and their papers taken away. They are then forced to work until their debts are paid off. In many cases this is impossible. According to a feature in *Time Out* (28 November 2001), they may get as little as £6 out of the £60 paid by a customer, and they have to buy condoms out of that. Police believe that of the estimated 300 women working from flats in Soho, 70 per cent are illegal immigrants. These newcomers are mostly Thais, Filipinas and Brazilians, but there are growing numbers of Albanians, Kosovans, West Africans and Hungarians.

This smuggling is changing the London sex trade in dangerous new ways. After a series of concerted police raids on Soho brothels in February 2001 the Home Office said the Albanian mafia had taken over much of the sex industry in the area. Inspector Paul Holmes of the Metropolitan Police clubs and vice unit said the Albanians had reached an accommodation with the Maltese and East End gangsters who have traditionally dominated Soho, and the transition had not been accompanied by the extreme violence seen when Albanians had taken over vice empires in Italy and Germany. 'The people who run these places want a set level of money and don't care whether the girls are from Albania or Mars. But we are concerned at what will happen when the turf is full and the Albanians start setting up their own places.'

APPENDIX 1:
Numbers of Prostitutes

Estimates for the number of prostitutes in London about the middle of the nineteenth century varied between 5,000 and 220,000. Paula Bartley says in *Prostitution: Prevention and Reform in England 1860–1914* that in the 1860s some people suggested that there were half a million prostitutes in England, yet police statistics suggested that the figure was around 30,000. The police figures were based on prosecutions, which were low. As Bartley points out, the discrepancies arose because of the different ways the figures were compiled. Colquhoun, who thought the total in London in 1800 was around 50,000, included 25,000 unmarried women 'who cohabit with labourers and others without matrimony', which wouldn't meet our definition of prostitution today, although presumably some of these women were also prostitutes. J B Talbot, secretary of the deeply puritanical London Rescue Society, reached the conclusion that there were 80,000 prostitutes in the capital. This was based on his own observations 'and the evidence of eight different investigators' in the 1830s and 1840s. The figure came to be widely accepted, although there was little hard evidence for it.

Henry Mayhew was another expert witness who believed the figure of 80,000 prostitutes. He wrote that in 1857 'according to the best authorities' there were 8,600 prostitutes 'known to the police', but felt that this figure 'scarcely does more than record the circulating harlotry of the Haymarket and Regent Street'.

The doctor and writer William Acton, an authority on the subject, did not agree, although he suggests that the true total was far in excess of the lower estimates. In his book *Prostitution Considered in its Moral, Social and Sanitary Aspects*, published in 1857, he wrote:

> I can merely give a few of the more moderate [estimates] that have been handed down by my predecessors. Mr Colquhoun, a magistrate at the Thames Police Court, rated them at 50,000 some sixty years ago. The Bishop of Exeter spoke of them as reaching 80,000. Mr Talbot...made the same estimate. The returns on the constabulary force presented to Parliament in 1839, furnished an estimate of 6,371 – viz., 3,732 'known to the police as kept by the proprietors of brothels', and 2,639 as resident in lodgings of their own, and dependent on prostitution alone for a livelihood. It was estimated by the Home authorities in 1841, that the corresponding total was 9,409 – which, I hardly need point out, does not include the vast numbers who regularly or occasionally abandon themselves, but in a less open manner...
>
> The police have not attempted to include...the unnumbered prostitutes whose appearance in the streets as such never takes place; who are not seen abroad at unseemly hours; who are reserved in manners, quiet and unobtrusive in their houses and lodgings, and whose general conduct is such that the most vigilant of constables could have no pretence for claiming to be officially aware of their existence or pursuits.
>
> The 1869 Report on the Contagious Diseases Act enables us for the first time to show the proportions of common prostitutes to soldiers at Aldershot. Thus Inspector Smith gave in a report proving that there were, in June 1869, 243 recognised prostitutes to about 12,000 troops. This paucity of prostitutes, according to Dr Barr, causes some of them to have intercourse with 20 or 23 men in one night. I may here call attention to a lesson taught us pretty clearly by these returns, which is, that to attempt to put down prostitution by law is to attempt the impossible...

Tom Hickman says in *The Sexual Century* that there were 80,000 whores in Edwardian London, although he does not say what the figure is based on. Gosling and Warner in *The Shame of a City* estimate that in 1958 there were 1,000 full-time streetwalkers in the West End, and about 3,000 in the whole of London. They believed that in addition there were between 6,000 and 10,000 women they called 'hidden prostitutes', that is women who did not solicit openly on the streets.

APPENDIX 2:
Prices

Comparison of prostitutes' rates over the centuries is difficult. The poet and playwright Thomas Nashe (1567–1601) says he visited an expensive whorehouse where the asking price was a steep half a crown although the customers could try to negotiate a better rate. The going rate for what Pepys called a 'bout' was 6d. in the country and up to 20d. in the city. Christopher Hibbert writes in *The Road to Tyburn* that eighteenth-century street prostitutes, many of them little more than children, would hire out their bodies for sixpence. Boswell wrote of 'the splendid Madam at fifty guineas a night down to the civil nymph with white thread stockings who tramps along the Strand and will resign her engaging person ... for a pint of wine and a shilling'. A better guide to average prices in the mid-eighteenth century is Jack Harris's *List*, where the eighty women who advertised in one edition charged an average of two guineas. This was about two weeks' wages for a working man.

The Victorian prostitute Swindling Sal got as much as £5 or as little as a few shillings, depending on what the customer could afford. The diarist 'Walter' would pay widely different rates according to the state of his finances. When they were low he often paid 5s. When he could afford it he would pay a guinea (21s.), although he said ten shillings would get 'as nice a one as was needed' from among the streetswalkers. According to Walkowitz, in *Prostitution and Victorian Society*, West End streetwalkers could expect £1 and upwards 'from well-heeled customers', although as we have seen even the West End had its worn-out whores who would accept what they could get. The sailor's tarts of the East End might have to accept shillings or even pence, or just a drink.

The gangster Arthur Harding described in *East End Underworld* the prices the local girls charged around 1900:

> There were two kinds of girl. Those who went up West and mixed with the toffs. They would get as much as ten shillings a time or even £1 and they would ride home in hansom cabs... the girls who stayed at Spitalfields were very poor. That was what you called a 'fourpenny touch' or a knee trembler' – they wouldn't stay with you all night...Even if you stayed all night with girls like that it was only a couple of shillings.

After the First World War wages fell rapidly and many of the women who had been attracted to prostitution during the conflict could no longer find customers. In the 1930s when the average wage was about £3. 5s. street prostitutes in the better areas of the West End were charging 10s. or £1, which was more than most men could afford.

In the 1950s police who arrested the ponce of a Soho prostitute found a notebook kept by the woman's maid. In it were day-by-day records of the prostitute's earnings. These showed that in a six-hour period each night she would have about thirty customers. Her income over twenty days was nearly £1,000 – amounting to an enormous tax-free annual income of more than £18,000. The prostitute Edna Kalman told the Attilio Messina trial in 1959 that in eight years she earned about £40,000 working her beat in New Bond Street.

By the 1960s streetwalkers in Mayfair were charging between £5 and £10 for brief sex, in Soho the range was between £4 and £6 and the girls in South Kensington, Maida Vale and Bayswater were said to be charging from £3 to £5. Girls in Hyde Park charged £1 for sex standing up, and £2 for it lying down. The Hyde Park women also used taxis for sex, and charged between £2 and £3.

Call-girls at the top of the profession were said to charge up to £50 for the night, and girls further down the scale up to £30. As indicated in the chapter 'Sex in the City in the 21ˢᵗ Century', women at King's Cross charge around £30.

Endnotes

1. Edward VI is believed to have suffered from congenital syphilis, as did his sister Mary. H W Haggard in *Devils, Drugs and Doctors* (1929) says that 'Queen Mary shows in her facial expressions a typical congenital syphilis'. P McLeod Yearsley states in *Le Roi est Mort* (1935) that it was a 'syphilitic rhinitis' and quotes a lady-in-waiting who said there was 'a disgusting smell from her nose'.

2. The condom was probably invented by Gabriele Falloppia (1523–63), a professor at Padua who claimed to have examined the genitals of 10,000 syphilitics. He gave his name to the uterine tubes.

3. The twelve great livery companies or guilds which dominated the City of London.

4. The publisher of a modern-day version of the Harris's *List*, the *Ladies' Directory*, was prosecuted in 1962. He was convicted of, among other things, living on the earnings of prostitutes, since they paid for their advertisements. He was jailed for nine months.

5. To 'peach' was to inform on someone. A little pamphlet entitled *The Humours of the Flashy Boys at Moll King's*, in the form of a putative conversation between Moll and a customer named Harry Moythen, who was later murdered, gives us an idea of how flash sounded.

Harry: To pay, Moll, for I must hike.

Moll: Let me see! There's a Grunter's Gig, is a Si-Buxom; Five Cats' Heads, a Whyn; a double Gage of Rum-Slobber, is Thrums; and a quartern of Max is three Megs. That makes a Traveller, all but a Meg.

Harry: Here, take your Traveller, and tip the Meg to the Kinchin... But Moll, don't Puff, you must tip me your Clout before I Derrick, for my Bloss has Milled me of mine. But I shall catch her at Maddox's gin-ken, Sluicing her Gob by the Tinney. And if she has Morric'd it, Knocks and Socks, Thumps and Plumps shall attend the Froe-File-Buttocking bitch...

And so on. To 'hike' meant to go home; a 'Grunter's Gig' was a hog's cheek; 'Si-Buxom' was sixpence; a 'Cat's Head' a ha'penny roll; a 'Whyn' a penny; a 'Gage of Rum-Slobber' a pot of porter; 'Thrums' was threepence; 'Max' was gin; 'Kinchin' a little child. 'To Puff', to impeach; 'Clout', a handkerchief; 'Derrick', to go away; 'Froe-File-Buttock', a woman pickpocket-prostitute. Dickens uses 'kinchin' in *Oliver Twist*, where Fagin explains the Kinchin Lay, the art of stealing from tiny children:

The kinchins, my dear, is the young children that's sent on errands by their mothers, with sixpences and shillings; and the lay is just to take their money away – they've always got it ready in their hands – then knock them into the kennel [gutter] and walk off very slow as if there's nothing else the matter but a child fallen down and hurt itself.

6. The practice of forcing inexperienced girls to pay exorbitantly for their working clothes was widespread among bawds. George Alexander Steevens says in his *Adventures of a Speculist*, 1788:

On bulks and in alleys we often meet with girls of twelve and thirteen years of age lying in a most despicable condition: poor objects with a pretty face. A pimp will pick them up and take them to a bawdy-house wherein the poor wretch is stripped, washed and given clothes... The pimp gets paid a pound or two for his trouble: the girls have thus been bought and must do as the purchaser pleases . . . I have known a girl pay £11 for the use of a smock and petticoat which when new did cost only six guineas.

7. The *Essay* was probably written by the Medmenham club member Thomas Potter, with notes by Wilkes. It is partly a parody of Pope's *Essay on Man* and partly an attempt to ridicule one of Wilkes's enemies, Bishop William Warburton. There is a copy in the British Library. Pope's essay begins:

> Awake, my St John! leave all meaner things
> To low ambition and the pride of kings.

The opening lines of the parody are:

> Awake, my Fanny, leave all meaner things:
> This morn shall prove what rapture swiving brings!
> Let us (since life can little more supply
> Than just a few good fucks, and then we die)
> Expatiate free o'er that loved scene of man,
> A mighty maze, for mighty pricks to scan . . .

There is a story that one reason for Sandwich's hatred of Wilkes was a joke the latter played on him when they were both members of the Medmenham fraternity. Wilkes acquired a baboon and dressed it up to look like the devil. One night when the monks were holding a Black Mass, prancing about among the candles in the darkened abbey and calling on the devil to appear among them, he released the beast from a cupboard where he had hidden it. It jumped on to Sandwich's shoulders and by the time it had been driven off Sandwich was almost insensible with fear. He never forgave Wilkes.

8. This story is widely believed, but not, alas, by the curator of Apsley House, the Duke's fine London mansion which is now a museum.

9. One of the informers for the Society for the Reformation of Manners was Frank Rigg, who had once 'peached' on Sally Salisbury and had also been one of the informers leading to Mother Clap's arrest and the subsequent hangings of homosexuals.

10. Hemyng believed that Kate Hamilton's Cafe Royal was owned by a Jewish family, who also owned several other night houses. This may have been David Belasco and his associates, who were known to have wide interests in brothels. Belasco went bankrupt, and according to Chesney in *The Victorian Underworld* was later reported to be working as a waiter. This is one of the few glimpses we get of the shadowy figures behind the chains of brothels.

11. In 1987 the Met said that 'only about six or seven specific areas' were involved. In November 2001 *Time Out* reported that it was 'booming' in Streatham, Tottenham, Brixton, Stoke Newington, Paddington, Whitechapel and King's Cross. 'Residents...are well used to seeing prostitutes plying their trade with the associated delights of creepy punters propositioning schoolgirls they mistake for whores, kerb-crawlers and drug dealers scenting a lucrative market – not to mention the muggers and thieves who trail in their wake.'

Sources

Records of prostitution in London are patchy, and the reticence of professional historians hasn't helped. Until well into the last century the blight of Victorian hypocrisy made the subject taboo. Fortunately for writers on vice in London there are the works of the splendid amateur historian E J Burford, the most important of which cover the period from Cromwell to the end of the Regency. Otherwise, with the exception of a few writers such as Bloch, we have to consult fabulous rarities at the British and Guildhall libraries or read now-neglected memoirs, plays and novels. The Elizabethan playwright Robert Greene was an early chronicler of the London underworld, and his pamphlets on *Coney Catching* (1591 and 1592) are valuable guides to the tricks of swindlers and whores. John Garfield's *The Wand'ring Whore*, 1660–3, is perhaps the earliest list of whores and bawds, a genre of which Jack Harris's *List of Covent Garden Ladies* of the mid-eighteenth century is the most important and also the most amusing example.

The diaries and memoirs of Pepys, Boswell and William Hickey help establish for us the moral tone of Stuart and Georgian London, as do contemporary records of whoredom such as *The Nocturnal Revels* of 1779. Defoe's novel *Moll Flanders* is an unflinchingly realistic account of the life of an upwardly mobile whore. Cleland's notorious *Fanny Hill* is an optimistic novel of erotic entertainment. There are biographies of courtesans, such as Captain Walker's *Authentic Memoirs of the Life, Intrigues and Adventures of the Celebrated Sally Salisbury*, 1723, and the anonymous *Memoirs of the Celebrated Miss Fanny Murray*, Sally's successor and the foremost Toast of the Town in the middle of the eighteenth century. The Regency courtesan Harriette Wilson's memoirs are still worth reading. 'Walter', whose *My Secret Life* chronicles his encounters with 1,200 women of pleasure, is an invaluable guide to Victorian vice, and D Shaw's *London in the Sixties* describes many of the high-class haunts of of such women, including Mott's, Kate Hamilton's and the Argyll Rooms. It catches something of the dangerous glamour of upper-class gallantry in the mid-nineteenth century. Two general histories, both called *The Victorian Underworld*, by Kellow Chesney and Donald Thomas, are well-written and informative.

The modern age is poorly served. The memoirs of the bawd Marthe Watts cover the war and post-war years, and the brief surveys of Tiggey May and her collaborators of the contemporary scene, and Professor Roger Matthews' *Prostitution in London*, make you hope they will attempt something more ambitious.

Fernando Henriques' three-volume *Prostitution and Society*, a comprehensive survey of vice through the ages, is still useful, as are, in their various ways, the books listed in the select bibliography. Stephen Inwood's *A History of London* is the best general history of the capital.

Some time in the middle of the eighteenth century, magazines and newspapers became aware that there was a public avid for news of the great courtesans and their lovers. In pursuit of circulation they turned them into the first media celebrities. The *Town and Country Magazine*, which ran from 1769 to 1797, carried erotic engravings and gossip of amatory and sexual adventures. A very popular feature, said to have pushed the journal's circulation to an unlikely 14,000 copies per issue, was the Tête-à-Tête series. This consisted of side-by-side engravings of a well-known woman, usually a courtesan, and a man, usually an important public figure. The accompanying text was sometimes well-informed, sometimes out of date. In Goldsmith's *She Stoops to Conquer* the absurd Mrs Hardcastle reads it avidly to keep abreast of events in the capital. There were calls for its suppression, to which the magazine replied: 'The suppressing of this publication would be depriving posterity of a very curious piece of biography.' The issue of February 1769 has a description of Charlotte Hayes's brothel. The *Covent Garden Magazine* (1772–5) is interesting on sexual manners in high and low society. Its formula was copied, among others, by the *Rambler's Magazine*, or the *Annals of Gallantry, Glee, Pleasure and the Bon Ton* (1783–90). Daily newspapers were also a rich source of gossip about courtesans and their lovers. The *Public Advertiser*, the *Morning Post*, and above all the *Morning Herald* recorded their movements and their *mots*, if any.

Select Bibliography

Anon. *A Genuine History of Sally Salisbury alias Mrs S Prydden.* London, 1723

Anon. *The Life and Character of Moll King.* London, 1747

Anon. *The Poor Whores' Complaint to the Apprentices of London.*

Anon. *The Nocturnal Revels – The History of King's Place and other Modern Nunneries, by a Monk of the Order of St Francis.* 1779

Anon. *LOW LIFE, or, One half of the World knows not how the Other Half Lives, being a critical account of what is transacted by People of almost all Religions, Nations, Circumstances, and Sizes of Understanding, in the Twenty-four hours between Saturday-Night and Monday-Morning.* London, 1752

Ackroyd, Peter. *London: The Biography.* London, Chatto and Windus, 2000

—*Dickens' London.* London, Headline, 1987

Acton, William. *Prostitution Considered in its Moral, Social and Sanitary Aspects.* London, 1857

Archenholz, J W von. *A Picture of England.* London, 1789

Bailey, Paul. *An English Madam: The Life and Work of Cynthia Payne.* London, Cape, 1982

Bartley, Paula. *Prostitution: Prevention and Reform in England, 1860–1914.* London, Routledge, 2000

Bloch, Iwan. *Sexual Life in England Past and Present.* London, 1958

Booth, Charles. *Life and Labour of the People in London.* 1902–03

Boswell, James. *London Journal 1763* (ed. Frederick Pottle). Edinburgh University Press, 1991

Bristow, Edward J. *Vice and Vigilance: Purity Movements in Britain Since 1700*. Dublin, Gill and Macmillan, 1977

Brome, Vincent. *Havelock Ellis, Philosopher of Sex*. London, Routledge, 1979

Burford, E J. *The Orrible Synne*. London, Calder and Boyars, 1973

—*Royal St James's*. London, Robert Hale, 1988

—*The Synfulle Citie*. London, 1990

—*Wits, Wenchers and Wantons, London's Low Life: Covent Garden in the 18th Century*. London, Robert Hale, 1986

Burford, E J, and Wotton, Joy. *Private Vices, Public Virtues*. London, Robert Hale, 1995

Butler, Josephine. *Personal Reminiscences of a Great Crusade*. London, 1896

Champly, Henri. *The Road to Shanghai*. London, 1934

Chesney, Kellow. *The Victorian Underworld*. London, Penguin, 1991

Cleland, John. *Fanny Hill or Memoirs of a Woman of Pleasure*. London, Penguin. London, 1985

Colquhoun, Patrick. *Treatise on the Police of the Metropolis*. London, 1796

Cunningham, Peter. *The Story of Nell Gwyn*. London, 1903

Davis, Godfrey. *The Early Stuarts*. London, Clarendon Press, 1959

Dawson, Nancy, *Authentic Memoirs of the Celebrated Miss Nancy Dawson*. London, 1762

Dickens, Charles. 'On Duty with Inspector Field', in *Reprinted Pieces*.

Dormer, Joseph. *The Female Rake or a Modern Fine Lady*. London, 1763

Dryden, John. *Satire on the Players*. London, 1691

Dunton, John. *The HE-Strumpet, A Satyre on Sodomites*. London, 1707

Evelyn, John. *Diary* (ed. William Bray). London, 1951

Finch, B E and Green, Hugh. *Contraception Through the Ages*. London, Owen, 1963

Fraser, Antonia. *The Weaker Vessel*. London, Mandarin Paperbacks, 1993

Garfield, John. *The Wand'ring Whore*. London, 1660–3

Geijer, Erik. *Impressions of England 1809–10* (trans. Elizabeth Sprigge and C Napier). 1932

Gosling, John, and Warner, Douglas. *The Shame of a City*. London, W H Allen, 1960

Gramont, Comte de. *Memoirs* (ed. Horace Walpole, trans. 1714, revised Sir W Scott 1814).

Greenwood, James. *In Strange Company: The Notebook of a Roving Correspondent*. London, 1873

—*The Seven Curses of London*. London, 1869

Harris, Jack. *List of Covent Garden Ladies or The New Atlantis*. London, H Ranger, 1764

Hazzlewood, Charlotte. *Secret History of the Green Room*. London, 1790

—*True and Entertaining History of Charlotte Lorraine, Afterwards Mrs Hazzlewood*. London, 1790

Head, Richard, and Kirkman, Francis. *The English Rogue*. London, 1665

Henderson, Tony. *Disorderly Women in Eighteenth-Century London*. London, Longman, 1999

Henriques, Fernando. *Prostitution and Society* (3 vols). London, MacGibbon and Kee, 1962–8

Hibbert, Christopher. *George IV, Prince of Wales*. London, Longman, 1972

—*The Road to Tyburn*. London, Longmans Green, 1957

Hickey, William. *Memoirs*. 1948

Hickman, Tom. *The Sexual Century*. London, Carlton Books, 1999

Higgs, Mary. *Glimpse into the Abyss*. London, 1906

Holloway, Robert. *The Phoenix of Sodom: or, the Vere Street Coterie*. London, 1814

Huish, Robert. *Memoirs of George IV*. London, 1831

Inwood, Stephen. *A History of London*. London, Macmillan, 1998

Jesse, J H. *Literary and Historical Memorials of London*. London, 1847

Kelland, Gilbert. *Crime in London*. Bodley Head, 1986

Low, Donald A. *The Regency Underworld*. Stroud, Sutton Publishing, 1999

Macauley, Thomas Babington. *History of England*. London, Heron Books, 1967

Masters, Brian. *The Mistresses of Charles II*. London, Blond and Briggs, 1979

Matthews, Roger. *Prostitution in London: An Audit*. Middlesex University, 1997

May, Tiggey, Harocopos, Alex, and Hough, Michael. *For Love or Money: Pimps and the Management of Sex Work*. Home Office, 2000

May, Tiggey, Harocopos, Alex, and Turnbull, Paul J. *Selling Sex in the City*. South Bank University Faculty of Humanities and Social Study, June 2001

Mayhew, Henry and Binney, John. *The Criminal Prisons of London*. London, 1862

Mayhew, Henry, Hemyng, Bracebridge, Binney John and Halliday, Andrew. *London Labour and the London Poor*. London, 1861–2

McCall, Andrew. *The Medieval Underworld*. London, 1977

McLynn, Frank. *Crime and Punishment in Eighteenth-century England*. London, Routledge, 1989

McMullan, John L. *The Canting Crew*. Rutger University, 1984

Meyrick, Kate. *Secrets of the 43*. London, John Long, 1933

Misson, H. *Memoirs and Observations of his Travels over England*. London, 1719

Murray, Venetia. *High Society in the Regency Period*. London, Penguin, 1998

Nead, Lynda. 'The Girl of the Period'. *National Art Collections Fund Quarterly*, autumn 2001

Pepys, Samuel. *Diary of Samuel Pepys 1660–8* (ed. Robert Latham and William Matthews). London, HarperCollins, 1995

Picard, L. *Dr Johnson's London*. London, Weidenfeld and Nicolson, 2000

Porter, Roy. *English Society in the Eighteenth Century*. London, Pelican.

—*The Greatest Benefit to Mankind: A Medical History of Humanity from Antiquity to the Present*. London, Fontana Press, 1997

—*London, A Social History*. London, Hamish Hamilton, 1994

Rees, Sian. *The Floating Brothel*. London, Headline, 2001

Roberts, Nickie. *Whores In History*. London, HarperCollins, 1992

Salgado, Gamini. *The Elizabethan Underworld*. London, 1992

Sanger, William. *A History of Prostitution*. New York, 1859

Shaw, D. *London in the Sixties*. London, 1908

Smithies, Edward. *Crime in Wartime*. London, George Allen, 1982

Stow, John. *The Survey of London*. London, Everyman

Tanner, Anodyne. *Life of the Late Celebrated Elizabeth Wisebourn, Vulgarly called Mother Wybourn*. London, 1721

Thomas, Donald. *The Victorian Underworld*. London, John Murray,1998

Thompson, Edward. 'The Meretriciad', *A Satire*. 1765 and 1770

Tobias, J J. *Crime and Industrial Society in the Nineteenth Century*. London, Pelican, 1972

Tomkinson, Martin. *The Pornbrokers*. London, Virgin Books, London, 1982

Tristan, Flora. *Promenades dans Londres*. 1840

Uglow, Jenny. *Hogarth, A Life and a World*. London, Faber and Faber, 1997.

Walker, Captain C. *Authentic Memoirs of the Life, Intrigues and Adventures of the Celebrated Sally Salisbury*. London, 1723

Walkowitz, Judith R. *Prostitution and Victorian Society: Women, Class and the State*. Cambridge, 1980

Waller, Maureen. *1700: Scenes from London Life*. London, Hodder and Stoughton, 2000

Ward, Edward. *The London Spy*. London, 1698–1709

Watts, Marthe. *The Men in My Life*. London, Christopher Johnson, 1960

Weinreb Ben, and Hibbert, Christopher. *The London Encyclopaedia*. London, Papermac, 1993.

Wilmot, John, Earl of Rochester. *A Panegyrick Upon Cumdums*. 1674

Wilson, A N. *The Faber Book of London*. London, 1993.

Wilson, Harriette. *Memoirs* (Folio Society edition). London, 1964

Wilson, J H. *All The King's Ladies*. Chicago, 1958

Wilson, Mary. *Exhibition of Female Flagellants*. London, 1777

Ziegler, Philip. *London at War*. London, Mandarin, 1996

Picture Credits

Guildhall library, Corporation of London: pp. 72, 80, 85, 295

© Hulton Archive: pp. 341, 364, 367, 369

Mary Evans Picture Library: pp. 89, 211, 275, 285

By courtesy of the National Portrait Gallery, London: p. viii
(Artist: C Spooner); p. 127 (Artist: John Smith after Godfrey Kneller).

Mirrorpix: p. 361

See plate section for details of plate section picture credits.

All other pictures from author's private collection.

Index

Figures in italics indicate captions.

399

Holland, Mary 84
Holland's Leaguer, Bankside 19–23, 71
Holloway, Robert: *The Phoenix of Sodom: or, the Vere Street Coterie* 193
Holmes, Inspector Paul 378
'Holy Land' (St Giles) 224
Holywell Street 349, 350, 351
Home Office 378
Street Business: The Links Between Sex and Drugs Markets 376
homosexuality 189–96
    clubs 83, 189, 190
    harbouring homosexuals 6
    of James I 15
    marriage 193
    mollies' houses ix, 83, 90, 95, 189, 192–3
    red-light district 5
    Wolfenden committee 343
    see also buggery; lesbianism; sodomy
Hopton Street 23
Hosier Lane 6
Hospital Rents, Fleet Street 5
hostess bars 373
hotels-cum-brothels ix
Hotten, John Camden 351
Hough, Michael 375, 376
Houghton, Mrs 119
House of Commons 121, 287, 288, 298, 300, 307, 321, 323, 330, 368
House of Correction 74
House of Lords 65, 117, 297, 302
    Select Committee (1881) 207, 241–2, 245
    Select Committee (1888–90) 270
Howard, Lucy 53
Huguenots 78
Huish, Robert: *Memoirs of George IV* 52
Hume, Donald 335

Humphreys, Jimmy 352, 353–4, 355–6
Humphreys, Rusty 353, 355, 356
Hundesmor, Thomas de 6–7
Hungarians 377
Hunt, Inspector 224, 225
Hunt, William Holman: *The Awakened Conscience* 139
Hyde Park 139, 142, 199, 304, 320, 325, 326, 342, 384
hygiene, and venereal disease 36, 37

illegal immigrants 377
Imperial Protestant Mercury, The 77
incest 146
Independent 344
informers 175
Inns of Court 160
Inwood, Stephen 272
    A History of London 229, 269, 271
Irish population 224, 244, 268–9
Islet Town Club, Curzon Street 339
Islington 12
Ivanov, Captain 367, 368

Jack the Ripper murders 269, 279–80, 305
Jacobs, J (condom seller) 31
James I, King 15, 20, 22
    Touching on Disorderly Houses in Saffron Hille 16
James, Mrs 250
James II, King 47, 48
Janson, Hank 352
Jarrett, Rebecca *299*, 302
Jeffries, Mary 297, 298, 299, 302–3
Jenkins, James 175
Jenkins, Roy 357
Jennings, Frances 61
Jermain, Mr 190
Jersey, Lady 53–4
Jesse, J H: *Literary and Historical Memorials of London* 154
Jewish Board of Guardians 269